Selling Words

Critical America

General Editors: RICHARD DELGADO and JEAN STEFANCIC

Taxing America
Edited by Karen B. Brown and Mary Louise Fellows

Notes of a Racial Caste Baby:
Color Blindness and the End of Affirmative Action
Bryan K. Fair

Please Don't Wish Me a Merry Christmas:
A Critical History of the Separation of Church and State
Stephen M. Feldman

To Be an American:
Cultural Pluralism and the Rhetoric of Assimilation
Bill Ong Hing

Negrophobia and Reasonable Racism:
The Hidden Costs of Being Black in America
Jody David Armour

Black and Brown in America:
The Case for Cooperation
Bill Piatt

Black Rage Confronts the Law
Paul Harris

Selling Words:
Free Speech in a Commercial Culture
R. George Wright

From *Adbusters* magazine, Vancouver, Canada

Selling Words

Free Speech in a
Commercial Culture

R. George Wright

NEW YORK UNIVERSITY PRESS
New York and London

NEW YORK UNIVERSITY PRESS
New York and London

Copyright © 1997 New York University

Library of Congress Cataloging-in-Publication Data
Wright, R. George.
Selling words : free speech in a commercial culture / R. George
Wright.
p. cm. — (Critical America)
Includes bibliographical references and index.
ISBN 0-8147-9315-0 (acid-free paper)
1. Advertising laws—United States. 2. Freedom of speech—United
States. 3. Popular culture—United States. I. Title. II. Series.
KF1614.Z9W75 1997
342.73'0853—dc21   97-4899
                                    CIP

New York University Press books are printed on acid-free paper,
and their binding materials are chosen for strength and durability.

Manufactured in the United States of America

10 9 8 7 6 5 4 3 2 1

For Jim, Nancy, and Andrew George

c o n t e n t s

acknowledgments

The author's thanks go to Michelle Curci, Richard Delgado, Michael Froomkin, John Garvey, Lori Hackleman, Gina Hunter, Andy Klein, Ed Martin, Judy McAlister, Richard Moon, Michael Perry, Niko Pfund, Richard Pollay, Roger Shiner, Jean Stefancic, Mark Tushnet, and Mary Wright.

Acknowledgment is also hereby gratefully extended to the Denver University Law Review for permission to reprint a revised version of R. George Wright, "Freedom and Culture: Why We Should Not Buy Commercial Speech," *Denver University Law Review* 72 (1994): 137, as well as to the Media Foundation, publishers of *Adbusters* magazine, for the cover art and frontispiece. The chapter epigrams are from Sinclair Lewis's *Babbitt*.

. . . the Babbitt whose god was modern
appliances was not pleased.

introduction

It was observed some years ago that the bright lights of Times Square
must be a magnificent spectacle to those unable to read. Indeed, our
commercial culture seems a marvel to us, to the extent we lose sight
of the possibilities of human development, well-being, and genuine
freedom.

Our survey begins with a brief excursion through the perpetually
cash-strapped Arrid-Mentos Junior High School. Arrid-Mentos, formerly named for President Franklin Delano Roosevelt, is located on
a small section of Minerva Street now officially redesignated as Ford
Bronco Drive. As you now may suspect, the school has entered into a

series of Faustian bargains in return for modest, but desperately needed, cash payments.

To this end, the school's morning homeroom announcements over the PA system are sponsored, appropriately, by Vivarin. And in an attempt to reduce the number of untoward incidents in the hallways, Blockbuster Video has installed several continuously running TV monitors at selected points. Most of the wall space is occupied by lower-tech, lower-budget ads, currently in various stages of defacement. Hallway audio speakers provide a democratically negotiated mix of rock, country, and urban contemporary music, interspersed with commercials for products of special interest. For example, the French classes are sponsored by Yves St. Laurent, with a variety of products advertised so as to avoid monotony and maintain interest. Today's American history lesson consists of a classroom video plus a not unmanageably difficult, self-scoring quiz sponsored by Hershey. Not surprisingly, the video features the intriguing history of chocolate manufacturing in the United States.

The students have their lunch in the food kiosk area, next to the ATM machines and the newly expanded vending machine area. The accoutrements—from trays to cups to napkins—are emblazoned with the familiar Pepsi logo and instructions on how to win desirable prizes. But given the quality of even the name-brand food kiosk items, the students joke that Tagamet would be a more appropriate sponsor. On their way back to class, the students check out the Certs Interactive Social Calendar. When afternoon classes are over, the students return briefly to their homeroom for a series of PA announcements, highlighted by the Masterlock detention list. Many of the students will be returning that evening for the basketball game in the Old Spice–New Balance Gym against traditional rival Charles Revlon Junior High.

The school's symbiotic relationship with various commercial sponsors has been, not surprisingly, controversial. At first, many people objected to the ads for tobacco and distilled liquor, but in light of these companies' generous financial terms, they found it hard to argue against the Galweed Tribute to American Women and the Kentucky Guzzler First Amendment Display. After a while, both those particular displays lost their novelty, so when Kentucky Guzzler switched to a display emphasizing the responsible use of its products by persons of legal age only, the students' reaction was, at best, ambivalent. Eventually the "Kentucky Guzzler: For Adults Only" campaign was regarded as tiresome and stale. A sense of freshness thus pervades the latest series of Kentucky Guzzler ads, focused on fun, humor, sociability, social competence, success, and excitement, with only a few references to underage drinking and safe driving.

The effects of our commercial culture are important. But commercial advertising and commercial speech do not strike like natural disasters, leveling an established cultural landscape in a moment's fury. Instead, our commercial culture affects us gradually and incrementally, often in unnoticed ways. No manifestation of our commercial culture ever seems unprecedented, a departure from all that has gone before.

This book explores how the familiarity, pervasiveness, and incremental development of our commercial culture help insulate it from reasonable legal regulation. Let us return briefly to the example of distilled liquor advertisements, on television and elsewhere. Some people find such commercials objectionable, dangerous, offensive, or, to some degree, immoral. But do such commercials lead to the sorts of harms to which a free and democratic government may properly object? What concrete harms can we definitively attribute to liquor commercials, as opposed to some other source? Has our social science really advanced to the point of being able to answer such complex causal questions with clarity and certainty?

In all likelihood, the effects of liquor commercials, if any, are diffuse, delayed, subtle, and easily confounded with those of dozens of other possible causes of the same alleged effects. Does it make a difference, for example, whether the liquor commercials are run at 7:00 P.M. or 9:00 P.M.? The time may make a difference in the balance of political forces on this issue, but do such commercials make a noticeable difference in the cultural effects? What if the ads were shown only at 9:00 P.M. for as long as it took most of us to become desensitized to their presence and then were shown also at 7:00 P.M.? Or at 2:00 P.M., during a professional football game? Could we show that any harm resulted from the ad's gradual expansion across channels or airtimes?

What if the evidence as to whether liquor ads even increased overall alcohol consumption were unclear? The producers would, no doubt, argue that liquor commercials only redistributed market shares among brands or increased their sales only at the expense of beer and wine. Perhaps, then, given the drop in consumption over the last decade, any rise in liquor consumption is only a natural swing of the pendulum. Perhaps the controversy itself over showing liquor ads on television has increased sales.

In addition, if we have legally tolerated some of these commercials, can we realistically object later if the number of liquor commercials aired gradually increases? Surely such trends reflect market forces. Where can we find a demonstrable and significant difference in the harm that an increase in such ads causes?

We can hardly ignore, furthermore, the question of the commercials' content. Suppose that many of the early liquor commercials emphasize responsible drinking. What demonstrable harm would there be in then switching, after a discreet interval, to the ads' emphasis on fun, humor, sociability, or personal gratification?

Beer and wine commercials are not governed by the same regulations. Can we prove that the differences between distilled liquor and beer and wine translate into significantly different levels of social harm? How can we take account, for example, of the fact that beer and wine commercials do not raise cultural eyebrows, merely because they are familiar and established in our culture? Given all these problems, attempting to regulate such commercials legally is likely to look arbitrary, puritanical, speculative, repressive, heavy-handed, or unprincipled.

Let us consider another cultural step. Even though we know that novelty is collectively prized, any predictions of future cultural developments will likely seem far-fetched and implausible. Part of the problem is—to exaggerate only slightly—that our commercial culture is divided between those events to which we have become inured and those predicted future developments to which we react with incredulity.

The point is that wherever the battle lines are drawn in individual cases of commercial speech, it already is too late. The basic problem is not the harms that may be associated with any particular product or category of commercial speech—and this book's central concern is not with allegedly harmful products. The basic problem also is not that liquor distillers, along with beer and wine and tobacco sellers, contribute enormous sums of money to both major political parties. Rather, the basic problem is the pervasiveness of the culture of commercial speech in general. That is, we should be more troubled by the dominance of the commercial culture than by any particular allegedly harmful instance of commercial speech.

If we must focus on particulars, however, we should recognize that the most serious harm caused by liquor advertisements in public schools is not, say, that some pattern of car wrecks can definitively be traced to those ads, to the exclusion of other causal influences. Instead, the most serious harm is that the school is teaching a generation of students that there is almost no place where commercial advertising, commercial relationships, and commercial values do not belong. This school is, in effect, ratifying the pervasiveness of our commercial culture.

The pervasiveness, and even the predominance, of our commercial culture is really not a matter of how much time, effort, or attention we devote to commercial matters. In an earlier day, we may have devoted more energy to acquiring and spending and yet have lived in a less pervasively commercial culture. We should therefore not assume that today, most people, whatever their station, are consciously preoccupied most of the time with purely commercial affairs. We may have our collective cultural obsessions, but pure commerce itself is hardly chief among them.

The pervasiveness of our commercial culture is, more important, a matter of the ways in which commercialism and commercial values affect how we experience the otherwise noncommercial elements of our lives. That is, personal relationships that might otherwise have been based primarily on friendship, love, respect, legitimate authority, or considerations of dignity have gradually been tainted and transformed, however subtly, by elements drawn from the commercial sphere.

It is impossible to say precisely how our commercial culture does and does not affect us. By now, it is difficult to imagine a preexisting, noncommercial self to be subsequently affected by the commercial culture. One possible misconception, however, can be set aside. There is no reason to assume that the primary effects of a commercial culture must involve our consciously focusing on money or productivity or even on acquiring commodities. We might instead find that our commercial culture has revised most of our valuations of novelty and permanence, glamour and reliability, depth and superficial excitement, fashion and dignity, self-indulgence and sacrifice, mind and body, short and long term, pleasure and well-being, style and substance, the coarse and the refined, the nature of maturity, or the proper scope of empathy and compassion. These sorts of effects might prove more important to our culture than any historical change in the degree to which we consciously focus on commercial consumption itself.

Excessive commercialization does have a variety of real consequences and is not automatically recognized or self-correcting. Some of the most thoughtful persons, including judicial authority figures, wind up hampering democratic efforts to reduce, reasonably and fairly, the excesses of commercialization. For them, the spread of commercialization by any means not involving fraud or deception seems to be a natural reflection of freedom and the pursuit of well-being. This book is intended as a response to this influential, but ultimately unsatisfactory, line of thinking.

Chapter One presents the book's major constitutional arguments and examines issues of freedom and well-being in the context of commercial free speech case law. It shows that commercial getting and spending is, except in the case of the poor, at best weakly correlated with happiness or well-being. In addition, current free speech law tends to overprotect non-misleading commercial speech from the standpoint of all the basic reasons for protecting free speech in the first place, including considerations of personal self-realization and personal autonomy. Free speech law in part reflects the current absence of any consistent, serious, appropriately scaled institutional counterspeech challenging the culture of commercial speech.

Chapter Two applies some of these constitutional arguments to a discussion of the logic of tobacco-advertising regulation and the socioeconomic-class dynamics of tobacco consumption. We also examine the difference between expressive and pragmatic justifications for regulating commercial speech. This chapter points out that under current free speech law, both government regulators and tobacco sellers have strong incentives to mislead us by centering the tobacco-advertising debate on smoking by underage consumers. Neither the government nor the tobacco sellers have much interest in recognizing the inconvenient truth that smoking is increasingly a socioeconomic class-linked phenomenon.

Chapter Three shifts the focus from a particular commodity to a developing medium of commercial speech, the Internet. The Internet is treated as a test of what we believe about the extent and inevitability of our culture's commercialization. In fact, the Internet may be, because of its rapid growth and mutation, a good illustration of the power of our commercial culture. That is, it may be in the process of transforming itself into an institution in which commercial considerations, while certainly not dislodging other elements, become pervasive and increasingly dominant in the case of any conflict, analogous to the powers and limitations of traditional colonial rulers.

Chapter Four shifts from medium to technique, concentrating on the functions of various sorts of intentionally controversial commercial ads. Some commercial enterprises are driven by the increasing "ad clutter" to produce more entertaining or more controversial, attention-getting ads. We sometimes assume that envelope-pushing controversy in advertising is politically progressive. This chapter explores a number of reasons that this assumption is unrealistic. In particular, we note the rise of ambiguous, pseudoprogressive ads that can be seen as either progressive or not progressive, depending on the viewer's own sympathies.

Chapter Five looks at several different categories of consumers, or the audiences for commercial advertising, and how those audiences are depicted, appealed to, and affected. In particular, we consider both the overlapping and the conflicting interests of advertisers and minority groups, women, and children and address the relationship between advertising and the freedom and well-being of these groups.

Finally, Chapter Six examines the elephantiasis of our commercial culture as a whole and describes some of the most common ideological reactions to that culture, such as the ambivalence and accommodation of various forms of liberalism and conservatism.

Before beginning, I should point out the limitations of any attempt to analyze the culture of consumption promoted by advertising and commercial speech in general. Precision and certainty in this matter are unattainable. Lab experiments are impossible. Control groups are unavailable. Indeed, it is hard even to imagine a society that resembled our own in all other major respects but was not significantly influenced culturally by commercial speech promoting commercial values. Such a society would seem not so much to be a control group, with only one key variable adjusted, but, rather, an alien society. Fortunately for our analysis, this limitation itself begins to tell us something about the role of commercialization and commercial values in our society.

We might also suppose that our concerns are far-fetched and overblown. Surely, we might think, our depiction of the commercialization of Arrid-Mentos Junior High is an absurdly unrealistic fantasy. Unfortunately, it turns out to be too well grounded in the logic of commerce and school funding to reside only in the realm of fantasy. Right after I wrote about Arrid-Mentos Junior High School, the *New York Times* reported that the encroachment of commercial pitches and sponsorships in the schools is already under way. The Hershey Foods Company, for example, sponsors a "Chocolate Dream Machine" video and curriculum guide.[1] Ads and radio-style commercials for various products can already be found in some schools. Some of our horror stories may still be fantasies, but reality is catching up with fantasy at an alarming speed.

Perhaps the pedagogy of consumption serves too many interests to be anything other than inevitable. And a corporate presence in the public school classroom is admittedly not a new phenomenon: short, self-serving, industrial films have been a classroom staple for decades. Still, such a corporate presence may be a matter of degree, and we should remain abreast of even inevitable trends.

The motives and temptations underlying the commercialization of the classroom are easily understood. The commercialization of the public school is nonetheless a betrayal of the students' basic interests. Public schools should reflect popular sovereignty and our democratically expressed will. Simultaneously, the public schools should honor, express, and embody our democratic values and aspirations. Finally, the public schools should, for the sake of those democratic values, retain some distance and critical detachment from all cultural institutions and forces only imperfectly embodying those values.

Pretending that a thickness contest between Prego and Ragu spaghetti sauce—another very real case, by the way—is the best way to promote a knowledge of, or even an interest in, real science is merely capitulating to powerful cultural forces. Commercial forces must be kept at a distance permitting critical examination. Students are usually subjects rather than targets. Schools should not be in the business of implicitly announcing that commercial forces are deservedly, or at least inevitably, everywhere and that no sanctuary, no perspective, no integrity, is possible.

Some students clearly recognize, and have mixed reactions to, public school commercialization. At some level, spaghetti sauce comparisons—to the intended advantage of one competitor—are more fun than real scientific experimentation. At another level, however, some students at least dimly appreciate that they are being devalued, manipulated, and deprived, and they may express their dissatisfaction. But it is neither fair nor realistic to expect students to be more mature and farsighted than the adults who make pedagogical decisions on their behalf. In the meantime, we are in the process of selling the students' birthright—autonomous, critical decision making—for gym shoes.

Commercial Speech in Context

These ... advertised wares ... were his symbols and proofs of excellence; at first the signs, then the substitutes, for joy and passion and wisdom.

c h a p t e r   o n e

Consider a typical car commercial, one emphasizing high performance or attractive lease terms. Were it not for the ad producers' technical artistry, the odd disclaimers and qualifications would stand out: This stunt was performed by a professional driver on a closed track. Always wear your safety belt. Do not attempt this at home. Or the stream of lease terms and conditions such as required down payments, interest rates, and total payments is delivered so quickly as to call into question whether the seller really wishes us to dwell on such matters.

Not all these disclosures are made by the seller voluntarily. The government, usually at the federal level, may have pressured or simply legally required the industry to incorporate such declarations into their commercials. How can the government do this? A car is not a bogus cancer cure. Certainly not all the regulated commercials can be claimed to be coercive, fraudulent, or deceptive. What happened to freedom of speech?

The government either is prohibiting the seller from saying what it wants to say, in its own way, or is requiring the seller to say what it does not want to say. Isn't free speech restricted in either case? Just as the government can't prevent us from saying what we believe, so it can't put words in our mouth. The government can't force us to salute the flag, recite a party platform, or, presumably, even sign our e-mail. Thousands have fought and died to establish these principles. Aren't similar principles at stake, to a similar degree and in similar ways, in car ads and in commercial advertising in general?

We expect the government to have the constitutional authority to regulate the production and sale of goods and services. The government can impound dangerous drugs and bar them from sale. But shouldn't we draw the line at regulation of speech? We expect mandatory recalls of dangerous drugs, but why should the government be allowed to regulate speech touting drugs that are not dangerous? Isn't that paternalism in the realm of thought? Surely we cannot say that speech touting commercial products is not important or is of little interest to us.

Some products are more controversial, and more dangerous, than others. Tobacco and alcohol products are examples. Nonetheless, these products are legally available for sale to adults. Why should adults' choices of what product to buy be any more subject to regulation than adults' choices of which political ideology to "buy"? Let us begin by considering the broader issue of commercial speech and culture.

We live in a remarkably commercialized culture, one that has constantly been changing but, for the moment, whose commercialization seems inevitable. Our culture does contain noncommercial elements, and some of our ways of living are less commercialized than others. Nonetheless, we can deny the cultural predominance of commercialism only in the way that a fish might deny the significance of water.

We need not focus on a single precise meaning of the idea of commercialism for all contexts. The boundary between the commercial and the noncommercial is often, though certainly not always, clear. The United States Supreme Court itself has been inconsistent in defining commercial speech, but to no great loss. Typically, our intuitions about what is more and less commercialized are adequate. Distinctions in kind and of degree usually are easy to make. However paradoxical it might seem, we even can often agree that some commercial purchases are less commercial than others and that the degree of commercialism varies among product categories. For instance, buying a copy of the Hindu Upanishads is in a sense a commercial transaction, but it may also be much more.

The importance of particular cultural institutions is not always mirrored by their degree of federal constitutional protection. Generally, we value institutions such as housing, employment, recreation, education, families, and friendship opportunities. But either these institutions are not specifically mentioned in the Constitution, or they are protected in only limited ways. The Constitution does, however, explicitly protect speech, and so we might simply consider commercial speech to be a subset of speech in general.

Until recently, the Supreme Court did not treat the government's regulation of commercial speech as different from its overall regulation of business activities, but that has now changed dramatically. Among other reasons, the Supreme Court has noticed or has been willing to admit that many of us care more passionately about our choices among competing brands of automobiles, running shoes, pharmaceuticals, hamburgers, antacids, malt liquors, and cigarettes than about the major political candidates for elective office or about which scientific or aesthetic theory is best.

The Supreme Court's initial embrace of commercial speech did not, however, equate the constitutional status of commercial speech with that of political, artistic, or scientific speech. That is, the Court was willing to distinguish false, deceptive, or misleading commercial speech from commercial speech without these attributes and to refuse to give protection to the former. Plainly, the Court would not tolerate government regulation of "misleading" political speech. But even commercial speech that was not false, deceptive, or misleading received at least slightly less constitutional protection than did, say, political speech.

In the past few years, the Supreme Court's treatment of non-misleading commercial speech has not been readily predictable or consistent. If there has been a discernible trend beyond the Court's fits and starts, backtracking, and ambiguities, it has been in the direction of greater constitutional protection for commercial speech not thought deceptive or misleading, at least not in any narrow or direct way. Showing merely that the government regulation of such speech can be said to be broadly reasonable is not now sufficient to save the regulation.

It seems fair to say that the Court is less likely to reduce significantly than to maintain or expand its protection of commercial speech, especially commercial speech that is not deemed misleading. It is possible that the Court will cease, in practice if not in theory, to offer less constitutional protection to commercial than to political speech.

We might not find troubling the trend toward increasing protection for commercial speech, especially when such speech is not considered deceptive. What's wrong with rigorous constitutional protection for such speech? Why shouldn't we welcome—and at least ratify if not extend—such constitutional protection?

This book seeks to answer that question and to provoke others to offer better answers. In brief, the costs and conflicts in the basic values at stake in commercial speech cases are much more serious than the Supreme Court has so far recognized. I am not arguing for elitism, or for a "high" culture as opposed to a "low" culture. Instead, I appeal to broadly shared values. We should not assume that we once lived in a golden age of pristine noncommercialism, but we also should not merely rationalize what appears to be inevitable. We should not suppose that the unwashed masses are helpless before the subtle manipulations of contemporary advertising; we are, as a people, too experienced, too distracted, or too cynical for that.

We should not be surprised if a commercialized society affords whatever protection to commercial speech seems necessary, whether that protection is at the level of the federal Constitution or of other sorts of legal protection, or at a broader cultural level. It may be that to some degree, these forms of protection are interchangeable. And certainly, many factors affect the degree of a society's commercialization other than its legal or constitutional regime. But it seems unlikely that the degree of constitutional protection for commercial speech really makes no difference to the greater society, even over the long term.

Thus it is not surprising that a commercialized society eventually extends to commercial speech a constitutional protection beyond requiring a demonstration of merely the reasonableness of the regulation. This seems even less surprising if the society as a whole is leaning toward increasing commercialization and commercial influence and if the government regulatory apparatus has also expanded in scope and power over roughly the same time.

Our best understanding of freedom of speech may emphasize instead the need to protect the speech of the outcast and the relatively powerless. It is clear that constitutional rights are often won not through political weakness, need, or logic but through political and economic strength. Commercial elements are generally capable of lobbying and litigating on behalf of their own interests, and the rise of the New Deal regulatory state provided them with incentives and opportunities to do so. Often, though certainly not always, the overall commercial interest has been to avoid or reduce the government's restriction of commercial speech, however much some commercial groups might profit from restrictions on commercial speech.

Currently, an odd coalition of social and ideological forces favors the rigorous constitutional protection of commercial speech. But there is really no convincing reason to believe that in our cultural context, rigorous protection for commercial speech promotes the overall freedom and well-being of the public. In our culture, reducing the current degree of constitutional protection of commercial speech would, in general, enhance both freedom and well-being in the long term, but not because some commercial speech is false or narrowly deceptive or misleading. Rather, beyond a certain degree of cultural pervasiveness, commercial speech tends to undermine freedom, autonomy, and well-being.

However much we might prefer to pretend otherwise, our contemporary culture offers no meaningful institutional challenge to the deep and pervasive influence of commercialism and commercial speech. No cultural institution is currently both able and inclined to offer a meaningfully scaled "counterspeech" to the broad intended or unintended "message" of commercial speech in its various forms. Any reasonable regulation of commercial speech may be based on a narrower, particularized justification, such as promoting conservation, nutrition education, the knowledgeable purchase of securities, health, or the safety of the consumer or third parties. But any such reasonable regulation also tends, if only in a minimal and indirect way, to contribute in broader ways to the citizens' overall freedom, autonomy, and well-being.

The reasonable regulation of even nondeceptive commercial speech implicitly questions the proper role of commercialism and commercial speech in our culture. This does not mean that the government itself can be relied on to counterbalance the influence of commercialism. Nor does it mean that questioning the cultural sovereignty of commercialism by itself effectively validates real alternatives to commercialism. Rather, the reasonable regulation of commercial speech is merely one step in a complex process of legitimizing and facilitating free choices of either commercial or less commercial styles of life, consistent with democracy, the free speech clause, and the rest of the Constitution.

The Supreme Court's expansion of constitutional protection for commercial speech has been controversial. Commentators, in fact, are divided on whether or precisely how to extend constitutional protection to commercial speech. Unfortunately, this debate has usually been poorly structured, with the commentators often falling into definitional traps. Typically they begin with either a broad or a narrow range of purposes and values underlying the free speech clause. They then characterize wider conceptions of the values underlying freedom of speech in such a way as to encompass commercial speech within the scope of protected speech. At the same time, they construe narrower understandings of the values underlying free speech in such a way as to exclude commercial speech. The problem, of course, is that whether one ends up protecting commercial speech depends almost exclusively on well-worn and perhaps interminable debates over the scope of the purposes underlying the free speech clause.

This trap can be avoided, though, if by adopting a larger cultural focus, we can accept a broadly inclusive view of the reasons for protecting free speech while still concluding that the restrictions of commercial speech need only be reasonable in order to pass constitutional muster. The idea is to show that a relatively restrictive approach to commercial speech need not rest on either unappealing values or a narrow construal of the reasons for protecting free speech in the first place. We can and should accept an expansive, accommodating view of the values served by free speech and, on that basis, limit the Court's current protection for commercial speech.

Let us begin our analysis with a bit of folklore that seems almost culturally universal. Many of us grasp this insight at some time or another, and the sages commonly confirm it for us. Simply put, we believe that the relationship between acquiring market-produced goods and services and achieving the sort of happiness or well-being we most desire is, at best, dubious.

This insight antedates the anxieties of postindustrialism. We find essentially this thesis in the *Discourses* of Epictetus and in the *Analects* of Confucius. Similar themes are echoed by Jean-Jacques Rousseau in the *Discourse on the Origin of Inequality*, by Henry Thoreau in *Walden*, by Thoreau's colleague Ralph Waldo Emerson, and by the poet William Wordsworth. Karl Marx explored similar ideas in his *Economic and Philosophical Manuscripts*.

It is possible to dismiss each of these writers as somehow outside the mainstream. Epictetus was a Stoic given to asceticism. Confucius was denied familiarity with the miracles of modern industrial productivity. Rousseau, Thoreau, Emerson, and Wordsworth were at least vaguely Romantic figures, inclined toward the cult of the natural. Marx's attitude toward capitalism divided civilizations.

But a hasty dismissal of these writers is unwarranted. Their strictures reflect moments of common experience. Rousseau, for example, convincingly notes that we convert former luxuries into "negative" necessities whose absence creates a sense of deprivation and unhappiness but whose presence has largely lost the power to please. Our inevitable, and often rapid, psychological adjustment to the possession of most goods means that we derive only minimal satisfaction from them while at the same time becoming vulnerable to losing them, or to the fear of losing them. Rousseau thus recognizes a certain tread-mill-like, or vaguely addictive, quality in many consumer purchases.

The process that Rousseau describes does not apply only to commercial goods and services. Even though a promotion at work, for example, is not a tangible good or service, we may expect to be permanently happier if it is given to us. The promotion may in fact bring with it a sense of euphoria, followed by an upward adjustment in our expectations, thereby leaving us no better off.

Even though it may seem true at first, it is ultimately wrong to assume that getting what we want never makes us happier over the long term. This assumption may apply to commercial goods and services—does a heart transplant count?—and even to most noncommercial desires, including a promotion at work. Suppose, however, we want a stable, loving relationship on which we can rely without reservation. If we are happier as a result of creating such a relationship, should we assume that our happiness will be only temporary? Is the happiness of a deep, mature friendship really as transient as that derived from a coveted toy? Can't it be self-renewing, or at least decay more slowly than the happiness obtained from acquiring commercial goods?

We also cannot attribute this argument to Rousseau's idiosyncratic views, as we might also have cited Erasmus, Montaigne, or Durkheim. Immanuel Kant, no less than Rousseau or Henry David Thoreau, argues in his *Lectures on Ethics* that as our wealth and purchasing power increase, so do our wants and that the act of "satisfying" those wants is ultimately illusory, in that our appetite for more is quickly sharpened.

Marx was, of course, deeply interested in the possibility of non-commodified standards for human relationships. This idea, along with his interest in various forms of authenticity and alienation, was developed by later writers under the ambiguous rubric of "commodity fetishism." In an informal sense, *commodity fetishism* refers to excessive dependence on the ownership or market exchange of objects and services in the pursuit of self-respect or happiness. In this nontechnical sense, commodity fetishism means expanding the sphere of market exchange in ways that eventually impede the fullest and highest development of one's personality.

It is possible—if not true by definition—that market exchanges tend to maximize the wealth of the transacting parties. Market exchange is commonly thought to presume, embody, or maximize freedom in some sense and thereby to remove the necessity of government restriction of the voluntary exchange of non-misleading commercial information.

None of these arguments shows, however, that restraints on commercial speech undermine well-being or freedom in the fullest sense. The commodity fetishism theorists rightly observe that market theory does not establish that freedom and well-being are maximized when markets convert the broad range of different kinds of social relationships into market-based relationships. Freedom and happiness may well not be maximized when the logic of market exchange affects the nature and quality of nonmarket relationships by making them seem peripheral or ineligible.

Attempting to satisfy social needs—including those often fulfilled by friends or family—through commodity exchange may not so much maximize our wealth as convert us into different if not incommensurable people—who seek beneficial economic exchanges at the expense of worthier and more fulfilling goals. That is, we may not be better off but, instead, worse in all but a narrowly pecuniary sense.

Perhaps it is impossible to avoid our culture's gradual shift in emphasis from production—initially driven in part by otherworldly considerations—to the immediacy of consumption. Production requires consumption, of course, and increasing production requires that the act of consumption be legitimate and unstigmatized. But we are not necessarily made freer or happier by commercializing our lives, even if all our choices are voluntary and not narrowly coerced.

Through its eventual pervasiveness, commodification is largely self-justifying. Commodification as a lifestyle of persons and societies is a matter of degree and proceeds almost imperceptibly. But once commodification becomes sufficiently widespread, any substantial departure from exchange as the primary vehicle of satisfying human needs comes to seem unnatural, risky, sentimental, outdated, confused, alien, lonely, deviant, utopian, sacrificial, or simply inconceivable. Once commodification is sufficiently ubiquitous, it assumes an entrenched, loosely monopolistic character and may even reduce our ability to imagine, pursue, or appreciate other ways of living.

This entrenching process takes place even if the logic of the market fails to maximize human fulfillment. Writers such as Thorstein Veblen, R. H. Tawney, John Maynard Keynes, and John Kenneth Galbraith have variously argued that the modern emphasis on fulfillment through consumption has been less successful than the economic textbooks might lead us to imagine. We can test this view not only by introspection and reflection but also by social science, especially survey evidence.

Adam Smith, a writer usually sensitive to the virtues of markets, concluded:

> Wealth and greatness are mere trinkets of frivolous utility, no more adapted for procuring ease of body or tranquility of mind than the tweezer-cases of the lover of toys; and like them too, more troublesome to the person who carries them about with him than all the advantages they can afford him are commodious.[1]

We may fairly conclude that doubts about the relationship between consumption and happiness are not confined to those least sympathetic to the market economy.

Let us now consider some of the evidence regarding the relationship between consumption and well-being. Our well-being or happiness—insofar as it is affected by consumption—depends not only on our own lifestyle choices but also on those of others. We might, for example, be happy with what we might call a consumptive lifestyle for ourselves, but only if many other people choose another lifestyle. We may individually benefit in certain ways if most of us focus on consumption, but these effects may not necessarily predominate. Perhaps we all will demand the same goods, for which there may be no good substitutes, thus driving up their prices faster than the expansion of supply or the economies of scale can reduce them. This is not to argue what is likely, only what is possible, and it is possible that most of us will suffer if most of us focus on commercial consumption. Our own welfare as consumers may suffer if too many persons similarly emphasize consumption as their source of happiness. We may well be happier as consumers, for example, if more of those around us devote their lives to nurturing, virtue, noncommercial creativity and invention, or public service in a broad sense. Are we really better off with fewer heroes, saints, and friends and more shoppers?

This effect does not by itself show that there is anything intrinsically wrong with a consumptionist lifestyle. There is nothing inherently wrong with being devoted, say, to one's farming operation as a source of happiness. This would mean concentrating on production as opposed to consumption. But we might be chagrined, and clearly worse off, if we discovered that too many other people were taking up farming, thereby making our other material and nonmaterial needs were more difficult to meet. The market, of course, usually reduces the number of farmers to some economic if not cultural optimum, but some persons may be much happier as farmers than in some alternative role into which the market steers them.

It is possible that just as the price of medical services tends to drop when the number of physicians rises, so the rewards of a consumptionist lifestyle could diminish—perhaps through something like congestion or mutual interference—if too many of us focused on consumption, thus providing incentives to reduce our concentration on consumption as the key to happiness. If we all can afford, and actually buy, the most fashionable sunglasses, running shoes, and the like, such items will lose their appeal. Indeed, we derive almost no gratification from owning numerous appliances that would be beyond price for Louis XIV.

Likewise, we may assume that the market process works reasonably well in the case of physicians, but we cannot extend the logic of this process by means of assumption. The decision to become or remain a physician, for example, and to seek fulfillment through consumption are clearly different. No one becomes a physician without consciously and explicitly choosing to go to medical school, however ill informed or casual the decision and however unfamiliar the alternatives may be. At least we are aware of the alternative of going or not going to medical school. In many cases, we choose with reasonable freedom to go to medical school, even if others would be disappointed by a contrary choice.

Few of us, nevertheless, consciously and explicitly weigh our choice to emphasize consumption as the main road to happiness. There are no application forms to fill out. There is no particular moment of decision. We may not even be aware that we have made, or are repeatedly reinforcing, such a choice. How, after all, would we know that we are emphasizing, or even overemphasizing, consumption? Compared with whom? What if most of the people around us seem roughly as consumption oriented as we are? How would we know that our consumptionism is making us pay an unnecessary price? How could we do more than guess at the real costs and benefits of lessening our emphasis on consumption? What would this transition involve?

In our society, the alternatives to emphasizing consumption may seem unrealistic. In fact, once we reach a point at which consumptionism seems normal for us and is widely exhibited by our peers, it may be too late. That is, the costs of reducing our focus on consumption may at that point be quite large, psychologically, socially, or financially. For example, it may be hard for us to acquire skills that we have abandoned or never learned, like trying to learn a foreign language without an accent. We may be locked into daunting financial commitments, leading us to rationalize away alternatives that no longer seem feasible. We do not calculate how easy it would be to quit smoking, taking addictive drugs, or overindulging in food or alcohol simply by comparing two static pictures of ourselves, before and after. The fact that we would have been better off had we never started down a consumptionist path does not mean that it is practical now to turn back. This goes to the problem of real freedom.

The problem is rather a deep one. Even if we were free to move our focus from consumption—once we have become habituated to consumption—it may not be worthwhile to attempt to change. It is possible that a life of consumption may actually enhance the psychological rewards of de-emphasizing consumption. Perhaps the shock of contrast once we abandon consumptionism would make the transition more enjoyable. But this is hardly guaranteed. Any lifestyle involves sunk costs, unanticipated commitments, loss of certain potential abilities, and personality changes. A life oriented toward consumption affects our capacities, whether or not we recognize those effects. Some of the capacities, aptitudes, and skills necessary to enjoy nonconsumptive ways of living may be irreparably impaired or permanently stunted through disuse.

To the extent this is so, we would have to face the unpleasant realization that as consumptionists, we are both less free and less happy than we could have been but that for some of us, it is not realistically possible to improve our circumstances or even to capture much of what we have lost. In a pervasively commercialized culture, perhaps this point of no return commonly arrives at a surprisingly early age, and perhaps we all sense that this is the case.

In any event, we need not choose between optimistic and pessimistic scenarios in this regard in order to examine some of the evidence of the links, or lack thereof, between consumption and well-being. Much of the survey evidence does not pertain directly to consumer spending but, instead, to income or wealth and happiness. In the abstract, therefore, it seems improper to treat income as a proxy for consumer spending. But what is unfortunate for American retirement prospects is fortunate for our inquiry. Unlike some other societies, ours does not radically distinguish in practice between income and consumer spending. Our collective private savings rate is both historically and internationally low. In fact, more than 90 percent of American incomes are devoted to consumption.

Given these generally low savings rates, those people who save an even lower percentage of their income may be unhappy or insecure about that very fact. But at least they are obtaining more consumer goods, presumably, than they would have if they had set aside more money for savings. In any event, we take advantage of our current general inability, or disinclination, to save privately, by treating income as a proxy for consumer spending.

For many economists, the voluntary consumption of goods and services is not the beginning but the end of any serious inquiry into the relationship between consumption and happiness. Any disturbing gap between consumption and happiness is assumed to reflect matters such as force or fraud, changes in taste, or unexpected defects or

dangers in the products consumed. Many of us generalize and sim-
plify such an outlook by assuming in practice that money and
spending money are associated with happiness. Many of us suppose
that if our incomes and expenditure levels were, say, 20 percent
higher, we would be significantly happier over the long term.

According to most of the available social science evidence, however, these beliefs are likely to be wrong. Consider first the undeniable
general and quite substantial increase in American living standards in
the decades following World War II, despite the various periods of
recession, stagflation, and low wage and productivity growth. For
long periods, real income rose substantially, but during the same
periods, reported levels of satisfaction remained the same or declined
slightly. During some of this time, the number of respondents
describing themselves as "very happy" steadily decreased, a trend that
was most pronounced among the most affluent.

We might be tempted to dismiss these results as the reflection of
unique historical events. Naturally, we might imagine, a pre-*Sputnik*
America with few economic rivals would, all else being equal, be
happier than a post-Vietnam, post-Watergate America. In response,
however, we could contend that, first, the trends in reported subjective satisfaction have not recently been reversed. As the data questioning the link between consumption and happiness are further
extended in time, it becomes increasingly implausible to dismiss
them as merely reflecting unique historical events.

Second, anyone who tries to explain the data on consumption and
happiness by appealing to broader historical or cultural events comes
perilously close to undermining, rather than rescuing, the claim that
consumption leads to happiness. Why not suppose, for example, that
collective happiness is affected by an unpopular, divisive, or unsuccessful war on the scale of the Vietnam War, independent of the war's
effects on our collective income or spending? This is not to endorse

such a thesis but to point out that it is of little service to those who maintain that consumption is associated with happiness.

Third, the weakness of the relationship between income or spending and happiness is supported by a surprisingly large and diverse number of studies and perspectives. The evidence extends far beyond the American context. The minimal connection—if not the lack thereof—between income and well-being apparently applies to most developed countries, even though some studies, or interpretations of studies, reach the opposite conclusion.

In fact, though, some evidence suggests that the link between income and happiness in the United States is growing weaker over time. It has been found, as well, that despite the geographic regional differences in income levels around 1970, the residents of southern states judged the quality of their lives slightly more positively than did the residents of other regions. Far less decisively—but nonetheless intriguingly—a survey of twenty-two winners of large lotteries found no significant difference between their happiness levels and the happiness levels of controls. More broadly, the research suggests that wealth does not tend to reduce the amount of worrying in which one engages; wealth instead simply changes the subject of the worrying.

As a general rule, then, though with some qualifications, happiness does not appear to be meaningfully linked in our culture with income and wealth or, presumably, with consumer spending. But this general finding is less plausible in the specific case of the poor, whether at the level of relatively poor nation-states or of the relatively poor in a particular nation-state. Surely the poor would be better off with higher levels of consumption, whatever other reasons there may be for relieving poverty.

There is actually some controversy over whether poor societies are significantly unhappier than rich societies. In any event, because the United States does not fall into the former category, seeking to increase our collective happiness by raising consumer spending does not seem like a promising strategy. Of greater interest is the relationship between income and happiness among the poor in our own society.

Abolishing poverty is among our foremost public moral duties, whether or not such actions have any effect on reported levels of subjective happiness. In any event, any declining marginal utility of wealth is of limited relevance to the poor, and the spending of money can at least relieve some forms of physical distress, such as extreme hunger, pain, and cold. It is thus not surprising that poor people in our society report greater unhappiness. Perhaps they compare themselves with the better-off more readily than the citizens of poor countries compare themselves with foreigners.

Assuming some negative correlation in our society between poverty and happiness, however, does not carry the analysis very far. For example, we should not lose sight of the obvious. A person who is both cold and poor typically benefits more from actually obtaining a warm coat than from unfettered commercial speech about coats, even when the indirect benefits of advertising in enhancing quality and driving down prices are considered.

Undoubtedly, the poor benefit from, say, the vigorous advertising of prescription drug prices, at least under some health insurance and welfare policies. But there also are costs for the poor in uninhibited commercial speech, even in this narrow sphere. Prescription drug price advertising may impair the commercial viability of small, independent pharmacies owned by persons with a long-term stake in a poor community. There may thus be some trade-off between price and the availability of a pharmacist who has ties to the poor, knows their needs, recognizes them as individuals, and can establish the sort of caring relationships that may be important to their health or personal happiness.

We should also bear in mind that not all the nondeceptive, non-misleading advertising targeted to the poor encourages price competition among prescription drugs. Disproportionately, billboards and other forms of advertising aimed at poor neighborhoods push items such as tobacco, alcohol, and the latest but soon obsolete versions of athletic apparel loosely, albeit expensively, associated with a celebrated sports figure. Whether the uninhibited hawking of hundred-dollar athletic shoes to the poor actually promotes their well-being is not beyond dispute, issues of paternalism and condescension aside. The poor do not exercise perfect control over the nature of the commercial messages to which they and their children are exposed daily. It may be difficult not to be part of a nearly "captive audience" for broad commercial themes, and the underlying message of consumptionism may, on balance, be socially harmful.

As we have seen, the typical inability of consumption to generate lasting satisfaction among the wider population has been variously diagnosed. When contemporary writers discuss consumption-based lifestyles, they typically return, with some of the classic writers and the introspections of many others, to ideas such as self-defeat, the "hedonic treadmill," being "trapped," or being "addicted." These and similar ideas clearly do not reflect conditions of either happiness or freedom. When we manage to do well economically, we typically rediscover Rousseau's insight that a short-lived sense of gratification gives way gradually to an adjusted level of expectation and aspiration, under which we take our prosperity for granted and derive no further happiness from our elevated status.

If happiness for most of us turns out not to be a matter of getting and spending, we can still appreciate some of the stronger correlates of happiness. Culturally, we have not been able to advertise ourselves out of the fact that happiness, or the lack thereof, is more affected by matters such as the nature and character of our work, leisure, basic beliefs, and social relationships, including family and friendships. Heredity may also play some role. These sources of satisfaction often do not depend on the market-based consumption of goods and services. Of course, neither social factors nor wealth and consumption can dictate levels of happiness if, as is sometimes argued, our typical range of happiness and unhappiness has biological limits.

In a way, it is surprising that a society as pervasively commercialized as ours has not unwittingly deformed itself so as to become more sensitive to the pleasures of consumption and less sensitive to those of, say, lifelong friendship. After all, a commercialized society would at least superficially thrive by increasing the payoffs for the options toward which it steers its members and by reducing the payoffs for the options it marginalizes. Yet we still feel, at least vaguely and without prompting, the imbalances in our lives. Of course, it is not in our interest to be so consumed by consumption that we find unemployment, layoffs, or a lower income to be overwhelming, because this may also reflect nearly inescapable differences between consumption and, say, friendship or stimulating work as sources of satisfaction. Although wealth and income may be subject to a law of diminishing returns, friendship or stimulating work do not seem to fade at the same rate, whether or not we appreciate this difference. The positive effects of a strengthened friendship do not fade in the same way that those of a salary increase might. Our usual experience seems to be that friendship, work, or leisure does not generate entrapping, self-defeating "treadmills" analogous to those we experience with consumption.

It is not easy to measure the "quality" of work or friendship, but we should not use measurement problems to rationalize away the basic message. We can assess our friendships and family relationships even if we have increasing difficulty imagining what deep, permanent friendships might be like. Incidentally, the evidence seems clear that casual visits between neighbors, family conversation beyond mere interpersonal coordination, and time spent jointly at family meals all have diminished in the United States since midcentury. No doubt these losses were in part the by-product of healthy, or at least inescapable, cultural and economic changes, including greater physical mobility. But their unintended or unexpected character and their connection with other social changes do not prevent their harmful effects on subjective well-being.

Some of these social losses are compensated by increases in other forms of basic sociability that would otherwise be unavailable. An adult may spend less time with friends, neighbors, or family because he or she has, perhaps for the first time, obtained employment with an interesting and rewarding social dimension. These sorts of jobs may more than make up for the other sociability losses involved. Of course, not all employment, whatever the income level, has this socially redeeming character.

Why we remain on the hedonic treadmill is a complex question with many partial answers. Most of us make large ongoing financial commitments, such as a mortgage on a house. One fragmentary but plausible explanation is that our short-term time horizons may play a role. Some relationships, creative work, and leisure activities with enormous potential payoffs over time carry a stiff price over the short term. Nonetheless, we might be better off in the long term if we did commit ourselves to doing something initially painful, like learning a foreign language, learning how to use a computer, or taking up the reading of music or a musical instrument. These activities are investments. Even if they are not unpleasant, they may be more uncomfortable at first than is some passive recreational activity. In that sense, they may require a short-term sacrifice. And this assumes that we have not already culturally deformed ourselves to the point of losing our aptitude for, or even the long-term capacity to enjoy, the activities in question.

There are other explanations of our inability or unwillingness to get off the hedonic treadmill. We do not live in a culture that offers neutral commercial and noncommercial solutions to life's anomalies. If we did, we all could simply brush off, for example, contradictory cultural messages to eat fast food and be fashionably thin. For many persons, especially the young, such incompatible commercialized messages are difficult to dismiss or to reconcile. If too many messages and choices concern commercial consumption, we may simply not be able to build a healthy identity or self-image not tied to commercial values.

We should not deny, however, the beneficial effects of commercial speech in general or of commercial advertising in particular. Even though wealth may be inequitably distributed, there is typically more of it in a commercial society in which such speech is screened only for fraud or deception, narrowly defined. Society as a whole benefits, for example, not only from news stories about a new drug that provides a unique and safe cure for a serious disease but also from accurate commercial advertisements regarding that drug.

Likewise, it would be difficult to deny the adverse effects on wages and employment if many of us abruptly abandoned our customary levels of consumption in favor of communing with nature or writing poetry. The specter of mass unemployment caused by a burgeoning interest in poetry readings does not seem likely, however, and reducing the level of constitutional free speech protection for commercial speech also does not seem likely to lead to such consequences. Those who find themselves burdened by excessive disposable income may wish, for example, to augment the effective market demand of the poorest among us.

For some persons, searching for and selecting consumer goods is itself utility enhancing. Indeed, we can sometimes overcome our sense of social fragmentation not through our increasingly rare common entertainments but through common ad campaigns. One way of coping with depression is to go shopping. Whether shopping amounts to a general solution to the problem of a lack of well-being is, however, doubtful. In any event, we can go shopping under all sorts of commercial speech regimes, including those upholding any reasonable government regulation of even nondeceptive speech.

More important, we need not endorse any alleged distinction between natural, healthy, authentic, or uncontrived consumer needs and their opposites. At least for our culture, disentangling the natural from the contrived or the artificially stimulated seems difficult and perhaps even unrewarding. For instance, the desire to have an air conditioner may seem like a contrived, cultivated need until we go to live in a sweltering climate. It seems that most of our desires have some minimal basis in the vaguely natural, along with a complex overlay of the more or less contrived and arbitrary. That is, we do not have a solely natural need for clothing in the form of Armani suits, or for Armani suits as opposed to some other equally fashionable or steeply priced suits.

We should not, however, stigmatize contrived or artificially induced desires and their gratification, even though there is something rather circular about a commercial culture's claiming to be able to fulfill the particular forms of desires that it has itself largely cultivated. In a sense, it hardly matters how efficient an arsonist is in putting out his own blaze. Our commercial culture accommodates our desire to, as it were, fill in the perceived holes in our lives. It sells us the shovels, and we buy them voluntarily. But it is also our commercial culture that has in large measure convinced us that the holes exist, that we ought to fill them, and that shovels are just the thing for that task.

Once the culture of commercial speech becomes too pervasive, it turns into a closed, self-perpetuating, self-reinforcing, self-validating system. Choice becomes a choice among commercial alternatives, often more alike than dissimilar. Although this outcome reflects the logic of the market more than a conspiratorial plot, the result is to impeach the logic of insisting on strong free speech protection for commercial speech, given the broad values or purposes underlying free speech in the first place.

If our responses to truthful commercial speech are not often manipulated in any crude or narrow sense but also are not really autonomous or independent of our pervasive commercial culture, why is such unregulated speech more consistent with, say, the free speech value of autonomy than with the regulation of commercial speech aimed at enhancing autonomy? Some people may suppose that no regulation of nondeceptive commercial speech can promote autonomy. But in a thoroughly commercialized society, this argument begins to lose its plausibility, even if we assume, unrealistically, that we created our commercialized society freely and with complete knowledge of all its consequences. For example, a regulation requiring cigarettes to refer to disease or the likely difficulty of quitting may be said to promote, as much as to impair, the autonomy of potential consumers, if not of the cigarette sellers.

Finally, we need not overestimate the power of commercial speech. Even when backed by the resources and visibility of a McDonalds Corporation, the power of commercial speech campaigns is limited. Neither particular advertisements nor broader advertising campaigns are always effective, even when they have been well researched and well financed: the majority of prospective new brands that are test-marketed are not marketed nationally. The battle of the marketplace has many casualties.

Even when advertising affects behavior, the effect may be temporary. And when the effects are more enduring, they may amount only to switches among rival brands by established users, rather than new consumers for any of the rival brands. Some advertising—consider the various recent plans and pricing claims of the leading long distance telephone carriers—is widely disliked. As a result, many ads are simply drowned out, unnoticed or unremembered in the ongoing daily proliferation of commercial speech.

This conclusion does not mean, however, that commercial speech, or commercial advertising more narrowly, does not have important long-term effects, intended or unintended, on American culture and decision making. Commercial advertising is in some sense a zero-sum game, with one product's gain being another's loss. The proliferation of ads, however, does not lead simply to a process of mutual conflict, let alone mutual annihilation.

Commercial advertisements that compete or conflict at one level may, at a more basic level, mutually reinforce one another. Such effects may not be intended or even recognized. Consider that physical waves in the natural world may interfere with and cancel one another out if they arrive out of phase but may also reinforce one another, thereby heightening their impact, if they arrive in phase.

Note, for example, that an advertisement for a particular drug is reinforced not only by advertising and commercial speech in general and by ads for noncompeting drugs, but even by ads for directly competing drugs. An underlying message of such speech, explicit or implicit, intended or unintended, is that medical, psychological, and even social problems can and should be addressed by taking drugs. Competing drug manufacturers agree on the preferability of drug to nondrug solutions to a remarkably wide range of problems. Indeed, a drug manufacturer who failed to act on this belief would be inviting a competitive disadvantage.

This process of mutual reinforcement and "generalization" seems to operate whether it is intended or even recognized by anyone, including the audience. The sellers' state of mind in this respect is of special interest. A seller who consciously intends to promote consumptionism as a style of life and who wishes to establish consumption as the preferred solution to personal and social problems should arouse some public concern. On the other hand, a seller who intends no such message but only a narrower commercial message less obviously or less deeply implicates the values and purposes underlying our desire to protect freedom of speech.

Thus even when an ad fails to sell a product, it still may legitimize and support commercial consumption as a way of living and of addressing various sorts of problems. Consumers must reject or ignore most of the ads to which they are exposed. But they may be less resistant to, if not gradually overwhelmed by, the predominance of the broader implied message touting commercialized consumption. That message cannot be reduced to what brand of what good to consume.

The typical viewer, we are told, will have seen two million television commercials by the time of his or her retirement. It is said that we will have devoted a full year and a half of our lifetime to watching commercials.[2] With a figure of this magnitude, it can hardly matter if we do not absorb each commercial. Accordingly, commercial sponsorship is now increasingly interwoven into programming and the underlying televised event. Even though we may be out of the room or electronically suppress many of the traditionally distinct commercials, we should note that many children's television programs are themselves only thinly disguised commercial advertisements pitched to an audience whose values are not yet well formed.

The forces seeking to engender commercialized values are powerful. We are told that each day, 12 billion display ads, 2.5 million radio ads, and 300,000 television commercials are generated. The formerly largely commercial-free Internet is being opened to advertising. Commercial underwriting announcements on public television are longer now. The proliferation of ads has driven commercial sponsors further afield into many previously unsullied territories, in a collectively self-defeating attempt to avoid ad clutter.

This near ubiquity of commercial speech—in public parks, on every exposed inch of sports in general, in public schools, inside spacecraft, on clothing, on the sides of rockets, on the Internet, and even projected onto cathedrals—would not be so troubling were it not for our culture's lack of any reasonably proportionate counterspeech. This disparity is enhanced by the political, noncommercial—and hence not subject to regulation—speech of commercial enterprises. Philip Morris and Seagrams, for example, promote their corporate interests by means of commercial speech as well as political speech and political quasi speech, largely in the form of massive contributions to, and lobbying of, both major political parties. But in our culture, no established institution currently devotes much energy or resources to providing a proportionate counterspeech for the broad implicit messages of our commercialized culture.

Some elements of many cultural institutions speak against consumption-oriented styles of life. But even their message is mixed and is overridden by the larger culture. Public television and public radio are increasingly dependent on commercial messages. Even though universities are traditionally skeptical of commercialism, they do not wish, for a number of reasons, to oppose it unequivocally. University courses' content, grading, and selection policies have an increasingly commercial favor. Most mainstream environmentalists attack waste in consumption or seek to ensure that resources will be available for future consumption.

Few dissident religious or political movements in the United States actively and explicitly target consumptionism. Furthermore, any local religious leader who speaks out against excessive commercialization may offend or annoy all those whose livelihood depends on commercial sales. Ultimately, financial donations to church institutions, programs, and charities must derive from commerce.

Churches and other religious institutions may decry the commercialization of various religious holidays and sometimes express broader concerns. But protestations against the commercialization of Christmas are, by now, harmless and ineffective. Indeed, the phenomenon of the commercialization of Christmas has become so familiar that it is now beginning, paradoxically, to raise new issues. We are, for example, unsure how far the commercialization of Christmas can go without becoming self-destructive. Consider the analogy to a parasitic organism and its biological host. The parasite wants to thrive relative to, or at the expense of, the host. But if the parasite draws too much energy and resources from the host, or otherwise weakens it, the parasite itself may suffer.

Ironically, the commercialization of Christmas has prospered while draining the holiday of religious meaning. It is unclear, however, how far this process can continue without commerce itself beginning to suffer. We have become willing to overspend in connection with a holiday. But if Christmas becomes solely a commercial event, would that really be good for commerce? What if the season evolved into a freestanding cultural imperative to feel generous and mildly euphoric? Would that be enough to sustain the compulsion to overspend on gifts?

There has never been a close logical connection between the message of peace on earth and shopping till you drop. Once the sense that the Christmas season is special is gone, why should we all participate, with undiminished enthusiasm, in the often-unappreciated consumptionist frenzy? Perhaps there is a point at which the commercialization of Christmas will begin to limit its own expansion, but we do not seem to have reached it yet.

It will be interesting to see how the celebration of Kwanzaa fares in this regard. From the beginning, the founders of Kwanzaa have repeatedly emphasized its noncommercial character. Can this continue? Or will Kwanzaa be gradually changed through commercialization, with the only issue being who profits from the commercialization process?

Parenthetically, we should note that the commercial parasitism-biological host issue does not arise only in the context of religious holidays. The evidence is as yet unclear, but one can easily argue that from the standpoint of the athletic contest, commercial influences on various professional and college sports have become so repellant, distorted, and arbitrary that there may soon be less money to be made in this area. Beyond some point, it may be difficult to undermine the sport without undermining the desire to spend money related in some way to that sport.

Families typically do not sell goods and services within the family unit. But parents can in various ways transmit commercial values, just as they can and often do reinforce noncommercial values. Most people do not spend most of their day doing this; rather, they bring their socialized commercial values to the family, thus commercializing the family itself.

The current and foreseeable future balance of cultural institutional forces thus seems reasonably clear, based not so much on the formal gathering of evidence as on a casual observation of the common culture. Many defenders of strong constitutional protection for commercial speech would not deny the pervasiveness of commercial speech. Fewer people accept the stronger claim that genuine freedom of speech requires at least a rough equality of resources among contending forces. But all that we need to acknowledge here is that in our current circumstances, no single cultural institution or set of institutions is both able and inclined to provide any substantial "countervailing" speech to offset the broad, reinforced, intended, or unintended influences of commercial speech. A "bias"—in the sense of a distinct, significant vector of cultural forces—toward some form of consumption of commercial goods and services is characteristic of our society. Some persons are, for various reasons, less affected by this cultural bias than others. This would be true, however, of even the most dominant cultural tendencies in any society.

This state of affairs is not the outcome of a struggle between opposing camps. We live in a highly commercialized society, which may or may not reflect the actual desires of the major commercial speakers. In this respect, there may be a gap between the desires of the commercial speakers and the effects of their commercial speech. Commercial speakers intend and welcome the eventual purchase of whatever good or service they are trying to sell, and they may not deny similar opportunities to other commercial speakers. But in the extreme case, the collective result of all this commercial speech may not be desired or intended by any commercial speaker.

This is not a complex argument. Presumably, no one sheep herder wants everyone's sheep, collectively, to overgraze and destroy the commons. But a sheep herder as an individual may find that it does not pay to make alternative arrangements. Likewise, farmers as individuals may find that allowing their pesticides to wash into the common stream is the best solution. No individual farmer, we may assume, contributes enough pesticides to the stream to significantly impair the water's quality. If every farmer follows this logic, though, the stream may become dangerously polluted. The interesting point is that this outcome may not have been intended by all, or even by any, of the farmers, even if they all foresaw the aggregate result.

Similarly, we could imagine that some, if not all, major commercial speakers face a conflict between their preferences for their own enterprises and their preferences for the direction and character of their society. Each commercial speaker may believe that if she does not speak for her product whenever and wherever her individual advantage dictates, her product may eventually fail in the competition of the market. Others, after all, are currently touting products that can be readily substituted for hers. The logic of the market may thus require her to speak commercially.

From this argument, though, we cannot infer that she wishes, for herself or for future generations, to live in the culture that will result from all commercial speakers' following a similar market logic. In the extreme, no commercial speaker may wish such a collective outcome. Each commercial speaker may, without any inconsistency, wish both to promote her particular product and to live in a culture less commercialized than our own.

To avoid misunderstanding, we should specify that a culture of consumption need not be biased toward what Veblen called *conspicuous consumption*. That is, it does not have to be biased toward consuming the most ostentatious or most expensive goods. Instead, we should expect fluctuations in society's consumption patterns over time, in which the emphasis switches from the exotic to the plain and functional and back again, in accordance with fashion and economics.

Let us consider an interesting objection, based on an analogy between economics and politics. One might claim that a parallel argument could be made for the political sphere, particularly for the competing electoral candidacies of opposing parties or ideologies. Don't competing electoral candidacies, like some physical waves or most commercial speech, tend, at least unintentionally, to reinforce certain basic, shared political themes so as to "bias" public thinking in ways not challenged by other institutions? If so, isn't there a case for political reform or regulation to limit these biasing effects?

A debate continually dominated by a range of similar ideologies may tend, intentionally or unintentionally, to delegitimize our other political options. How to respond to this possibility so as to promote the underlying logic of democracy is a crucial question. But because the cultures of electoral politics and the commercial market are different, it is a question that we will not answer here.

Most commercial advertising in all media does not refer invidiously to, let alone focus on, a competitor's good or service. When ads do make comparisons, they often do so with a light touch, only rarely implying that a competitor's product or service is in any sense unworthy, shoddy, or dangerous. Parenthetically, we might note that some of the major players in the long distance telephone service market have come close to "negative" commercial advertisements. Not surprisingly, the viewers' responses to these sorts of commercials have been unsympathetic. Accordingly, the content and tone of some of the more recent ads then shifted in a positive direction. Perhaps the telephone carriers' behavior started with the market dominance at the time by a few competitors, combined with a sense that most viewers would choose from among those few competitors and be unlikely to reduce the volume of their long distance calls, whatever their reaction to the advertising.

More typically, though, matters stand as they did decades ago, when the advertising pioneer Claude Hopkins observed in *Scientific Advertising* that it simply does not pay to knock the competitor's product. It is fair to say, however, that this practice is not as regularly observed in electoral politics.

In American politics, invidious comparisons are common. The precise effects of "negative" or "attack" ads in political campaigns are complex and difficult to track, but there is little doubt that generally they repel the public. Such ads contribute to voter disenchantment, apathy, cynicism, and a low turnout on election day. Many attack ads convey the idea that one's electoral opponent is unworthy of office, whereas most commercial ads, including most comparative ads, do not suggest, by analogy, that one is better off doing without than buying the competitor's product.

Overall, electoral speech by competing candidates is not as mutually reinforcing as in the case of competing commercial ads. In some ways, the lack of parallelism is easily understandable. Pepsi's goal is not to sell more sodas than Coca Cola does, whatever the dollar volume involved. Even if Coca Cola is by far the market leader, it cannot be happy with outselling its rivals, but at low volumes. For electoral candidates, on the other hand, the analogous outcome may be acceptable; indeed, winning on the basis of an abysmally low voter turnout may be deemed a success.

The nearly exclusive exposition of the mainstream political ideologies makes any alternative seem unrealistic if not inconceivable. This is a central problem for democratic theory, but one that need not be resolved here if we accept one of two views: First, mainstream political speech delegitimizes some or all non-mainstream political speech, and in the name of democracy, we should do something about this. Or second, there is a difference in the ways in which commercial speech marginalizes noncommercial speech and the ways in which mainstream political speech marginalizes non-mainstream political speech, and these differences justify regulation of commercial speech that would be unacceptable in political speech.

Many advertisements can be described as *propositional*. For instance, a full-page newspaper ad for a particular grocery store chain features a particular brand of pork and beans at a particular volume and price. Although not all commercial ads are based on this model, most have some similarities. But advertising has undergone some noticeable qualitative changes over time. Some ads, including many of the most prominent, are now largely imagistic or atmospheric, seeking only to create a mood. Some may attempt to link a product with a celebrity, an appealing noncelebrity, or even a not particularly appealing but somehow interestingly depicted noncelebrity. No proposition, promise, or representation is expressed or implied.

Such ads are neither true nor false, at least not in any narrow sense. They are not descriptive or misleading in any similarly narrow, traditional sense. In fact, they may attempt to leave the true and false behind rather than embrace falsehood.

To the extent that freedom of speech is a matter of seeking some propositional truth, even of a commercial sort, protecting ads that do not implicate truth or falsity is, in this respect, misguided. Many ads do not follow this model, and even the most vaguely imagistic ad can be misleading. The seller always believes that at least some of us should eventually buy the touted product, or a related one, that the product will somehow redeem itself to us as consumers, and, in particular, that buying, using, displaying, or even just thinking about or being associated with the product will make the consumer better off.

In some cases, it is the commercial itself or its ambience that is the real product. Sometimes references to earlier commercials are emphasized. The more tangible product at the store is secondary. In addition, the multimedia ad campaigns, and not the entertainment programs, may cross group barriers. In the era of digital television, we will be linked not by the common viewing of the *Ed Sullivan Show* but by the new McDonalds or Pepsi campaigns. The product is a reminder or a claim of association with the commercial. But even though this kind of analysis can be illuminating, it has limitations. The market requires that more than the commercial itself be consumed. Consuming the commercial itself is a choice and has opportunity costs. Consuming the commercial may have various intangible good consequences for the sponsor. But our consuming these commercials does not, by itself, line the pockets of their producers. Rather, we must eventually buy something associated with the commercial, or else the producer of the commercials cannot survive.

For our purposes, it really does not matter whether consumers are said to consume the commercial or the underlying product, as there is always the implicit claim that the product, if not the commercial itself, will justify the outcome. If the advertiser is trying to change the consumer's tastes or standards, he will appeal to those consumer standards. At least up to this point, even the most exotic commercial implies that the consumer will not get a raw deal, based on those standards. What is usually foremost in consumers' minds are matters such as their happiness and well-being, which are, however, standards that a culture of consumption may fail.

Even if commercials or the act of consumption made us happy according to our own standards, we would still wonder whether such happiness came at a price in freedom. Certainly, we cannot dispute the superiority of a well-stocked American supermarket over a shortage-ridden, Soviet-style food emporium. But increasingly, there is a danger of confusing a diversity of choice among market goods and services with freedom itself, in the form of a diversity in basic ways of living and thinking. Being able to choose among brands and products is a poor sort of freedom if our culture prevents us, realistically if not formally, from seriously considering less consumption-oriented ways of living.

More particularly, if we participate in consumption fads simply on the basis of their popularity or of a "bandwagon" effect, we are not choosing autonomously. We may instead be trading our autonomy for subjective enjoyment, reassurance, or a sense of community. But this sort of faddish consumption community, however tempting, falls short of the deeper, worthier, more stable community we may really be seeking.

In a culture in which consumption is dominant and only occasionally challenged, commercial speech may well change our basic tastes, capacities, and judgments in ways that we do not even recognize, let alone anticipate. This can be a freedom-destroying process. Some of these changes, such as expecting more rigorous standards for product warranties, may be benign. Other changes, including a loss or stunting of our capacities to value, enjoy, or even envision nonmarket solutions to problems, are not.

To claim that a "free market" in nondeceptive commercial speech makes us freer raises serious problems of measurement and commensurability. Why are we supposed to be unequivocally freer if we have lost our range of options, however much well-being they might have afforded or still be capable of affording? Why are we unequivocally freer if our sense of what is desirable and feasible readily matches what commercial markets can easily supply? Why must a democratic society interpret its constitutional guarantees of freedom to confirm these largely unintended, unconscious, and often unrecognized effects?

Our freedom would also be diminished if we lived in a culture that uniformly disdained consumptionist lifestyles. According to the evidence, even though we might well be happier in such a culture, we would have lost the option of pursuing happiness, however ineffectively, by getting and spending. Our freedom would be maximized, in this respect, only where both consumptionist lifestyles and their counterparts had lost their dominance. But our culture does not now offer this degree of openness and neutrality.

Think of a typical consumer good—hamburgers. The interests of both the producers and the consumers may be served by expanding the market and economies of scale if the variety of consumer tastes can first be modified in the direction of some less diverse, more nearly homogeneous common denominator. If this can be done, restaurant expenses and prices will fall, and consumers will not object to the homogenization to the degree that their tastes have actually been changed. Indeed, such consumers will see themselves as simply benefiting from certain assembly line-style cost efficiencies.

Currently, the world's most popular hamburger—as judged by volume sold, if not by taste test—arrives with a number of standard "default" choices already made. Some consumers, through either advance specification or manual deconstruction, may try to modify those default choices. The cost of advance specification may be a longer wait for their hamburger, and the cost of manual deconstruction may be unpleasantness or mild social disapproval. Some customers may even go elsewhere—after all, it is impractical to change the taste of the basic burger itself, and some other burger chains may offer hamburgers that cost nearly the same and that are sometimes rated better tasting by many adults, if not by children.

All this consumer assertiveness is healthy in a cultural, if not in a nutritional, sense. But it is not the whole story. To some extent, we resign ourselves to eating hamburgers that do not really match our preferences; we simply accept them as good enough to be paid for and eaten. More insidiously, though, another process may be at work, involving dissonance reduction, habituation, maturation, or a culinary Stockholm syndrome. In any event, our tastes are changed—gradually, unintentionally, and perhaps without our awareness.

Our tastes change for many reasons. We may decide to become vegetarian. Or we may have eaten so many hamburgers that they have lost their appeal, temporarily or permanently. Our taste for fat and salt depends on what we are used to. Certain food items—one thinks here of items such as the Klingons' *gagh*—would not likely become favorites of most fast-food devotees, even after repeated exposure. But the phenomenon of taste adjustment through habituation is real. We may come to find that our initial tastes are now foreign to us and no longer appealing.

Again, habituation may drive down costs, enhance at least some competitors' profits, and draw no objection from consumers. After all, a change in tastes in this context means that we have somehow come to prefer what is offered. There need be nothing narrowly deceptive or coercive about this process, in that no literal force or fraud is applied. And of course, fast food is not the only example and probably not the most extreme one.

To put it more dramatically, our experiences and taste histories can, to a degree, undermine our freedom. Consider, for example, that in our culture, jazz and classical music are relatively unpopular. This fact is obscured by their residual prestige and the affluence of many of their aficionados, but their limited appeal is easily documented. It seems evident that it is not a matter of their intrinsic inferiority as musical genres. Rather, their unpopularity is better explained on the basis of our generally infrequent exposure to them as children and young adults, apart from their unidentified, unpursuable, snippet-like incorporation into movies and commercials. It is, of course, more complicated than that. Jazz and classical music are relatively complex and may be perceived as odd or different. Understanding them there-fore requires more initial effort—even discomfort—and a bigger investment than do more popular forms of music. As a culture, we currently may be less inclined to make that initial investment, even if it would pay off over our lifetime.

This is precisely the point, that most adults do not go through life regretting their tastes in music or wishing that jazz or classical music meant more to them. The preferences of those adults for whom these forms of music have always been at the margins were not violated and overridden by some external agency. But we should not conclude that this sort of taste formation and reinforcement process in our culture maximizes freedom. Perhaps all choice histories influence our future choices. Perhaps all expressed preferences are fed back to us, changing our basic tastes and our very identity to some degree. All choices have costs, and perhaps all choices preclude certain possibilities. Freedom, however, is achieved to different degrees in different cultures.

Freedom in general and freedom of speech are not equivalent, so we cannot develop a theory of free speech by focusing exclusively on freedom in the broader sense. It is hard to believe, though, that we could be satisfied with a freedom of speech that constrains freedom in the broader sense. The idea of promoting self-realization or self-fulfillment is commonly cited as one of the goals or values underlying freedom of speech. It also is quite natural to see something like self-realization or human fulfillment as central to why we value freedom more broadly. John Stuart Mill, for example, argued in just this way.

So even when we set aside all cases of false or deceptive commercial speech, it is far from clear that freedom in general or the values underlying freedom of speech are maximized by stringent constitutional protection for commercial speech. Ultimately, what tips the balance is a realistic assessment of the vector of institutional forces and the absence of any substantial, institutionally based challenge to the dominance of the culture of consumptionism. Any reasonable governmental restriction placed on commercial speech may be said to reduce—if only symbolically or minimally—the cultural bias in favor of consumptionist ways of living. Reasonable people may disagree, but we do not need to prove this claim. Rather, the issue is whether the courts should overrule democratic decision making that places reasonable restrictions on commercial speech, in the absence of other legal issues. Our claim is not that those democratic decision makers are right to act as they do because our theory can be proved to be correct. Instead, we need only argue that in such cases, the courts should generally defer to reasonable democratic decisions based on plausible theories.

Some commercial interests seek to capture and use the democratic political process to promote their own selfish ends by restricting the commercial speech of others. One gasoline retailer, for example, may benefit if no competitors are allowed to advertise. But such acts may, on balance, undermine the public interest. Therefore, the courts should be able to reject such schemes simply as being unreasonable.

Other federal or state constitutional or other legal challenges, including civil rights or antitrust claims, may be used in such cases. But remember that along with the general public, the victim in such cases is another competing commercial faction. Neither victim is a historically despised, powerless minority, with no chance of influencing the democratic process. Although it may be too costly or impractical for the public to rise up in organized electoral or legal protest against such schemes, the public interest can often be upheld by the better-organized commercial victims of unreasonable, anticompetitive restrictions on commercial speech.

What sorts of values or purposes, then, underlie freedom of speech? This question has often been at the heart of disputes over commercial speech. The leading modern free speech theorist, John Stuart Mill, was ambivalent about the degree of protection, if any, to be accorded to some forms of nondeceptive commercial speech. Contemporary writers, though perhaps not ambivalent as individuals, are at least divided on the subject.

One broad and influential camp favors some degree of special or rigorous First Amendment protection for commercial speech. Writers in this camp recognize that many commercial ads are less propositional than vaguely imagistic or mood evocative. They note, however, that such ads may intentionally or, more often, unintentionally promote recognizable styles of life, such as materialism, consumptionism, or short-term hedonism, as indeed fully protected noncommercial speech might. Other ads, of course, clearly convey information of great interest to many people, and some ads have evident artistic value.

The failure to protect commercial speech might even be dangerous. As long as there is a significant difference in the level of constitutional protection accorded to commercial and noncommercial speech, including political speech, there is a risk that government and the courts might succeed in classifying political or ideological speech as mere commercial speech. This misclassification might then be used to suppress unpopular political or ideological speech.

In contrast, another group of writers is more skeptical of the desirability of special protection for commercial speech. They sometimes argue that such protection may actually endanger, rather than strengthen, political and ideological speech. If we offer equal protection to commercial and noncommercial speech, we will risk diluting free speech protection for political speech if we are repeatedly asked to apply stringent free speech protection for venal, mundane, self-interested, or trivial commercial purposes. The thinking is that we might be willing to fight and die for free speech in certain realms but not in others. Other people contend that commercial speech ordinarily generates fewer "external" benefits that go "uncaptured" by the speaker than does political or ideological speech. But then, as we noted, commercial speech may create the important externality of a culture of consumption.

The battle between these two camps is typically played out, albeit inconclusively, over the relationship between commercial speech and one or more of the values and purposes thought to underlie the free speech clause. Unfortunately, there currently is no consensus on the range or scope of these values. Some judges and writers cite a broad range of values, others a narrower one, differences that often are translated into disagreements over the constitutional status of commercial speech. Those who recognize a broad range of values underlying freedom of speech accord greater constitutional protection to commercial speech, and those who recognize only a narrow range of free speech values give it less protection.

This sort of persistent, apparently unresolvable, controversy is paralleled by a narrower debate over the relationship between commercial speech and the more particular value of self-realization.

Some writers believe that commercial speech encourages self-realization, whereas others are more skeptical. The debate remains unresolved largely because of the intractable ambiguity surrounding terms such as *self-realization*, *self-expression*, and *autonomy*. Roughly, self-realization—in the sense of acting as one currently happens to wish to do with regard to receiving commercial messages—is promoted, at least at that moment, by uninhibited commercial speech. But this is not the only familiar way of thinking of self-realization. If we think of it instead in terms of human dignity, the fullest and richest development of human powers, or the highest development and flourishing of the human personality, the connection between generally unregulated commercial speech and such self-realization will seem much more tenuous. Whether generally unregulated commercial speech promotes self-realization in a third sense—that of subjective happiness or well-being—also is controversial. As we have seen, the available evidence suggests that it does not.

As a practical matter, if we want to make a case for the reasonable regulation of commercial speech, we will gain little by adopting narrow or controversial theories of free speech. We should not, if only for reasons of persuasion, assume that free speech theory should focus only on, for example, the freedom of the speaker and not on that of the audience. Nor should we assume that even as speakers, corporations (or some carefully defined subset of corporations) fall outside the scope of the free speech clause. Even if for-profit corporations are constrained, in some sense, by the need to turn a profit, this does not tightly constrain the content or tone of commercial speech consistent with the corporation's survival. Benetton, Nike, Coors, Pepsi, Calvin Klein, Boeing, Cadillac, McDonald's, Ben & Jerry's, and Exxon may be subject to profitability constraints, but these constraints are compatible with interesting differences in their advertising messages. Profit-constrained enterprises enjoy a meaningful zone of indeterminacy within which the tone and content of their speech, as determined by one or more human agents of the corporation, may safely fall.

Our approach, in contrast, is to endorse a broad range of values or purposes underlying the free speech clause. The idea is to avoid limiting constitutional protection for commercial speech on the grounds of a narrow, crabbed, or controversial understanding of why we protect free speech in the first place.

Let us turn to the problem of distinguishing between commercial and noncommercial speech. Up to this point, we have set aside this question, relying when necessary on uncontroversial examples. A precise and easily applied definition is not possible. But we need not throw up our hands in despair, concluding that we will not be able to tell commercial and noncommercial speech apart—which might lead to stringent protection for both or, less attractively, to less stringent protection for political speech. Instead, we have reason to believe that the vague borders of commercial speech need not lead to implausible or harmful judicial results.

In this respect, the Supreme Court has been of limited assistance. The leading commercial speech case, *Virginia State Board of Pharmacy v. Virginia Citizens Consumer Council*, referred to commercial speech as "speech which does 'no more than propose a commercial transaction.' "[3] On the other hand, the Court also, in the influential case of *Central Hudson Gas and Electric Corp. v. Public Service Commission*, referred to "expression related solely to the economic interests of the speaker and its audience."[4]

If both these formulas are intended to be definitions of commercial speech, the first thing we should notice is that they may be inconsistent with each other. Separately, neither is very satisfactory. Consider first the "no more than propose a commercial transaction" approach. The problem here is that much commercial speech does more than, or something different from, proposing a commercial transaction. Is speech that accepts or rejects a commercial proposal usually itself a commercial proposal? We also should be a bit nervous that this assumed definition of commercial speech itself relies on, without further specifying, the idea of "commercial."

If our problem is distinguishing the commercial from the non-commercial, this definition is, by itself, of limited help, but the task of distinguishing the commercial from the noncommercial cannot be avoided forever. Even if we abandon this distinction in free speech cases, we will have to make a similar distinction for commerce clause purposes, unless we consider everything to be commerce. And if we regard all possible human relations as commercial, we have lost already.

This first definition of commercial speech is helpful in some contexts, however. It may often be used in cases of, for example, commercial advertising, securities offerings, and structurally similar cases. But other intuitively commercial forms of speech often do not fit neatly into the category of proposals. For example, many proxy statements, SEC filings, security interest filings, corporate financial statements, reports to shareholders, commercial contracts, accounting or budget reports, product safety brochures, warranties, prospectuses, product labels, consumer warnings, and product recall statements are not considered to be proposals.

The alternative, the "solely economic interests" approach to defining commercial speech, has faults as well. It does have the virtue of including some instances of commercial speech beyond mere proposals, but it leaves out much that is ordinarily considered commercial speech. Imagine a typical commercial advertisement for a perfume, an elaborate exercise machine, a hair replacement technique, cigarettes, or athletic shoes. These and similar ads may well relate to the economic interests of the consumers as well as to those of the sellers. Far more is at stake, however, than "solely" economic interests in the purchase of these and many other products and services. Self-improvement, relationships, mood, image, and fantasy may be crucial elements as well. It is easy to conclude that both these definitions of commercial speech are in some respects less than ideal. But no simple and satisfactory alternative definition is available.

Consider the distinction between the market for goods and services and the metaphorical "market" for ideas. Of course, we only figuratively buy and sell ideas. Buying an idea need not leave us with fewer resources with which to "buy" more ideas, even if buying an idea involves commitments and has opportunity costs. Selling an idea does not reduce the seller's supply of ideas, or even of that idea. What the seller receives in exchange for the idea, if there is an exchange at all, is often hazy. Legal rights in ideas—beyond copyright, patent, and trademark—are themselves hazy. Often, as with political or ideological ideas, the seller's goal seems merely to disseminate the idea rapidly, aside from the price or rate of return. Authors of political books occasionally seek royalties from their publishers. But royalty payments are, in many cases, not among the author's primary interests or motivations. In other cases, determining the profit motivation or other personal interest is simply impractical.

Nevertheless, the contrast between markets for goods and markets for ideas is useful in certain respects. Again, we cannot, for various reasons, simply disregard the distinction between the more and the less commercial, so that being a samurai and selling a Samurai are deemed equally commercial activities. We need to be reminded, in particular, that often speech about markets, or even about a particular market, and about how, if at all, such a market should be regulated, clearly transcends commercial speech.

Commercial speech may not have a unique, distinct essence. Perhaps the only thing that links all instances of recognizably commercial speech is a series of "family resemblances." We have seen that we should be reluctant to dispose of the distinction between the commercial and the noncommercial, in this or other constitutional contexts. But a pragmatic counterargument is possible. Suppose, the argument goes, we draw some reasonable distinction between commercial and noncommercial speech. This distinction would make a difference only if we allowed the government to regulate the two categories differently. It is common to distrust the government's ability to regulate political or ideological speech on the grounds of the speech's alleged harmfulness. The particular area of hate speech regulation is more controversial, but the general idea is familiar enough. But why, the argument concludes, should we imagine that government regulation of commercial speech will be fairer, less biased, or otherwise more defensible? Why shouldn't skepticism about government regulation of political speech extend into the realm of commercial speech? If it does, fussing over the distinction between commercial and noncommercial speech might lose much of its point.

This argument, however, is not convincing. No doubt, as we have seen, some government regulation of commercial speech is driven by an industry's or an enterprise's desire to restrict the entry of potential competitors, by a wish to discriminate unjustly, or by other anticompetitive motivations. This is not the whole story, however. We should not be as distrustful of a government's ability to regulate reasonably all commercial speech as of its ability to regulate fairly the speech of the government's own rival political parties, political movements, and political ideologies.

Whether cigarettes cause a particular disease is, in some cases, a complex and controversial issue. Judgment is often required. But this sort of question may well be more objectively determinate than, for example, whether a particular political candidate, party, or ideology is socially pernicious and should therefore be regulated. The sitting government may indeed hold certain biases on commercial matters. Some of, if not all, the affected parties may offer campaign contributions. But these biases must—according to common sense and the writers of our Constitution—pale in comparison to the government's biases regarding its own merits. On the one hand, in many commercial controversies, the leading governmental actors may have, at most, a limited stake in the outcome. But on the other hand, few governments fully appreciate criticism of their policies or of their very existence as governments.

Let us state our position in a somewhat less familiar and somewhat narrower way. It is plausible to hold that in some cases, we should protect unpopular and perhaps even arguably dangerous ideas—perhaps for the sake of promoting the public virtue of tolerance. In contrast, few people would contend that we are better off protecting the advertising of potentially dangerous products. This contention would not change even if we added, in the latter case, the availability of counterspeech by *Consumer Reports*, the availability of the civil tort system, and the possibility of criminalizing the production of such goods to minimize the carnage. Nor would our conclusion change if we focused on the harms of nondeceptive commercial speech.

We are not trying to minimize the potential for abuse of the government's power to regulate commercial speech. But such abuse can be reduced by means other than rigorously protecting commercial speech. Virtually all criticism of attempts to limit competition by regulating commercial speech is itself fully protected political speech. Indeed, some attempts to restrict competition by restricting commercial speech might fail a judicial test of reasonableness.

More important, we should remember that a private party that is able to persuade the government to limit competition by regulating speech may well be able to achieve similar anticompetitive effects by means other than restricting speech. A private party that sees it cannot restrict competition through speech regulation is unlikely to give up, and it has no practical reason to do so. Many ways of limiting competition through legislation do not directly involve commercial speech.

Finally, let us recall that historically the most egregious restrictions on competition have often included conscious discrimination on the basis of race, ethnicity, and other group affiliation. We should not need the free speech clause to attack such anticompetitive discrimination. In such cases, the equal protection clause and a variety of state and federal civil rights statutes should be invoked.

In sum, then, there is no reason to suppose that permitting the reasonable regulation of even nondeceptive commercial speech could not provide long-term benefits. We should, of course, do what we reasonably can to prevent potentially valuable political or other social sorts of speech from being swept into the net of commercial speech regulation.

It is easy to think of cases that test the boundary between commercial and political speech. A cigarette manufacturer might conspicuously endorse the Bill of Rights. In a television commercial, a clothing manufacturer might take at least an ambiguous position on an important social issue. An advertisement might, with some irony, play off the attenuation of many social relationships, or of the general public trust, in order to offer consumption-oriented solutions. A poor person who is reduced to begging may thereby be said to engage in commercial speech or in broadly political speech. A magazine may seek to inform consumer purchases with no financial stake in the recommended goods and with or without related advertisements. Or scientifically based health claims may be made on behalf of particular products, sometimes in the context of an otherwise purely commercial ad.

We should not, however, overestimate the frequency or severity of these borderline cases. Most advertisements are classified as commercial speech according to any reasonable theory. But those speakers who want to convey a political message protected by the law can readily avoid entanglement with commercial elements. Thus the truly unavoidable costs of misclassifying political or commercial speech are limited. Often, the court is able to separate commercial and noncommercial speech, thereby giving greater protection to one than to the other.

If necessary, the court can devise special legal tests for particular kinds of borderline cases. For example, think of a claim that egg yolks are healthful precisely because of their cholesterol content. The court might wish to distinguish among proponents of this claim based not on the presence or absence of a financial interest but on a broader consideration of what reactions would logically please the speaker. A scientist who sees special health benefits in eating egg yolks presumably wants people actually to eat, rather than merely buy, eggs. A commercial egg producer, on the other hand, who makes precisely the same health claim may or may not care what the purchasers of eggs do with them. Instead, selling as many eggs as possible may be his main goal. The egg producer may indeed be most pleased by purchasers who consistently buy eggs, throw them away, and then buy replacements.

There is no guarantee that an acceptable method for deciding particular borderline classification cases of commercial and noncommercial speech will always be available. But there are ways of reducing the real costs, if not the risk, of incorrectly deciding close cases. For example, a court faced with a close case of classification may want to determine whether the speaker in question clearly had, but unreasonably failed to exercise, some control over his own classificatory destiny. Some speakers, after all, can easily present what they wish to say in a way that is as clearly noncommercial as reasonably possible under the circumstances.

The courts may therefore want to establish reasonable legal incentives to encourage speakers who might otherwise pose more difficult problems of classification between commercial and noncommercial speech. A judicial rule might take the following form: In borderline classification cases only, the court may treat speech as noncommercial if the speaker comes as close as reasonably and inexpensively possible under the circumstances to presenting it as noncommercial. What is reasonably possible must be considered in light of the speaker's actual resources and abilities, as well as the speaker's interest in not sending a distorted message or in addressing an undesired audience.

In borderline cases of commercial speech, therefore, the court might look to the speech alternatives available to the speaker and ask whether he ignored more clearly noncommercial speech alternatives. For example, a court might point out to a store that it is possible to express its views about the Fourth of July without describing items for sale in lavish detail. Finally, if the court decides that the harm of wrongfully classifying borderline political speech as commercial speech is generally worse than the harm of wrongfully classifying borderline commercial speech as political speech, it can establish another informal rule that the remaining close cases will be classified as political speech.

Let us assume that the speech in question is classified as commercial. What degree of constitutional protection does the Supreme Court currently accord to such speech? At least for the moment, the basic contours of the constitutional test for regulating commercial speech can be traced to the *Central Hudson* case briefly referred to earlier. *Central Hudson* involved a state's regulation of a utility company's promotion of electricity consumption. The basic idea underlying such regulation was one of conserving energy and natural resources.

The Supreme Court devised a four-part test that begins by specifying that the speech at issue must concern lawful activity and not be misleading. Next, we must ask whether the asserted governmental interest is substantial. If both inquiries yield positive answers, we must determine whether the regulation directly advances the governmental interest asserted, and whether it is not more extensive than is necessary to serve that interest.[5]

In practice, the *Central Hudson* test unhappily combines apparent rigidity with remarkable vagueness in such a way as to invite challenges to virtually any regulation of commercial speech, however reasonable and carefully considered the regulation may be. Often, application of this test is mainly the formal elaboration of subjective judicial preferences.

In reference to the elements of the *Central Hudson* test, it is important to remember that the general burden of proof in these typically hazy inquiries is placed on the government. Placing the burden of proof on the government is normally reassuring when political or ideological speech is being regulated. In commercial speech cases, however, this placement of the burden of proof commonly tends, at every stage of the test, to undermine reasonable government regulation.

Next, let us look at the initial *Central Hudson* inquiry into whether the commercial speech at issue is "misleading." The idea of speech being misleading or not misleading is a familiar one. The actual judicial inquiry into misleadingness, however, is often complex, multifaceted, and indeterminate. We have already alluded to the idea that commercial speech can be non-misleading in a narrow sense yet still be misleading in a broader sense.

The problem is also that many commercial claims may be narrowly misleading or deceptive, perhaps even predictably so, but to only a narrow or special segment of the intended audience. It seems unrealistic, for example, to support the claim that a commercial for a sugary breakfast cereal, featuring cartoon characters and aired on a Saturday morning, is not legally misleading because it would not mislead reasonably intelligent adults. This is true even if many adults watch the commercial and even if all cereal is bought by adults.

Below a certain age and level of maturity, children lack the life experiences and reasoning ability—or the cynicism, general suspicion, and social alienation—they will probably later acquire. They thus may accept claims and representations, express or implied, that adults would not. Or an advertiser may more deftly avoid making falsifiable claims while still conveying impressions of enormous product desirability to children. On the other hand, free speech law is often reluctant to hold speech hostage to standards that are appropriate only to children.

Further muddying the water is that in most deceptive advertising cases, the crucial question is not really the alleged misleadingness of the speech. Instead, the issue is whether the misleading claim can be fairly ascribed to the speaker. The speaker may thus simply dispute the accuracy of the government's interpretation of the ad for particular audiences. The government imputes one meaning to the ad, and the speaker imputes another. The speaker disclaims any intent to convey a misleading message and may fund survey research showing that few viewers interpret the ad as making the claim in question. A dispute might arise, for example, over whether a bread manufacturer is or is not claiming that one will grow up strong and healthy if one eats nothing but this bread. The problem of audience heterogeneity also is present here, with the results commonly indeterminate.

These sorts of complications are often played out through a complex judicial subdivision of the idea of misleading commercial speech. The Supreme Court has been known to consider merely whether the speech at issue is misleading "in the abstract."[6] One might suppose that it not entirely clear how a statement can be either misleading or not misleading in the abstract. What sort of audience is there in the abstract? Perhaps the idea is that some claims are more or less universally bogus and thus misleading in any context or to any audience. Is it misleading in the abstract to label an orange juice container as cholesterol free? Is it misleading at all? Some persons may find this label informative. On the other hand, no orange juice has ever contained cholesterol.

Accordingly, the courts have developed complex typologies of misleadingness and have varied their degree of scrutiny of commercial speech, depending on whether the speech is deemed actually, inherently, potentially, necessarily, demonstrably, or possibly misleading. The Federal Trade Commission makes further, more specific, inquires. All these characterizations take us in different directions.

None of these characterizations, however, bypasses the need for only loosely constrained judgments about the presence, extensiveness, degree, and consequences of misleading speech. In some cases, the misleadingness of the speech is or can be reduced to some degree by means of a disclaimer or a warning. But the courts must then judge whether the phrasing, prominence, and clarity of the disclaimer are sufficient or whether the disclaimer itself creates undue confusion.

Let us assume that the issues of the speech's misleadingness have been resolved. The court must then consider whether the government can identify a substantial interest underlying the regulation of commercial speech, which is not a trivial or easily resolved issue.

In particular, the government's burden in this respect "is not satisfied by mere speculation or conjecture; rather, a government body . . . must demonstrate that the harms it recites are real."[7] Whether a substantial—and, of course, a morally and constitutionally legitimate—government interest is at stake can often be contested. Depending on the degree of their sympathy for the state regulation, the courts may identify the interest at stake in more and less favorable ways. Adding to the indeterminacy is that government regulations rarely pursue single-mindedly and exclusively any particular interest. Like most other complex human activities, government regulation seeks at least to balance the interests, to take the edge off the most bothersome trade-offs, and to pursue, if not rank, a range of varied goals. Judges can often fault a regulation for not even trying to maximize a particular cited aim.

The idea of "demonstrating" the reality of a harm should be daunting. Many social harms cannot be rigorously demonstrated to flow from any particular cause. It is not even clear that the criminal law requires a prosecutor to demonstrate the presence of all the criminal elements in a case. Of course, the idea of demonstration need not be interpreted in a rigid, deductive sense. Instead, the term *demonstrate* may be used with greater and lesser degrees of rigor. Its very adaptability, though, means that the "demonstration" requirement is available for use by any court inclined to derail the regulation of commercial speech. The combination of literally rigorous language and the lack of authoritative, specific guidance by the Supreme Court invites the litigation of any reasonable regulation of commercial speech and opens the door to judicial rejection of such regulations by any court so disposed.

This general problem is made worse at the next stage of the judicial inquiry. Here, the government is required to "demonstrate" that the regulation of the commercial speech will "in fact" advance the specified government interest "in a direct and material way." As we might imagine, just what counts as "directly" promoting a government interest is often open to dispute.

In this context, directness may refer literally to an immediacy or simplicity of connection between the regulation and the assumed government purpose. But directness is often interpreted as referring to the degree or magnitude of the effect produced by the regulation. Thus directness has been contrasted with tenuousness, speculativeness or high speculativeness, ineffectiveness, conditionality of support, marginality of support, remoteness, or limited, incremental support.

In large measure, the ideas of, say, direct versus speculative or limited support operate merely as opposing end points on a continuum. Is the degree of effectiveness of most government policies beyond dispute? This inquiry's potential for affixing conclusory labels in the process of upholding or striking down reasonable regulations should be evident. Can the government show, for example, that it will achieve some useful goal by distinguishing—if and when it does—between beer or wine commercials and liquor commercials on television?

The judicial focus on directness or immediacy versus indirectness is surely misconceived. Why should we care whether the regulation advances the government interest directly or indirectly, as long as the effect is sufficiently positive and substantial and the other parts of the constitutional test are met? Surely some problems are best approached indirectly. The Supreme Court's choice of the "directness" terminology is surprising because it rejected, in a well-known line of basic commerce clause cases, just this terminology. The Court has learned to focus on the substantiality or magnitude of relationships, as opposed to their directness or indirectness.

Finally, in these commercial speech cases, the government must show that the regulation is not more extensive than is necessary to promote the government interest at stake. But this is an extremely demanding requirement. So construed, this formulation would allow courts to strike down reasonable regulations on the basis of some real or imagined, slightly less restrictive means of achieving presumably the same or sufficiently similar goal. How a court is to decide whether achieving a somewhat similar goal through an alternative regulation—or 90 percent of the government's original goal—is reaching the same goal is left unclear. It is not difficult for the courts to envision such regulatory alternatives if they are so inclined. They need not weigh the real feasibility, degree of effectiveness, or cost in other values—including the free speech interests of other persons—of whatever alternative regulation they may consider.

In several cases, however, the Supreme Court specified that the "not more extensive than necessary" requirement is not to be interpreted with literal rigor. The government, it stated, need not discover and use only the presumed absolutely least restrictive means of promoting the government's interest. The scope or burdensomeness of the restriction—assuming, interestingly, that *scope* and *burden* mean the same thing—must somehow be reasonable or in proportion to the interest served by the regulation.

A bit of residual haziness from this requirement lingers here, which becomes murkier when we take a more realistic view of things. Surely there often will be graduated trade-offs between the scope or burden of two possible regulations and their degrees of effectiveness. The law should therefore recognize that a slightly less burdensome regulation may well be slightly, though hardly dramatically, less effective. Does this suffice for constitutional purposes? Or we could say that the slightly less burdensome regulation achieves a slightly different goal or mix of goals than does the more burdensome regulation? How different must an effect be before it no longer is the same effect for free speech purposes?

Less obvious are the often unarticulated problems in determining whether one commercial speech regulation is really broader, more burdensome, or more restrictive than another. For example, how do we trade off a decrease in the numbers or kinds of speakers regulated against an apparent increase in the severity of the regulation? Which is more important to assessing degrees of burden: financial cost or a very slight distortion of one's message? These problems will exist even if we ignore the free speech and other interests of third parties not before the court. Let us focus, therefore, only on the free speech interests of the commercial speakers, ignoring even the free speech and other interests of the audience itself.

Realistically, it is often difficult to say whether one regulation is "worse" overall for a commercial speaker than some other regulation is. This is partly a matter of the unpredictability of future consequences. But the problem is deeper than that. Bad consequences for one's free speech have various dimensions, which are not easy to compare. Two possible speech regulations may, for example, have different effects on the size of one's audience, and this may be important. But so may the composition or demographics of one's audience. One may or may not prefer a smaller but more affluent or a more substantively targeted or receptive audience.

By themselves, the alternative regulations may impose different financial costs in reaching one's audience, or each may require that one change one's message to some degree. How is the court to determine whether a slightly altered message is fully compensated by a somewhat larger or somewhat different audience? How are differences in the required media, audience mood, or time of day to be factored in when the courts decide that one regulatory scheme is broader or more burdensome than other? For free speech purposes, the breadth of a regulation simply cannot be read off the text, that is, intuitively inferred. A regulation that "looks" broader may, to the speaker, be less burdensome.

Which, then, is more burdensome—to be denied all use of a particular medium or to be allowed the use of all media, but only with an embarrassing warning label or disclaimer? It is clear that many courts either ignore or resolve these sorts of issues in a self-serving way. Those courts inclined to find a regulation unconstitutional can often, given the indeterminacies involved, simply point to some arguably narrower alternative.

Matters would be simplified a bit if the courts could rely on the individual speaker to explain which regulatory schemes are, at least from its own perspective, more and less burdensome. Such an approach would, however, be unreliable even with regard to that speaker's own, largely subjectively determined, free speech interests. For several reasons, speakers often have strong incentives to be less than candid in this regard.

Suppose, for example, that in the eyes of the court there are only two ways of achieving a given governmental interest. One method, actually adopted and enforced in the case at hand, is the one less burdensome on the speaker's free speech rights. The other method would be more burdensome but has, from that speaker's standpoint, a saving grace, that it could probably be blocked politically. Therefore, it is unlikely to be enacted for one or another arcane reason. Or if it were enacted, it could in practice be rather easily evaded by the speaker; that is, it might be difficult to enforce. Under these circumstances, the speaker is better off with what is in some sense the more burdensome regulation. The speaker may, therefore, have a strong incentive to argue for a potentially more burdensome regulation. The court, certainly, may not be privy to the practical politics of enactment and enforcement in this area.

The problem is actually broader than these examples suggest. After all, commercial enterprises care about more than degrees of burden on their free speech rights. Shareholders do not judge a company's performance solely on its tenacity in resisting threats to corporate free speech. It is fair to say that most commercial enterprises would prefer greater restrictions on their commercial speech rights to being forced into bankruptcy and liquidated as unprofitable.

Yet current free speech doctrine encourages commercial speakers to pretend otherwise. As the Supreme Court recently recognized, the government's power to close down a business for health reasons does not automatically imply a government power to impose any and all forms of commercial speech regulation on that business. The power to force anyone to say or not say anything the government wishes is not a lesser power included in the governmental power to close down the business itself for appropriate reasons.

The commercial free speech test considers only a particular kind of regulatory burden—the burden on freedom of speech. Thus, those burdens imposed on a commercial enterprise that do not currently count as burdens on speech—which sometimes include huge losses in profits or even insolvency—simply do not matter for free speech purposes, however much they may matter to the commercial enterprise. A business therefore has a current judicial incentive to contend that a regulation that would more severely burden its speech would not do so if the less speech restrictive regulation were riskier or more costly for reasons deemed unrelated to commercial speech. That is, it is better to pretend that a rule is less burdensome on one's speech than to go out of business.

Curiously, some industries may have a real incentive to pretend to prefer commercial death to restriction of their commercial speech. An industry that senses it cannot realistically be closed down or rendered unprofitable has every incentive to argue that the government has the constitutional power to close the industry, even without paying compensation, but does not have the power to impose particular commercial speech regulations on the industry, because they are too burdensome or insufficiently narrowly tailored.

In any event, it is a mistake to assume that the courts will uniformly allow governments broad discretion in the degree of tailoring, proportionality, or "fit" between the breadth or burdensomeness of the regulation and the government interest at stake. The Supreme Court insists that the scope or proportionality of the regulation be "carefully calculated." This formulation, given the inherent indeterminacies involved, again encourages judicial second-guessing of reasonable commercial speech regulations.

Whether the Supreme Court will soon modify any elements of the current commercial speech test is unclear. At least some current members of the Court seem receptive to strengthening the constitutional protection accorded to non-misleading commercial speech. Their inclination now seems to be to strengthen, rather than to weaken, the requirement that the regulation be no broader than reasonably necessary. The Supreme Court might rewrite, or merely interpret more rigorously, this element of the commercial speech test. Although it also is possible that the current test will not be strengthened in any respect, there is, at this time, little support on the Court for weakening the commercial speech test.

Protecting commercial speech currently appeals, interestingly, to both conservatives—especially to economic or laissez-faire, as opposed to some cultural or Burkean conservatives—and the relatively liberal members of the Court. The latter apparently see no prospect of collision between the increased protection of non-misleading commercial speech and the modern regulatory and consumer protection state they also clearly favor.

The idea, for example, of promoting health, nutritional, or environmental goals by restricting advertising that is not narrowly misleading is currently viewed with great suspicion by most of the Court. The justices view as more constitutionally attractive the alternative regulatory schemes, including special taxation, mandated disclosure of information, and even prohibition of the product in question. Such schemes are assumed—dubiously, however—to be less paternalistic, and the Court seems to assume also that they will ordinarily be practical.[8] We have already seen, however, some reason to doubt the universal truth of that assumption.

What initial conclusions may we draw concerning the regulation of commercial speech? We have every reason to believe that commercial speakers can generally take care of their own interests without rigorous free speech protection, beyond a requirement that the regulation be reasonable. In our culture, the broad, implicit, and often unintended messages of advertising and commercial speech in general are not significantly contested by any substantial coalition of cultural forces. Reasonable regulations of commercial speech, whatever their more immediate particular justifications, tend at least minimally—and if only symbolically—to reduce the cultural preeminence of commercial consumption. There is no reason in the logic of the free speech clause, broadly understood, not to pursue this course. The largely inadvertently accrued power of commercialism could be fairly reduced for the sake of greater cultural freedom, well-being, and broad range of values underlying the free speech clause. A constitutional democracy should at least be judicially permitted to embark on such a course.

The current level of constitutional protection for commercial speech is disturbing enough, and there is some indication in the most recent cases that even that level of protection may be raised. Things could get worse, however, even if the Court's test is not changed. The present levels of free speech protection may make more difficult the reasonable state and federal regulation of many sorts of ordinary businesses. We are not thinking here of restrictions on tobacco and alcohol advertising but, instead, of government regulation of environmental claims made by product sellers, the sale of securities, or even nutritional labeling.

After all, to be told how to express one's environmental claims of biodegradability or recyclability or how to convey the saturated fat or cholesterol content of one's product is to restrict one's commercial speech. Many free speech cases in other contexts indicate that compulsory or standardized speech, or even rules prescribing how one must express one's ideas, may violate the free speech clause. Why can't a seller offer evidence that its way of talking about recyclability or health hazards is as good as the government's mandatory scheme and thus should be accommodated on free speech grounds? Can the government show that making such accommodations would undermine the regulatory purpose? Aren't there other ways of promoting conservation or nutritional awareness that do not restrict commercial speech, or at least not so severely? Can the government demonstrate, in advance, that all the alternative rules would be less effective? Why can't the market, the tort system, or criminal law decide on acceptable levels of recycling? Already this logic is at work in Supreme Court and other federal court opinions.

Without arguing that commercial speech should always be valued as highly as political speech is, the Supreme Court recently equated, in some respects, the constitutional value of both kinds of speech. No doubt there are grounds to do so, as long as we focus on whether persons normally care at least as much about commercial speech as about political or electoral speech. In an increasingly commercialized culture, commercial speech becomes in some sense more important.

The Court held, for example, that a city may not attack problems of safety or aesthetics by limiting commercial but not political speech, if commercial speech is no worse than political speech in the relevant respects.[9] In such a case, the Court would prefer that the city promote its chosen interests by also restricting political speech.

Thus the Court in effect has created something of an equal protection clause for commercial speech. Unless commercial speech is more closely related to the underlying harm than political speech is, it cannot be restricted more severely than political speech is. This may seem like evenhanded justice. But it is actually, given our constitutional history, a rather curious result. Let us consider a brief hypothetical example.

Imagine that we are on a ship that will sink unless two units of weight are jettisoned. We of course want to avoid sinking, but we want to do so at low cost. It is therefore better to toss over two unit weights of glass than of diamonds, or, for that matter, of human beings. Let us suppose, though, that on board instead of diamonds or glass are a number of discrete, separable, one unit weights of commercial speech and of political speech. Tossing overboard any two units of speech will save the ship. As perhaps befits a highly commercialized society, the Supreme Court has in effect forbidden us from tossing overboard two units of commercial speech in order to save most of the commercial speech and all of the political speech.

This result, however, is not required by a reasonably broad view of our reasons for protecting speech in the first place, especially given our present cultural circumstances. Instead, such a result protects commercial speech at the expense of the broad range of free speech values, of democratically expressed and well-founded views of freedom itself, of well-being, and of the proper scope and limits of purely commercial values.

Before we begin a survey of some of the dimensions of contemporary commercial advertising, let us ask one final preliminary question. We have argued that in general, the regulation of commercial speech should be constitutionally tested only for whether it can be said to be reasonable or unreasonable. At this level, it does not much matter which party bears the burden of proof. Surely the government will want to offer some account of the reasonableness of the regulation. The placement of this burden will not be objectionable if the courts defer to the government on matters such as the weight of the relevant evidence or that of competing public policy concerns.

But what sorts of policy goals or interests count as reasonable in regulating commercial speech? As we suggested, even nondeceptive commercial speech can sensibly be regulated in the name of environmental protection or nutritional education, for example. A more interesting question might center on the claim that a culture of commercial consumption does not promote freedom and well-being as much as we had hoped. Could a government cite that very belief, by itself, as reasonable grounds for regulating commercial speech?

In such a case, the government would not be making the more specific claim that the commercial speech in question was associated with some narrower harm, such as the failure to optimize recycling. Instead, the government's claim would be merely that the regulation at least minimally legitimized the alternatives to what we have called consumptionism or that it made consumptionism seem less naturally inevitable. The point, however, is not to advance a particular view of consumption but actually to promote freedom and happiness.

In a proper case, the latter sort of restriction should be upheld as reasonable. It is too late to pretend that a liberal society can somehow be completely neutral in its effects on all possible ways of pursuing what people see as good ways of living. The constitutional test should not be whether the reviewing court finds the critique of consumptionism to be convincing but whether a reasonable person or a government could find it persuasive. Nonetheless, it will always be reassuring to a court for the government to be able to offer an additional, more specific justification for regulating commercial speech.

What, though, would be a proper case of regulating commercial speech solely to encourage alternatives to consumption, along with the resulting effects on freedom and happiness? We should certainly respect the equal protection rights of particular commercial speakers not to be arbitrarily burdened. We must—without doubt if not without some irony—rule out regulating speech that intentionally endorses broad consumptionism as a way of living. This sort of claim is clearly not pure commercial speech. Instead, it is a broader social or cultural claim that is not always made, as a matter of the speaker's intent, in every commercial advertisement. Such claims deserve greater protection than an inquiry merely into the reasonableness of the regulation.

No doubt it is possible for the viewer of any ad to conclude—as a result of viewing that and other ads—that consumption is the most preferable way of living. But we do not and cannot protect speech based merely on what it may inspire persons to conclude, apart from the speaker's actual intentions. Inserting a daisy into the barrel of a soldier's rifle will, in the circumstances of a protest rally, usually amount to protected speech. But the mere growing of the daisy does not rise to the level of speech, even if the sight of the daisy predictably inspires broad reflection on, say, conservation of the environment, peace, beauty, or the fragility of life. To advertise a product is roughly to seek to promote the sale or profitability of that or some related product, now or in the future. This is not necessarily to seek also to convey the desirability of a consumption-focused way of living generally. As we have seen, some advertisers may in fact disagree with this latter, broader idea. To say that we should buy a particular good does not necessarily mean that we should generally pursue happiness through consumption, any more than performing music implies a belief that we should listen to music more often.

So the regulation of commercial speech in proper cases, for the sake of validating or reducing the accumulated cultural bias against less consumption-oriented styles of life, remains open. Most governments are unlikely to undertake such regulation as a practical matter. If they did, however, the reviewing courts would rightly want to consider matters such as the severity of the burden on the regulated party and hence any arbitrariness in singling out for regulation the speaker or the particular industry.

The goal of legitimizing less consumptionist lifestyles would not, for example, justify prohibiting all advertising by Coca Cola while leaving Pepsi's advertising untouched. This would rightly be seen as unduly burdensome and arbitrary—so clearly so that the presumed intention of the regulation itself would in all likelihood be undercut. Such an inexplicably biased rule would impeach the claim that we are really trying to validate less consumption-oriented lifestyles. Not all lines of division need to be so arbitrary, however. Some products, for example, may be more closely associated with consumptionist lifestyles than others are. In principle, therefore, commercial speech is subject to regulation according to a generalized lifestyle theory, but commercial speakers are not defenseless against biased and unfair regulation.

Some people might argue that it is possible to promote noncommercial ways of living not only by regulating commercial speech but also by a government subsidy of noncommercial or anticommercial speech. Speech subsidies are well known to the legal system. Commercial advertising costs may be tax-deductible business expenses, and much commercial marketing material, commonly referred to as junk mail, is delivered at a subsidized postal rate. But then, some noncommercial speech is also subsidized under the current system. A religious organization, for example, whose major tenet is the repudiation of commercialism, could qualify for various tax advantages.

The main reason for not relying more heavily on the subsidization of either anticommercial or noncommercial speech is the practical problem of direct or visible financial costs. Regulating commercial speech—say, tobacco advertising—doubtlessly has indirect costs, at least to consumers or investors. But in a time of concern for government budget deficits, it may seem less politically appealing to incur the more direct costs of subsidizing some additional selected portion of anticommercial or noncommercial speech.

Tobacco and Patronizing Speech

He stopped smoking at least once a month.

c h a p t e r   t w o

For some time, a battle has been under way between tobacco sellers and government regulators of tobacco advertising. It is not surprising that the tobacco sellers' arguments are patronizing, superficial, self-serving, and hypocritical. But perhaps more surprisingly, the counterarguments by the government regulators of tobacco advertising are equally so. Tobacco sellers contend that the purchase of cigarettes by adults is normally a free and voluntary choice, no more reflective of addiction or a lack of consent than the desire to continue to live in the same house or to go to the same job day after day. Although it would not violate the tobacco sellers' free speech rights

78

simply to shut down their business as a health hazard, as long as tobacco can be sold legally, the rights of willing adult buyers and sellers to exchange nondeceptive, non-misleading information and imagery must, the sellers believe, be respected.

Government regulators of tobacco advertising, on the other hand, see the evidence as reasonably clear that restrictions on tobacco advertising can substantially affect the purchase of tobacco. Accordingly, they believe that if advertising is restricted, significantly less tobacco will be bought. The problem, according to government regulators, is that too many persons—and too many young persons in particular—are unaware of or underestimate the serious long-term health risks of tobacco, especially given the addictivity of smoking.

In fact, however, neither of these two sets of arguments is fully acceptable. Both give themselves, overgenerously, the benefit of the doubt. Both, in their own way, are unduly patronizing. Both miss crucial points, with neither remotely approaching what is increasingly the core of the problem of tobacco consumption. Instead, we offer the alternative of a class-based analysis to the argument's standard focus on age.

Much of the attention in the current debate is on tobacco advertising and young people. At first, this seems sensible; after all, most people do not begin smoking at age thirty. For the tobacco business to remain financially healthy, tobacco sellers as a class must either increase the amount or value of tobacco consumed per person or, in the long run, recruit new smokers to replace those who, for one reason or another, have stopped smoking. Their solution has been to concentrate their efforts on young potential smokers.

Given our commercial free speech law, as well as the nature of our economic system, both government regulators and tobacco sellers have an interest in retaining this focus on the young. For government regulators, the advantage is the ability to center the discussion on the most objectionable practices, particularly the illegal sale of tobacco to minors. Constitutionally and politically, government regulators are most comfortable condemning sales that are already illegal under state law, along with advertising that is said to encourage such illegal sales. Government regulators may even try to treat all tobacco advertising as proposing one or more illegal transactions, in the form of illegal sales to minors. Nonetheless, this ingenious argument can be refuted by the tobacco sellers' merely adding to their ads "you must be eighteen."

The tobacco sellers do not, moreover, object to this attention to the young. After all, tobacco sellers need not defend illegal sales to minors. All they need to do is deny that particular forms of advertising are intended to promote such illegal sales or that the advertising does in fact significantly enhance such illegal sales. This is, at the very least, a surprisingly complex and difficult empirical claim, the burden of proof of which is on the government.

It is easy to allege that restricting tobacco advertising in some way will substantially reduce illegal sales. But proving this allegation, in the court of either social science or law, is another matter entirely. Remember that as a constitutional matter, the government must prove not only that the advertising restriction will substantially reduce such sales but also that a similar reduction could not be achieved by any means substantially less restrictive of the tobacco sellers' free speech rights. The potential effectiveness of alternative regulatory measures, such as educational schemes and the more rigorous enforcement of existing laws, are, at best, debatable. For the tobacco sellers, then, this is hardly unfavorable terrain on which to fight.

Neither side, in contrast, has an interest in shifting attention to the uncomfortable truth that tobacco consumption is becoming more and more a socioeconomic class-based phenomenon. For government regulators, emphasizing this truth would suggest that smoking now reflects not only the superficial manipulation of advertising imagery but also the real and perceived hardships and inequalities in basic life prospects and that greatly reducing smoking would require mitigating those hardships and inequalities. For governments, it is usually more politically attractive to try to require a disease-generating industry to change merely how it talks than to address basic inequalities in various economic classes' life chances. Think of the analogy here to how some governments, dependent on revenues from lottery ticket sales, awkwardly underplay the economically regressive character of this revenue source.

Likewise, the tobacco sellers have little interest in acknowledging that smoking has become a class-linked phenomenon. In principle, a major American industry could explicitly sell itself as the refuge of the distinctively disfavored or as the dubious consolation of the less affluent. But this approach would contradict the tobacco industry's long-term commitment to associating smoking with glamour, sophistication, carefree and uninhibited enjoyment, recreational activity, and self-sufficiency and independence. And there are obvious risks in changing a broad-based commercial appeal to a narrower, less positive appeal, especially when the new target consumers would generally be less affluent.

The politics and commerce of emphasizing that tobacco is by now largely a class-related matter are thus rather inconvenient, except, of course, to the less affluent themselves. Our following account of the changing economic demographics of smoking does not deny the addictiveness of cigarettes and does not view the decision to smoke in the first place—let alone to continue to smoke—as a gloriously free and uninhibited consumption choice by the less affluent. We also do not patronize the less affluent by claiming that their smoking reflects either their ignorance of the health risks involved—even if the likelihood of addiction itself is, at least publicly, underestimated—

or their seduction by commercial advertising ploys that could be restricted.

Smoking among the less affluent, we instead argue, may reflect not so much any hypnotic power of cigarette advertising as the real and perceived circumstances of life among the less well off. Admittedly, this means that the government's power to enhance people's lives in this respect is not principally a matter of regulating commercial speech. The motives for smoking among the less affluent will not evaporate if tobacco ads are further restricted or prohibited. Instead, and more fundamental, a structural redistribution of opportunities would be necessary.

We first consider the commercial speech regulatory worlds of Washington, D.C., and Ottawa and judicial reactions to the regulation of tobacco advertising. The constitutional provisions regarding freedom of speech in the United States and Canada were enacted during different historical eras and under much different cultural and historical circumstances. The texts of the two free speech provisions are not very similar. Yet in both countries, in practice, the same sorts of issues and inquiries are read into commercial speech cases. Surely this should tell us something about the actual process of constitutional interpretation.

These two regulatory and judicial worlds have been changing rapidly, and so we shall try to keep the discussion fairly general, concentrating on themes and broad ideas rather than focusing exclusively on detailed proposals, regulations, or specific elements of particular legal cases.

Let us look first at some elements of the regulatory measures proposed by the Food and Drug Administration (FDA) under the Clinton administration.[1] The headline story describing the proposed regulations was the attempt to alter the statutory and administrative status quo by asserting authority to regulate tobacco under the Food, Drug, and Cosmetic Act. The reasoning was that Congress authorized an FDA finding that tobacco products are intended to affect bodily functions and that cigarettes are intended as devices for the delivery of chemicals, such as nicotine, having those effects.

Although the jurisdictional question of the scope of the FDA's authority is important, it is not our central concern. We turn instead, for illustrative purposes, to some of the financial, packaging, advertising, promotional, marketing, sales, and other distributional requirements under the proposed FDA rules. The rules imposed both affirmative or "positive" requirements and prohibitions or "negative" requirements. It is clear that the express intent of the proposed rules was to discourage the illegal sales of tobacco products to minors. These means included attempts to reduce the appeal of tobacco to minors beyond merely supporting prohibitions of the illegal sales themselves. Issues such as governmental intrusion into legal lifestyle or consumption choices by minors, now and as future adults, and also those by current adults were thus a consideration.

In brief, the proposed regulations were aimed at barring some cigarette-vending machines, distributing free samples, and selling small numbers of cigarettes. Retailers would have to verify the buyer's age. Manufacturers would be required to pay for a public education campaign to reduce the appeal of tobacco to minors. Trade or brand names for established nontobacco products could not be transferred, along with their appeal, to tobacco products.

Most important, the regulations would require that tobacco ads in publications whose readership was either more than 15 percent youth or more than two million young readers be limited to text and to black-and-white copy. In addition, consumer items identifying a brand of tobacco, like caps and T-shirts, and the sponsorship of events such as automobile races and tennis tournaments would be prohibited. Additional health-related warnings would be required on all cigarette advertising. Finally, billboard advertisements of tobacco within one thousand feet of schools or playgrounds would be prohibited.

In this context, how have the cultural assumptions regarding classic free speech controversies changed? The purpose, for example, of the requirement that tobacco ads in periodicals be text only and in black and white is clear. Young people, indeed young magazine readers, are assumed to be uninspired by, if not allergic to, black-and-white text. This unflattering assessment and the resulting restriction would likely pose only an unusually interesting challenge to advertising agencies. Given these constraints, they would have to design a new sort of tobacco ad to capture the interest of both young people and adults. But such a challenge seems no more unmanageable than asking a jazz virtuoso to improvise an interesting theme based on several apparently poorly related musical notes.

The broader point is that in the past, requiring that disfavored messages be conveyed in black and white has not been thought an effective method of repression by those who believed those messages to be harmful. It is difficult, for example, to imagine Cardinal Bellarmine deciding that Galileo should be free to discuss heliocentricity as long as he did so using only black-and-white text.

In any event, because we have reached the historical point at which ordinary text is now regarded as vaguely aversive, we should review the constitutional status of the black-and-white text requirement for tobacco ads in magazines with a high proportion of youth readers.

Here we discover competing constitutional platitudes. On behalf of the regulation, we might argue that the form and the content of speech are largely separable and that the black-and-white text requirement primarily affects the form, rather than the content, of the tobacco sellers' commercial message. The regulation also makes at least some attempt to exempt from the scope of its restrictions those magazines intended mainly for adults.

Conversely, in at least some contexts, we have become increasingly distrustful of the distinction between form and content. How graphically or entertainingly a message is delivered has become a part of the idea or image conveyed. At least in part, the medium is the message. And in this case, one could argue, the restriction holds speech intended for adults hostage to what is fit for children.

Setting aside for a moment the issues of burdens and degrees of proof, the court would ask whether this sort of advertising restriction was effectively promoting a substantial public interest. It would then ask whether the restriction was sufficiently narrowly tailored, in the sense of accomplishing its purpose without unnecessarily restricting the tobacco sellers' speech. Can we envision other, significantly less speech-burdensome ways of equally promoting the same public interest?

These inquiries are part of the record of evidence before the court. They are also, however, a matter of judicial sympathy and predisposition and, to a degree, even of judicial speculation and fiat. If, for example, it seems to the court that under the restriction, adults are being told by the government that some legal products are good and others are bad, with the alleged harms being concentrated on consenting adults, it would probably rule against the regulation.

We should stress that our argument does not depend on any sense in which some tobacco advertising—for instance, of a healthy couple frolicking and smoking—might be said to be misleading or deceptive. Instead, we are using demonstrable medical harms of remarkable severity, chiefly to the smokers themselves but also to unconsenting third parties. Furthermore, we are seeking to regulate only commercial speech and not noncommercial speech endorsing tobacco.

One can easily envision such advertising restrictions being struck down as unconstitutional, even in the face of the argument that the adult purchase and consumption of tobacco will predictably affect the well-being of others, especially minor children, in the household. Two points are crucial here. First, despite what common sense tells us, it would probably be difficult for the government to demonstrate that the sorts of ads to be prohibited do in fact contribute significantly to smoking by children and adults. Second, it would be just as difficult for the government to show that the speech restrictions are narrowly tailored and that no significantly less speech-burdensome ways of promoting the public interest at stake are available.

It is surprisingly controversial whether, or how much, tobacco advertising actually induces children and young adults—or people in general, for that matter—to smoke. Tobacco companies spend enormous amounts of money on advertising, so it seems fair to assume that they believe that there is a good reason for doing so. Perhaps the ads reassure established smokers. The tobacco companies are well aware that generally, either persons start smoking when they are young, or not at all. Furthermore, children do have some awareness of cigarette advertising. One well-known study found that 30 percent of three-year-olds and 91 percent of six-year-olds were able to match the cartoon character "Joe Camel" with cigarettes.[2]

Even if we assumed, however, that Joe Camel has led to an increase in sales of Camels cigarettes among younger smokers, this would not prove the necessary point. The tobacco sellers maintain that the intention, and the only significant effect, of tobacco advertising is to maintain or increase the market share of legal customers. The idea is thus supposedly not to motivate tobacco use in the first place or to convert young nonsmokers but to affect rates of brand switching or brand choice.

If we had no empirical evidence, we might simply dismiss such claims as self-serving rationalizations. But generally, teenagers and adult smokers are not overly inclined to say that they would not have smoked if it had not been for tobacco advertising or that tobacco ads were a crucial element in their decision to smoke. Moreover, many of the motivations for taking up smoking or continuing to smoke do not seem to depend on tobacco advertising. Although some of the reasons to smoke, such as a perceived link between smoking and glamour or cowboy independence, may be dependent on advertising, others may not. For example, if a young person takes up smoking as rebellious or authority-defying behavior, restricting the ads for tobacco may only strengthen the association between smoking and rebellion and actually enhance the cachet of the former.

The social scientific evidence for whether tobacco advertising increases the rates of smoking in general is surprisingly murky, complex, and equivocal.[3] Studies in the United States and other countries reached conflicting conclusions, and it is not difficult to find possible methodological flaws and uncertainties in some of them.

For example, it often is not easy to decide even what counts as tobacco advertising or how to measure its presence or amount. Should one attempt to account for changes over time in what might be called the *antiadvertising* of tobacco, as in the release of reports by the U.S. surgeon general, or for changes in health warnings or public policy? Can some consumer goods act as a substitute for tobacco? Should one try to account for changes in the rate at which those goods are advertised or in their price relative to tobacco? What about advertising "clutter" in general or changes over time in the degree of ad clutter? Could these issues have any impact on the effectiveness of tobacco ads?

Should we assume that smoking is affected only by current advertising? Could significant time lags instead be involved? Could a surgeon

general's report or economic conditions work to reduce simultaneously both advertising and smoking, making the latter appear to be
causally linked? There is also the problem of the direction of causa-
tion. Is it possible that a brief period of increased sales, or even the
realistic expectation of increased sales—perhaps for economic,
demographic, or product-development reasons—would lead to
more advertising?

Other studies may either accommodate these concerns or show
them to be inconsequential. If, however, the Supreme Court continues to impose evidentiary and proof standards on the regulating
agency, the advertising restrictions may not survive if it is deemed
debatable whether they significantly promote the public interest in
question. If the evidence linking tobacco advertising and teen smoking is at least inconclusive, the Supreme Court may send the regulatory agency back to the drawing board.

None of this complex and occasionally heated inquiry into the
causal relationships between advertising and health should be necessary. Our political culture recognizes a role for both symbolic politics and causally effective, empirical problem-solving policies, but
the latter is more commonly the focus of our attention. As a pragmatic, achievement-oriented people, we usually prefer that problems
be solved rather than, say, some emotion be expressed, sympathy be
conveyed, or vows of solidarity be undertaken.

Our public health goal in this area is to persuade young people, if
not their elders, to choose not to start, or to quit, smoking. There is,
however, also a legitimate supporting role for what we might call
expressive policies, as opposed to pragmatic or teleological policies.
An expressive public policy expresses the public endorsement or condemnation of some idea, practice, or state of affairs. If the government condemns a state of affairs, the point of an expressive public
policy is not necessarily to eliminate or even mitigate the condemned

state of affairs. Instead, it is mainly to express disapproval, to dissociate the government from the state of affairs, or to refuse to give legitimacy to the disapproved state of affairs. There is an analogy here to expressive theories of criminal punishment.

By analogy, a disgruntled citizen might cast a blank ballot in an election in order to express his disapproval or to avoid legitimizing the choices, without having any real intention to affect the electoral outcome. Similarly, a government policy, even one involving a restriction on private speech, could reasonably be motivated by similar expressive concerns.

With respect to tobacco, the intent of restrictions on advertising, particularly that targeted to large numbers of young persons, might be largely symbolic, expressive, or deontic rather than pragmatic or teleological. The restrictions need not be intended to change the behavioral landscape directly and significantly. Rather, the primary idea might be to make a modest, if not defeatist, statement along roughly the following lines: Even if the causal relationships between advertising and tobacco consumption are unclear, it is irresponsible for tobacco sellers to risk the basic health, or possible addiction to an unhealthy substance, of large numbers of even voluntary consumers, whether or not those consumers are of legal age.

The focus here is on the sellers' irresponsibility in the form of the merely arguable, as opposed to demonstrable, health harms of advertising, precisely in order to avoid a currently inconclusive battle over the empirical evidence on a possible connection between tobacco advertising and any actual harm to health. Note that advertising can be irresponsible even if the effects allegedly flowing from that advertising are themselves not certain. For example, it is clearly—and not merely arguably—irresponsible to stab someone who may already be dead or be on the point of dying of unrelated causes. That is, risky behavior can be irresponsible even if it turns out later that no harm was actually even possible. Likewise, governments may, in some cases, both prohibit irresponsible tobacco advertising behavior with an eye to reducing possible medical consequences and also simply to express through such prohibitory legislation their condemnation of such irresponsible advertising behavior, whether or not the prohibition is effective in reducing the harms of smoking.

When such condemnation takes the form of a prohibition of speech, the practical effect on the speaker of an expressive condemnation of irresponsible advertising is largely the same as it would be in the case of a merely risk-regulatory speech prohibition without any special or additional expressive purpose. In that sense, the expressive condemnation adds little to the advertising prohibition itself. The possible health risk underlies the regulation in both cases. But it may be morally important for governments to emphasize the expressive, as opposed to the pragmatic risk-regulatory, dimension of the prohibition, and it certainly is important for government regulators to shift the focus away from whether tobacco advertising can be clearly linked causally to any of the harms of tobacco.

Can it be said that this mainly expressive restriction of tobacco advertising is really a restriction, based on viewpoint, of commercial, if not political, speech? Does such a restriction merely impose official sanctions on disfavored commercial ideas? Should expressive restrictions of tobacco advertising receive rigorous judicial scrutiny? It is true that restricting tobacco advertising limits commercial speech, whether or not we call the legal restriction expressive. But we cannot claim that restricting tobacco ads amounts simply to counterspeech on the same subject. Without taking into consideration the government's purpose in restricting the speech, most valid commercial speech restrictions have predictably adverse impacts on the idea that the product in question should be used. Any required warning label on a product, for example, undercuts the idea that the product should be used casually. No commercial or any other sort of speech restriction is idea neutral, but that is hardly the decisive point.

The expressive restriction of tobacco advertising is instead aimed not simply at a disfavored idea itself but at marketing practices or commercial speech or conduct that a government is reasonably justified in considering risky or socially irresponsible, in the sense of marketing that may involve frequent, extremely serious—if undemonstrable—harms with no proportionate social benefit. By analogy, to condemn without legally barring the selling of dangerous fireworks to children, even if the advertising itself is banned, is to condemn a behavior rather than, or at least as much as, an idea. The refusal, for pragmatic or other reasons, to criminalize tobacco sales does not add to the social responsibility of such sales or undermine the government's right and power to issue such a regulatory condemnation. Again, noncommercial speech endorsing tobacco consumption need not be affected.

The government would be making a clearer, more unequivocal statement in this regard if it chose to prohibit tobacco sales altogether. Again, the actual effectiveness in practice of such a prohibition would not be central to the message conveyed. Indeed, the clarity of such a statement would be enhanced by simply not federally subsidizing the growing of tobacco, whatever taxes might also be imposed at some stage. The failure to prohibit all tobacco sales, however, or even to end tobacco-growing subsidies need not hamper the expressive message sent by restricting tobacco advertising.

We all appreciate certain realities, whether political, economic, or physiological. It thus need not be hypocritical or inconsistent to acknowledge the practical impossibility of seeking to impose a Prohibition-style ban on tobacco sales while at the same time condemning as irresponsible the willingness of tobacco sellers to arguably, if not provably, jeopardize the health of even their originally freely consenting adult customers through advertising. One appropriate way to condemn this irresponsibility would be through something like the prohibition, or mere regulation, of tobacco advertising, perhaps in general-circulation magazines.

Earlier restrictions on tobacco advertising, including television bans and required health warnings, can be seen as conveying similar messages. Sometimes, however, such messages lose even their purely symbolic or expressive power because they become familiar or are treated with disdain. A new vehicle for the basically similar message thus becomes necessary. We might also consider the industry's continuing disregard of a prior message as a new and different moral or social offense, requiring a new and different government response. We might, by analogy, consider unduly loud music as one offense and the owner's refusal to turn down the volume as a second.

Thus the government might choose to view the tobacco sellers' continuing advertising practices—despite the conflicting evidence regarding advertising and consumption and the accumulating evidence regarding health and addictivity—as a new and different offense requiring a distinct response, perhaps along the lines envisioned by the FDA. Or more simply, the government might reasonably view colorful ads in mass-circulation magazines as a separate irresponsible act, even if no worse than some other activities. According to this view, restricting color ads in mass-circulation magazines would be an appropriate governmental response to just this one irresponsible practice.

Consider some possible responses to this expressive regulatory approach. First, to those people used to purely pragmatic justifications in narrow-tailoring inquiries by the courts, this approach seems like cheating, like refusing to go along with the game. The usual justification for a restriction on speech is supposed to be empirically disprovable, with the regulated party having a good chance to show that the regulation does not serve its purpose effectively or is not tailored narrowly enough to do so. It thus seems unsporting at best if the government alleges mainly an expressive or condemnatory interest and indeed one that, given a modest foundation in the social science evidence, by design fits precisely the commercial speech practice being restricted.

It is not hard to carry out one's expressive or condemnatory interest. Usually, one actually condemns what one also publicly, officially, and explicitly condemns, whether one merely condemns or condemns through legal restriction. This condemnation may thus not allow the customary room for counterevidence of ineffectiveness. The government may be enunciating—in the language of British philosophers—a performative, as in promising or vowing. Used in the right circumstances, performatives are often difficult to rebut. If the government says "we hereby condemn practice P" or "we hereby condemn as irresponsible the color advertising of tobacco in mass-market magazines," it actually is condemning these practices. There is not much room to argue that despite its expressed intentions, the government has failed to so condemn or that the fit is wrong. Again, that no one is provably deterred from smoking or that no harm is provably avoided by such condemnation is irrelevant to this purpose. Rather, the irresponsibility at issue is in running some significant risk that one's advertising and any possible sales attributable to such ads are harmful. As long as there is some evidence of a link between tobacco advertising and health, the case is roughly akin to regulating commercial speech touting a product that may well—but may not—blow up in the consumer's face.

Suppose that the purpose of the regulation is to condemn vigorously by means of a binding restriction on commercial speech or to dissociate a government from a sales practice or smoking itself, and not necessarily to motivate anyone to quit or refuse to take up smoking or to improve public health in any provable way. Can we say that such a governmental justification for restricting commercial speech is both legitimate and sufficiently important? Certainly the tobacco sellers can deny either the legitimacy or the weight of the merely expressive government interest at stake. But these arguments are actually less favorable, from the tobacco sellers' standpoint, than the standard claims that advertising restrictions cannot be demonstrated to be effective in significantly reducing smoking or that other, more narrowly tailored means of achieving that pragmatic goal are available.

A government might in some sense condemn tobacco advertising without also legally regulating it. But we are assuming that there is evidence suggesting that tobacco advertising is linked to tobacco consumption levels. For a government to condemn without regulating is therefore both to condemn in a different, arguably less serious, way and to fail to address pragmatically this possible, if unprovable, causal link to bad health.

In most cases, the tobacco companies can reasonably dispute the complex empirical evidence regarding advertising and tobacco consumption. When the government is intent on proving that advertising increases tobacco consumption, the uncertainties in the evidence accrue to the tobacco companies' favor. They can also argue that less speech-restrictive approaches, such as more rigorous enforcement of current laws against sales to minors or school tobacco education programs, would be just as effective and are therefore constitutionally required. In the case of the FDA regulations, the tobacco companies could point out that advertising would be restricted if it is available to populations that are 15 percent young persons and 85 percent adults—or a ratio of more than five adult potential viewers for every child potential viewer. Why would a court generally unsympathetic to commercial speech restrictions choose to view this arbitrary ratio as reasonably narrowly tailored to protect children and young adults? Why not some different, clearly less restrictive, ratio?

By contrast, consider the tobacco sellers having to argue, first, the illegitimacy of the government's regulatory condemnation of their behavior as reckless or irresponsible. It is difficult to see that the tobacco sellers are on their strongest ground on this point. Here, merely some evidence of a link between advertising and the obviously grave medical harms should suffice. The tobacco sellers can contend that they are not acting recklessly or irresponsibly in advertising in a particular way. But here, the judicial inquiry turns in part on the reasonable possibility, not the probability or certainty, of a link between advertising and tobacco consumption levels and on the more basic, less appealing inquiry into smoking, addiction, and health. Recklessness or irresponsibility turns not only on merely plausible causal links between ads and smoking but also on the ratio of the social benefits of tobacco to the social harms of tobacco, including disease, addiction, and death. Does the current, or at least the initial, consent of their young or adult buyers absolve tobacco sellers of the charge of irresponsibility? Or does it instead help provide the occasion for such a charge?

On this largely expressive battleground, the government need not prove that any tobacco advertising leads to tobacco consumption. Rather, the alleged irresponsibility of the tobacco sellers is in running any significant possible risk that this may occur, and this much is hard to deny. The legal debate is thus shifted closer to the merits, or demerits, of tobacco and tobacco selling under present circumstances.

If the government cannot, for a variety of practical, physiological, or political reasons, reduce tobacco consumption significantly, it remains a matter of moral importance for the government to condemn and anathemize at least some forms of tobacco advertising. Sometimes it is crucial to take a stand despite, if not because of, our hypocrisies. This may be so even if we know that the right will not prevail or that our stand will make no causal difference to its prevailing or not prevailing. By analogy, we would nonetheless expect a government that could not end or even reduce racial discrimination by private actors to legally condemn and attempt to regulate such private discrimination, and we would consider it a matter of high moral urgency and importance that it do so.

This is not to equate or even vaguely compare racial discrimination and the advertising of tobacco. The point is merely that there is a moral imperative to condemn both that depends, among other factors, on the nature and possible or demonstrable gravity of the associated risks and harms. And it is difficult to deny the importance of the risks and harms associated with smoking, however hazy the link between advertising and consumption.

It still is possible to object that it is not important to denounce tobacco in any particular way, such as through restricting color or pictorial ads in mass-circulation magazines. Indeed, it would be absurd to claim that it is important to condemn the general evils of tobacco in exactly this way and no other. But this is not the issue. Generally, a particular symbolic protest does not lose its importance once it is pointed out that other means of symbolically protesting the general harm may be available. The clarity and moral gravity of the condemnation—in general and in the particular case of tobacco—are not significantly undercut by choosing one theme, focus, or venue rather than another.

We have seen, though, that the government already condemns and supports tobacco in several respects. The FDA regulation in question is only one more such condemnation. Can such an additional condemnation carry moral importance? It certainly may, both by itself and in conjunction with other condemnations. As we have seen, each form of condemnation may have a different context, history, function, and purpose. Even if identical language is used, condemning loud music for the second time typically carries a message different from that conveyed the first time. In the case of cigarette advertising, the moral and social stakes are so high that almost every dimension of cigarette advertising, especially the most widely noticed, will be important.

Thus there may be real sense and a defensible logic in regulating tobacco advertisements on expressive grounds, even if we pessimistically assume that the number of smokers and their smoking histories are beyond our ability to affect through advertising regulation or even that additional advertising restrictions might add to the allure of smoking. That is, expressive statements may be worth making even if they may make things somewhat worse in practical terms. Using another analogy, an act of civil disobedience might be morally permitted, if not required, even if its only consequence was to provoke retaliation.

Modern governments, of course, do not remain in power by providing only a steady diet of symbolism. It is useful for governments to take a range of antismoking initiatives with the intention of actually reducing smoking among children and adults. We should, however, consider recent Canadian judicial experience as something of a cautionary tale in this regard. Courts generally unsympathetic to restrictions on commercial speech are often able to develop sufficient grounds, under current constitutional tests, to strike down serious limitations on tobacco advertising.

The crucial Canadian case is *RJR-MacDonald, Inc. v. Attorney General*.[4] Here, the Canadian Supreme Court addressed a statute that prohibited tobacco advertising in Canadian media but not in foreign publications sold in Canada and that restricted the promotion of tobacco products. Unattributed health warnings were required to be placed on tobacco-product packaging. In response, the Canadian Supreme Court issued a total of seven opinions that in their cumulative impact sorted out the restrictions, upholding some and striking down others.

The court was willing to concede the general importance of reducing tobacco consumption and its associated adverse health effects. Furthermore, it was not unduly troubled by the complex empirical problem of a causal link between tobacco advertising and consumption, generally requiring only a demonstration of the reasonableness of believing in some such connection. There is little indication, in contrast, that the United States Supreme Court is inclined to be similarly deferential.

The most important constitutional problem for the Canadian Supreme Court, then, was not the failure to demonstrate that the public interest was actually being substantially promoted by the regulations. Instead—and here following the U.S. pattern—the Canadian Supreme Court was more concerned with issues of narrow tailoring, or degree of fit between the scope of the regulations and the promotion of the public interest in health. In some respects, the court held, the regulations were unduly and unnecessarily intrusive, in that other, less speech-restrictive measures might have similarly promoted the public interest at stake.

The problem is that the government typically bears the burden of proof on the issue of narrow tailoring. It also is often a matter of barely constrained discretion whether a court chooses to believe that some supposedly effective and less speech-restrictive means of promoting the public interest is available. On the basis of conjecture alone, the courts often assume that a more narrowly tailored alternative does exist, and it is difficult for a government to anticipate all the possibilities that may occur to a court, let alone convincingly rebut all of them empirically, in some nonspeculative way.

In the Canadian case, the Canadian Supreme Court found measures such as a prohibition on the distribution of free samples to be justified, but it struck down the mandatory unattributed health warnings. The court also struck down a statutory ban on placing tobacco trademarks on nontobacco products, finding this ban to be unrelated to the statutory purposes. The court also objected to the breadth of the advertising ban, asserting that purely "informational" advertising should not be caught up in the same net as "lifestyle" advertising or with advertising clearly geared to underage smokers. Advertising that promotes low-tar cigarettes or that merely reminds consumers of a package's appearance also seemed to the court to be relatively innocent or otherwise justifiable.

These examples should show both the arbitrariness and, in this case, the typical hopelessness of any inquiry into the degree of the tailoring of tobacco advertising regulation. We can easily imagine why tobacco logos on glamorous or fashionable nontobacco products might be reasonably thought to risk glamorizing tobacco by association. This risk is hardly alien to the statute's purpose.

Some, presumably less sophisticated, citizens might wrongly ascribe to the manufacturer any unattributed health warnings. It is unclear, however, why this incorrect ascription is assumed to be more speech restrictive overall than a health warning specifically attributed to the government. Having words put in one's mouth is not the only way of having one's speech restricted.

This matter is, after all, partly empirical. To some people, an unattributed health warning might mean that the sellers were criticizing their own product. But if they believe that the warning was initiated by the seller, why not give the seller credit for candor? More important, why is it thought to be less intrusive to require sellers to print health warnings that serve as the official government condemnation of the safety of their product? By analogy, trial lawyers usually prefer to introduce adverse facts themselves rather than have a judge do so. Consequently, whether unattributed health warnings are more or less intrusive than explicitly official warnings are is not obvious. A credible, neutral, expert, official denunciation can cut rather deeply.

It also is an empirical matter whether purely informational advertising promotes smoking less efficiently than does lifestyle advertising, even assuming the two can be judicially distinguished. If one accepts the view that low-tar cigarettes tend to be smoked more frequently or more deeply or that their availability discourages quitting, then allowing the advertising of such cigarettes will entail real health risks. Such narrow-tailoring decisions thus involve rather complex judicial second-guessing of government judgments about their empirical effects. Consider a presumably purely informational advertisement that reads simply: "Cigarettes: two packs for a dollar." Can we really say that it is unreasonable to imagine that such steep price-discount advertising might promote sales at least as much as "lifestyle" advertising does? Is it clear that pervasive informational advertising would probably not legitimize smoking or discourage one from quitting?

The narrow-tailoring inquiry can be continued indefinitely by unsympathetic courts. Suppose that the regulatory response to a prior court ruling is a new prohibition of only "lifestyle" advertising of tobacco. Is it beyond the capacities of tobacco sellers to contend that some identifiable forms of lifestyle advertising may be less effective than others in promoting harmful behavior and are in fact no worse than some already approved "informational" advertising? Why should we assume that all lifestyle advertising constitutes a unique, narrowly tailored category not subject to further division? Why not insist on trying more elaborate tobacco education programs or more rigorous enforcement of existing sales restrictions?

At this point, those who want to regulate tobacco ads may either develop expressive arguments like those just described or be prepared to continue to pursue the more standard, if problematic, strategies.

In either event, it is important not to lose sight of, and thereby patronize in one way or another, tobacco consumers as they actually live their lives. Let us therefore turn briefly to the economic and social circumstances of actual smokers. In particular, let us return to the class, as opposed to the age, dimension of tobacco consumption and tobacco-advertising regulation.

Smoking is not just a pharmacological phenomenon; it also has important cultural and historical dimensions. Consequently, people smoke at different rates in France and in Vietnam, and Americans smoke at different rates than they did fifty years ago. Most important, in countries such as the United States, Britain, New Zealand, and Canada, there is now an important socioeconomic dimension to smoking; that is, smoking is no longer a class-neutral phenomenon. Smoking is now largely a matter of where one fits in one's society and of one's resources and prospects.

Consider some illustrative statistics. In *RJR-MacDonald*, the Canadian Supreme Court itself referred to a Canadian study indicating that in 1986, 60 percent of persons who did not attend high school reported smoking every day, whereas a mere 8 percent of persons with a university degree did so. This is both a striking figure and a striking development. Educational level is now plainly a significant consideration, but the phenomenon is even broader. Smoking is now increasingly correlated with lower socioeconomic status in general. Smoking is twice as common in the lowest British socioeconomic class as in the highest.[5]

This pattern shows that the higher socioeconomic classes have changed their behavior for the better but that the lower socioeconomic classes have not. In the late 1940s, nearly 80 percent of British

men smoked. Then, over roughly the past twenty years, more affluent British citizens roughly halved their smoking rate from about
four in ten to two in ten. Over the same period, however, roughly
half of the poorest British citizens smoked, despite the proliferation
of health warnings.

More particularly, a number of related factors seem to correlate
with smoking in present-day Britain, among which are being a single
parent, having limited education, having a blue-collar job, receiving
means-tested welfare benefits, being unemployed, and living in a
rental property. These differential smoking rates indicate not only
that different groups begin smoking at changing rates but also that
the more affluent groups give up smoking in greater numbers.

Roughly similar patterns can be found in the United States. One
complication is the finding that those with fewer than eight years of
school tend to smoke less than do those with more education but that
smoking generally correlates negatively with education for those with
at least nine years of education. One study estimates that by the year
2000, the overall smoking rate in the United States will be about 30
percent for those with a high school education or less and about 16
percent, or roughly half that rate, for those with at least some college.

Smoking in the United States is highest among those with
incomes below the poverty line, even though smoking means paying
heavy regressive taxes on tobacco and sometimes postponing or
doing without necessities. The influence of socioeconomic status
more generally on smoking in the United States is substantial. Smoking varies—at least fluctuates—in regard to age, race, sex, and geog-
raphy, but the difference between the smoking rates of white-collar
and blue-collar workers was found to be greater than that for any
other factor.[6]

As in the British case, these differences show that people at lower
income or educational levels have not joined those with more

income or education in reducing their smoking rates over time as the dangers of smoking become more widely publicized. The interesting question is, why not? Although we cannot fully answer this question, we can suggest a partial answer that is flattering to neither the cigarette sellers nor the current governments.

Cigarette sellers have a vested interest in asserting that the choice by the less affluent to begin and to continue smoking is a fully free and voluntary choice, reflecting a preference for the smoking lifestyle as opposed to the nonsmoking lifestyle. The smoking lifestyle is not the least risky lifestyle, but neither is a freely chosen but relatively dangerous occupation or hobby. We do not look askance at those who, after calculating the costs and benefits, become skydivers, rock climbers, auto racers, or firefighters. Naturally, these arguments apply most directly to adult smokers themselves and not to unconsenting third parties, such as dependent minor family members.

Governments, on the other hand, normally treat tobacco consumption as a problem of the user's ignorance, naïveté, or seduction. The theory, however rarely articulated, must be that at some level, the less affluent are unaware of the crucial health risks of tobacco or that they have somehow been manipulated by clever tobacco advertising into sacrificing their basic health interests. The government's answer consists mainly of consumer education about health risks, targeted at either the general public or particular demographic groups, along with increasing restrictions on tobacco advertising and some encouragement of groups and techniques oriented toward quitting smoking.

Neither the tobacco sellers' nor the government's perspective is completely convincing. The general risk of smoking's leading to disease and/or premature death has been widely known by all social classes for some time. Even before the first U.S. surgeon general's report, cigarettes were popularly referred to as "coffin nails," and their likely health effects were broadly disseminated by popular cultural figures such as Merle Travis. At the same time, however, celebrities also endorsed the benefits of smoking. Furthermore, people have a tendency to underestimate unspectacular or unreported risks of dying. But at this point, a large percentage of smokers in every socioeconomic class recognizes that smoking is associated with disease. In fact, many persons actually overestimate the risks of developing lung cancer.

A government might consider arguing that less affluent persons focus disproportionately on short-term considerations, unduly discounting the harms of smoking over the long term. Actually, it is not clear that the middle class and the governments themselves are any less oriented toward the short term, if we look at the retirement savings practices of the middle class and the budgeting practices of governments. And remember that poorer people pay higher immediate costs in smoking than do better-off people. For poorer people, the opportunity costs of smoking may mean, say, the loss of a varied diet, as opposed to the less severe trade-offs in smoking faced by more affluent persons.

Perhaps governments could contend that the problem with tobacco is mainly one of nicotine addiction and that social and economic classes differ in how they think about the nature and risks of addiction. Perhaps the less affluent do not fully appreciate what it is like to be addicted or the general likelihood of addiction, or perhaps they irrationally exempt themselves from the risks of addiction. Perhaps the poor are disproportionately confused about these matters. For instance, can poorly educated people explain what carbon monoxide or emphysema is, terms used in government health warnings?

No doubt, some social science surveys can find poor people who think in just these ways. But there is something unreal or at least incomplete about such arguments. A sense of personal invulnerability, of dispensation from risk and harm, or of control over one's future actions and outcomes may be characteristic of youth, but not of poverty. The poor may, for one thing, be more direct witnesses to the ravages of illegal drug addiction than many of the economically better-off are. More important, though, the life experiences of the less affluent have taught them lessons that contradict any ideas about being able to control one's fate or about personal invulnerability. They do not believe that poverty exempts them from personal suffering or ill health. If poor smokers claim that they, unlike other smokers, will not become addicted, this may reflect dissonance reduction, rationalization, or a touch of bravado. What else can one say to an interviewer?

In fact, many of the economically less fortunate have learned lessons that might be couched in opposite terms, under headings such as fatalism, pessimism, and a sense of lacking control, whether or not such conclusions show up on the social science surveys. The less well-off are usually aware of their general class position and economic prospects. Another problem they face is that ruling governments usually do not want to acknowledge ideas of fatalism, pessimism, or powerlessness among the less affluent.

Some people may find nicotine or the rituals and patterns associated with tobacco to be relaxing, stress reducing, or stimulating. But we must look beyond these physiological effects. Given the stresses and hardships associated with limited education, low income, single parenthood, or unemployment, smoking may serve as a coping mechanism or a way to change one's mood. For other people, smoking may be a legally permitted rebellion against fate or public indifference. In fact, tobacco, like alcohol, may actually have rather limited positive effects on one's ability to cope. One may soon smoke more because of addiction than because of any continuing free choice. We have not yet seen a fully thought out and convincing free speech theory for speech that promotes addictive products. Contrary to what the tobacco sellers may claim, for many persons, the first cigarette of the day—or the first cigarette after heart or lung surgery—is not like deciding to go rock climbing or even like deciding again to not sell one's car. The biochemistry of quitting, or of striving repeatedly to quit, is different from settling into a routine or resisting its disruption. In any event, even an ineffective coping mechanism is still a coping mechanism, and the physiological or psychological rewards of smoking can be real.

The less well-off are capable of realistically assessing their circumstances. They may see themselves as having less to lose by smoking than do the economically better-off, who tend to be in better general health anyway. There is a difference between retiring with a number of productive years remaining, being financially comfortable, being in good health, and holding a position of public esteem and respect—and the opposite. This is not a matter of irrationally discounting the future in favor of the short term or of being seduced by clever tobacco advertising. Instead, it is more a matter of recognizing the real differences in the opportunity costs for different socioeconomic groups. For some people, there is a less attractive future, and less of it, to discount.

We need not go so far as to suppose that any member of any economic class thinks of smoking as a form of slow-working suicide. Describing smoking in such dramatic terms, however, does show why neither most governments nor tobacco sellers are inclined to think realistically about tobacco and people's motivations to smoke.

What public policies would be necessary, then, if governments really wished to reduce smoking by the less well-off? Those who are interested in lowering the rate of smoking by the less affluent do not object to the standard antismoking policies and programs proposed. Nonetheless, because heavy excise taxes on tobacco are paid disproportionately by the poor, those tax revenues should be earmarked for the benefit of such groups, as opposed to the broader public, in a reversal of the Robin Hood legend.

Some demographic and cultural subgroups within the lower socioeconomic classes do smoke less than others. But governments are limited in their ability to encourage these subgroup patterns through publicity or by restricting anyone's speech. At some point, governments must face the consequences of economic class structure and do something more expensive than restricting the commercial speech of tobacco sellers. Governments must actually redistribute opportunities, resources, and prospects in a way that favors the less fortunate. Simply put, poor people must be made to feel that they have more to lose from smoking.

This is an expensive proposition. The moral case for substantially expanding the opportunities and resources available to the poor is much larger and more powerful than the subject of tobacco can encompass by itself. If there is any basis for optimism regarding the narrow issue of smoking and the poor, it is the evidence that fairly modest improvements in life circumstances are associated with measurable decreases in smoking rates. There should be no doubt, however, that the required public investment is greater than merely some modest further restrictions on tobacco advertising.

The Commercial Colonization of the Internet

We're all so flip and think we're so smart. There'd be—a fellow like Dante—I wish I'd read some of his pieces. I don't suppose I ever will, now.

chapter three

Ordinarily, we do not think of the Internet as the embodiment of commercial values. But some elements of the "traditional" or "original" Internet culture are conducive to the culture of buying and selling. Consider, for example, the freedom and plasticity of one's Internet identity or identities. The real, non-cyber, world, or "meatspace," tends to consign us to standard categories. Those who are, say, young or Asian or female or disabled are readily identified and perhaps even stereotyped. In cyberspace, however, we can reinvent or disguise ourselves according to our purpose, and we can assume or construct various identities. Finally, authoritarianism and rigid inflexibility have always been disfavored in cyberspace.

Once we have assumed an Internet identity, we can establish our Internet relationships on that basis. But since Internet identities can be discarded, perhaps out of boredom or distraction, as fast as they can be assumed, many such Internet relationships carry certain contingencies. Internet relationships typically do not require commitment and so often may lack a sense of depth, seriousness, and even subtlety. Perhaps because of the sense of plasticity of identity, impersonality, abstractness, and even anonymity in some Internet relationships, they offer a temptation to coarseness and disinhibition.

The point is not that these developments should be seen as undesirable. Rather, these Internet cultural phenomena seem to parallel features of our current commercial advertising culture. Although commercial advertisers do not lightly cast aside long-established brand identities, they are continually repositioning, updating, and refocusing their images. Why Coke is better than Pepsi—or vice versa—is, after all, largely a matter of arbitrary construction. In advertising, too, boredom and distraction are negative motivators. The relationship between advertisers and consumers is not characterized by depth, seriousness, and permanence. Given the need to be noticed amid the clutter of ads, a gratuitous coarseness of tone is not unknown in commercial advertising. In addition, authoritarianism and rigidity are no longer widely effective marketing techniques.

For these reasons, and certainly for the more structural and basic economic reasons discussed later, we should anticipate a generally commerce-friendly Internet. The commercialization of the Internet may be inevitable, but this may not mean that it is desirable. Note that we are not advocating the censorship or suppression of advertising or other commercial speech on the Internet. Indeed, censoring the basic commercial message of a major source of Internet funding is probably infeasible or, if not infeasible, would likely lead to a stunted, less interesting Internet.

In addition, there is a sense in which many if not all commercial encounters on the Internet are voluntary transactions between consenting adults. As a general rule, clicking is up to individual discretion. If one wishes, one can spend hours at a time on the World Wide Web, without being seriously distracted by prominent unsolicited advertising. The issue is not one of attempted censorship but of continually reevaluating the real cultural worth, and particularly the cultural costs, of the Internet and its commercialization.

Writing about the effects of on-line technology and the commercial culture on each other may be premature. Currently, the technology of the Internet and its more distinctively graphical component, the World Wide Web, is changing rapidly. Both technical problems and substantive opportunities seem to abound. Cost curves are shifting. Whether, or how, the problems are resolved and the opportunities realized seems impossible to predict. Much is at stake, in that the number of entities supplying and seeking information on the Internet and particularly on the web is continuing to expand.

The range of plausible future scenarios runs from collapse due to technical problems, war, or sabotage; to stagnation due to consumer fear, distrust, or loss of interest; all the way through the nearly universal adoption and displacement or absorption of other media. The Internet itself may be transformed into another sort of entity or entities. We may unite into a mutually understanding and tolerant global village, or we may wind up spending even more of our time with people who share our own narrow interests.

Most of what anyone thinks about the future of the Internet is, therefore, likely to be wrong. There are just too many uncertainties, and the sizes of the uncertainties are themselves uncertain. No one organization is calling the shots any longer, and the problems of coordination, collective goods, incentives, externalities, innovation, technology, and user psychology all are monumental. Predictions about, for example, web use in even several years vary greatly, and at best, any future relationship between commercial web sites and commercial sales or profitability is unpredictable.

But all this uncertainty is quite useful for our purposes. If well-informed persons cannot remotely approach agreement on even the short-term future of commercial activity on the web, this may actually shed light on the importance of commercial influences in our culture. If commercial culture is truly the most generally significant element of our broader communicative culture, we might be able to test and establish its dominance, in at least some crude fashion.

No rigorous, controlled test of the importance of commercial culture is possible. It is, regrettably, unclear what turn of events on the web would falsify the claim that commercialism is preeminent. Furthermore, to assert the relative preeminence of commercialism is not to claim that commercial forces always are successful. In any event, our broad commercial preeminence thesis is compatible with the failure of the commercializing forces to transform every locus of human interaction into a profit-generating enterprise. The web may never become fully commercial, or it may be only a temporary fad, for a number of reasons. The broad commercial preeminence thesis is thus consistent with a future in which marketers become disenchanted with the web or in which web users make most commercial presences on the web unprofitable. This might happen regardless of the general preeminence of the commercial culture.

Still, some possible cyberspace scenarios confirm or disconfirm a claim of commercial preeminence. If one or another commercial presence pervades the Internet, including e-mail and usenet discussion groups of, for instance, quantum decoherence, that would be one thing. But if, in contrast, anticommercial forces rise up in rebellion on principled grounds, against advertising or even against commercial web sites and drive them into obscurity, that would be another. There are other possible scenarios, of course, and probably more likely ones, between these extremes.

We often have more confidence in a theory if we can examine not only how well the theory can account for past events but also how accurately it can predict future events. It is better to predict future data, we think, than merely to explain past data.[1] This preference may actually rest on a confusion. Offering a superior explanation of the past should count as much in favor of a theory as does correctly predicting an unknown future. But in any event, we like to test theories prospectively, although much of what will eventually be true about commercial influences on the Internet has not yet taken shape.

It is sometimes suggested, inaccurately, that if the Internet is in the process of commercializing, it is doing so from a prior state of pristine noncommercialization. The idea that the Internet was invented by scientists wanting to communicate among themselves about scientific matters is an oversimplification. Rather, the Internet—or more likely, some segments of the Internet—may eventually be dominated by commercial influences, whether through visual obtrusiveness, rule writing, traffic management, publicity and hucksterism, subsidy, or prioritization. If this occurs, we should concede that commercialization did not start from zero.

Recall that in a former incarnation, the Internet was operated by the federal government's Advanced Research Projects Agency (ARPA) and then by the National Science Foundation (NSF). Heavy government subsidization, if not ownership, of the infrastructure long required some limits on unfettered commercial promotion. But even at the early stages of Internet use, some traffic consisted of large, high-tech industrial corporations talking to military and other potential customers about their products, both current and forthcoming. No doubt there is a difference between presenting a company's new technologies to a potential government customer and blatant huckstering. We do not, however, claim that even in its golden age, the Internet was free of commercial messages.

We also do not claim that the largely noncommercial ethos of the Internet, and of the World Wide Web in particular, is not changing. Quite the opposite. In particular, the commercialization of the web is currently proceeding rapidly on some, but not all, fronts. Let us look next at a current snapshot of these rapidly evolving circumstances.

The metaphor of a "range war" between commercial and noncommercial factions on the web is often used. More illuminating for our purposes, though, is the idea of colonization. Colonization, after all, implies an attempt at some form of domination, though not necessarily the physical displacement or complete suppression of the indigenous culture. Instead, the indigenous culture is suppressed only to the extent that it is incompatible with the colonial culture and its interests. And this subordination is imposed only to the degree that the colonial power finds it practical and cost effective to do so. Colonial powers do not find it in their interests to colonize all conquerable venues or to deny all local autonomy.

So we would not predict that in the future, the ongoing chatroom discussions of quantum decoherence will be interrupted for unrelated lengthy messages touting the virtues of a particular brand of sneakers. This would serve no one's interests, commercial or otherwise, even if the discussion were directly or indirectly subsidized by some commercial enterprise. It will likely be true in the future that ads widely perceived as alienating or intrusive will not be worth showing. We must remember, though, that over time—particularly as user experiences, costs, and demographics change—what Internet users now regard as intolerable will also likely change.

The intrusiveness of an ad on the Internet, as in the non-cyber-world, is a function of several gradually alterable factors. As the demographics of Internet usage change, the Internet user sentiment regarding advertising may change as well. The percentage of users, for example, who are interested in the Internet's hardware and software and their capabilities primarily for their own sake will probably decrease, and the percentage of users who, in contrast, are more interested in general shopping or in quick access to cultural news, visual materials, entertainment, games, music, or sports results will likely increase.

As these percentages change, the tolerance of advertising in general on the net will likely change, too. Perhaps the earlier net users were more receptive to technical ads for Internet-related products than will latecomers to the net. Resistance to commercialization will likely be different for different sectors of the net. Even the original net user cannot, at this point, claim to feel shock or intrusion, as opposed to disdain, regarding ads on the web. The sense of what one has tacitly authorized by voluntarily moving about on the net can gradually change, as can the cyberspace ethos of what sorts of solicitation or other commercial initiatives are permissible.

If commercial enterprise itself becomes more important to the net, in terms of either organization or funding, it will likely be reflected in the overall sense of propriety on the net. If commerce is paying the piper or is enabling many persons to join in the festivities, commerce should—or at least inevitably will—call the tune. Thus any increase in commercial involvement in and support of the net will legitimize net advertising and other marketing activities.

What net users find appropriate, or at least endurable, will to some degree reflect what they are used to. Those used to the absence of unsolicited advertising may be startled by even small, discrete banner ads. And those used to banner ads may be startled by larger or flashing, crawling, or movielike ads. Finally, those users who have never known anything else might assume that even a carnival atmosphere on the net is simply business as usual and accept the intrusion as the norm.

The degree of Internet commercialization may also reflect our expectations regarding the equipment involved. Some persons currently access the web not through computer monitors but through their television sets. Perhaps this will eventually make a difference, at least psychologically. We regard commercials appearing on our television screen as a natural, familiar, legitimate phenomenon. So through some process of association or generalization, we may, by extension, come to see web commercialization as similarly legitimate.

Net users, regardless of demography or location on the net, can become desensitized to commercial presences. Some "diehards" or "purists" may remain resentful, but they could easily be marginalized as technical elitists, and their real influence may wane over time. Consider the analogy to the increasing commercialization of the Olympics, of college and professional sports events, uniforms, arenas, stadiums, and sports broadcasting. The economics of sports, advertising competitiveness, and the broader culture all have changed within our lifetime. Virtually every moment and square foot of sports-associated time and space are now commercially sponsored. Professional sports franchises can be named after their owners' heavily marketed movies. Occasionally, we notice and decry this phenomenon, and we may think of sports commercialization as a public bad. But in the main, we now accept it. How else could we afford to pay players and owners millions of dollars? No single step in the commercialization process seems to be a dramatic departure. No force or fraud is involved. Other teams and other sports behave similarly. Surely one would not want one's favorite team to lose its competitive edge. Let us note merely that this desensitization process occurs gradually.

As a result, we may wind up with a commercial sports culture, or a commercial Internet culture, of which we earlier would have strongly, perhaps even unanimously, disapproved. Even if all choices and actions on the net are individually free and voluntary, the overall result may be one that many will find unattractive, or at least would have found unattractive at the start of the process, before their sensibilities became dulled and their tastes altered through repeated exposure to commercial influence.

No doubt there are limits to this process of adaptation to the commercial. If any single step in the commercialization process is too dramatic, it can be rescinded and at least temporarily shelved. Maybe next time the step will be less unthinkable, precisely as a result of the earlier, unsuccessful exposure. But advertising and commerce will never be permitted to do whatever they want, under all circumstances.

We can probably adjust, for example, to some kinds of unsolicited advertising in our e-mail, especially if we have the option of removing ourselves from some or all of the address lists. If, on the other hand, e-mail advertising reaches the point that people at work or at home are spending an intolerable amount of time each day reading or deleting unwanted commercial solicitations, something will have to be done. Note that wholesale unsolicited advertising faxes, as opposed to bulk advertising mail, have not become acceptable over time, given the delays and costs imposed on the recipients of junk faxes. At some point, other elements of the commercial culture step in to limit commercial excesses.

It should not be hard for advertising to find an entering wedge into even some of the least commercial Internet forums. Consider, for example, an on-line group consisting mainly of persons interested in a particular medical condition or disease. What would their reactions likely be if a pharmaceutical company offered to post relevant scientific, regulatory, and commercial news concerning the company's products? What if the company deemed it in its interests to support the group financially or to subsidize Internet access fees, perhaps in exchange for clicking on relevant ads or providing detailed consumer survey data?

Can we be sure that the group's members would rise up indignantly—conceding at most that pharmaceutical firms were entitled to their own web sites but could not intrude on preexisting, private usenet groups? A more interesting conflict of interest would be between the consumer-cultivating pharmaceutical companies and the physician who prefers not to discuss with his or her patients the merits of widely publicized alternative treatments.

More generally, what Internet users will adjust to depends in part on the power of the controlling images and metaphors. Is Internet marketing like interrupting a family dinner or a private conversation between friends? Or is it more like holding forth in a public park or on a downtown street corner? Could one argue that restricting commercialization on the Internet would be an act of social environmental conservation, akin to preserving a national park in its pristine form?

Or is principled opposition to the commercialization of the Internet likely to be seen by new users as merely stuffy, a sort of stodgy, old-fashioned, unrealistic paternalism akin to a restrictive dress code in a public school? There is already some Internet history to draw on, although cultural battles on the net will not simply recapitulate earlier battles, just as the commercialization of the net will not simply repeat the commercialization of television or any other medium. Generally, the developing net culture values privacy, but it also values what it regards as uninhibited, unrestrained discourse. Commercialization of the net will likely proceed furthest—financial issues aside—if it aligns itself with the libertarianism of the net. In contrast, commercialization will be inhibited to the extent that it is seen as raising serious privacy issues. If, to take the extreme case, commercial enterprises insist that they must bombard all prospective customers at will; not allow attempts to remove one's name from their lists; covertly track users' habits, finances, personal data, and net meanderings without their knowledge or consent; and sell such knowledge to all interested parties willing to pay the market price, again without consent, the issue will become one of basic privacy and security versus commercialization. None of these practices, however, seems essential to the net commercialization process.

Can we say that the federal government, as the former sponsor of the Internet before its privatization, has taken a neutral position in regard to commercialized and noncommercialized visions of the net? Consider the interesting remark of one official regarding the first Federal Trade Commission (FTC) crackdown on fraudulent Internet advertising. The director of the FTC's Bureau of Consumer Protection, Jodie Bernstein, stated that "cyberspace is a new frontier for advertising and marketing" but that "the Internet will not achieve its commercial potential if this new frontier becomes the Wild West of fraudulent schemes."[2]

This statement is not the authoritative administration position on the subject, and it can be interpreted in more than one way. The more culturally neutral interpretation would be that users of the net should be able to choose among an uncommercialized net; a thoroughly commercialized net in which the ads are not false, deceptive, or misleading; or something in between but whose ads are trustworthy. The less culturally neutral interpretation would be that the net should ideally be more or less commercialized but that we will not reach this desirable result if fraudulent advertisers louse things up for the rest. Hence the FTC's mandate to chase after alleged cyberspace versions of snake oil and patent medicine sellers for the sake of more respectable trade.

According to the latter interpretation, the government seeks to reduce fraud on the net as desirable in itself and also as a way of promoting the spread of commercial interests on the net. Even if this is an overreading of the government's attitudes, there is little reason to suspect that the government would place obstacles in the path of those trying to commercialize the net.

So why might commercial enterprises want to be on the net, and what might they want to do, given sufficient consumer demand for, or at least tolerance of, their activities? A commercial presence on the net can be simple or elaborate, inexpensive or costly. Ads can appear on another person's on-line service or off one's own server. An advertising presence can take the form of a banner with no other link to anything of much substance. Or an advertisement can contain text, color graphics, video, audio, interesting hyperlinks, and future enhancements.

But if the sponsors of commercial web sites are to make them worthwhile, they will have to go beyond these sorts of displays. A web ad with bright colors and fairly decent sound may have, for the moment, a certain cachet. But once the novelty wears off, visitors may notice that the sound and pictures are no better than those associated with a video game or commercial television. Commercial web sites must therefore do more if they are to pull their own commercial weight over the long term.

For commercial viability, web sites must combine the latest technical improvements with imaginative interactivity, across the full range of marketing tasks and opportunities. The site must be perceived as worth visiting over and over, even after the novelty and superficial appeal have worn off. From the commercial enterprise's perspective, a visit to the site should offer the commercial sponsor a range of useful results.

Consider the possible corporate benefits accruing from a well-designed, well-integrated web site. The actual ordering of goods has, at least until recently, disappointed the most optimistic expectations, perhaps because of technical, coordinative, and psychological problems in ensuring the security of Internet signatures, confidentiality, and the payment process. Ironically, the overall impact of this consumer distrust has not been enormous, given consumers' willingness to give their credit card numbers to complete strangers at the end of an 800 phone number or to toss credit card information into commercial wastebaskets. Cyberpayment may catch on, of course, when and if people come to trust the process. The issue may be partly psychological—remember that ATM machines were available for some time before they became widely popular. Given our accumulated experiences with ATMs and debit cards, however, the battle for cyberpayment may already be largely won.

Commercial web sites may be worthwhile even if no one directly orders from such a site, because they can make other contributions to overall commercial health. A corporation can, through a suitably elaborate site, accomplish a number of tasks: it can draw up and maintain e-mail customer lists; displace or supplement other, more expensive, traditional forms of advertising; keep track of its competitors and suppliers; and enhance its recognition and visibility in the market. Moreover, even if no one orders on-line, the overall speed of ordering and of product delivery may be increased.

In addition, some enterprises can keep their Internet stores open for business twenty-four hours per day, seven days a week. Internet stores also are accessible around the world, or at least to all sufficiently affluent customers who speak one of the languages understood by the site. Furthermore, property taxes on a web site enterprise may be quite low, so entrepreneurs can change their business practices, or even their entire business, at little cost.

Public relations and knowledge of one's customers should improve on the Internet. Companies can conduct on-line product surveys or solicit more open-ended customer feedback. Custom-tailored coupons can be generated and printed at home for store use, or some items of clothing could be custom-tailored on-line for those willing to participate in the design of their own fashions. The idea is to go beyond on-line versions of more familiar forms of advertising.

Suppose a bagel maker has reduced the sodium content of its bagels. Why not publicize that fact on-line, publish recipes, and have a nutritionist available on-line to discuss the expanding role of bagels in a sound nutritional program? Low-fat bagel customers could get sympathetic feedback and useful advice on dieting and weight loss. These suggestions are merely improved cyberspace versions of techniques used for many decades.

Some sorts of businesses are better positioned than others to profit from the Internet. For example, Federal Express and other delivery services have taken advantage of the Internet by enabling customers to arrange for shipments on-line and also to track package deliveries on-line. But other sorts of businesses cannot profit in the same way that Federal Express does. The bagel seller, for example, may find that only retailers, and not consumers, care where the bagel delivery trucks are at any given moment. Nor can bagels be taste-tested on-line.

Consumers of automobiles may or may not appreciate emotional support, bonding, and official discussion groups. It may eventually be possible, though, for prospective car buyers to take something like a test drive of an automobile on-line, as the video game technology for analogous pursuits has become quite sophisticated. Obviously, some key elements of a traditional automobile test drive, including real steering and road handling, cannot be duplicated behind the wheel, or joy stick, of one's browser. High-resolution color video images do not fly onto one's screen at breathtaking speed, at least not yet. But prospective buyers could get some sense of the location and use of the dashboard's features, of the visual elements of gear shifting, of the car's route-mapping and location systems, of its overall look and design, and of its internal components.

Suppose a hotel wants to emphasize the luxuriousness of its suites, its location, or the magnificent view from some of its rooms. This all could be done on-line on the Internet. Likewise, vacation spots or tourist areas could be advertised in a similar way. A variety of detailed maps could be made available to be downloaded by interested prospective visitors.

The issue is not whether it is impossible to do all these things without the Internet. Rather, it is whether it is deemed worthwhile for a business to provide these features on-line and whether potential customers want to pursue such possibilities on-line.

Consumers may also find merit in technically sophisticated responses to competing commercial enterprises on the net. Suppose a consumer wishes to buy tickets to *Aida*, replace contact lenses, arrange for a hotel room in Palo Alto, fill a prescription for tetracycline, or find a new translation of Homer's *Odyssey* through an on-line source. Most prospective customers are neither sufficiently Internet savvy nor sufficiently knowledgeable of the relevant market to properly explore the options, even if they had the time. But cheap and effective electronic intelligent agents can be subtly instructed as to one's real priorities and trade-off rates—they do not have to be crude proxies or foolishly absolute rules—and sent off to do one's bidding. Even given their cost, the intelligent agent might make on-line shopping a more attractive option for the individual consumer and help drive down prices more generally.

One might assume that web sites for big-ticket items would be more cost effective than those for smaller purchases. Prospective car buyers might ask a dozen meaningful questions, whereas those choosing among soft drink brands probably would not. As we have seen, though, even inexpensive, diet-related items might be associated with a flourishing web site. There may even be a certain logic, beyond sheer novelty, to having a soft drink web site. The leading soft drink manufacturers often compete, after all, not so much on the basis of price or taste as on perceived coolness. Establishing one's coolness compared with that of one's competitors can, however, be something of a dicey, subjective business. Certain kinds of commercials may assist in this process, as may accoutrements such as pagers or a well-chosen celebrity endorsement. Celebrities, however, may be vulnerable to injury or unfavorable publicity. If celebrity status can establish coolness by association, perhaps a cool web site for one's product can do the same. It may be easier to engineer perceived coolness into one's web site than into one's underlying product.

Net commercializers will, in general, do best by not seeking to deny basic, ingrained cultural patterns. Some markets have strong sensory elements beyond that of sight; thus many shoppers appreciate the chance to squeeze the melon or kick the tire. Eventually, such sensory elements may be virtually available. In addition, sometimes we look forward to the social, breeze-shooting aspects of shopping. Surely this is currently electronically possible, whether with real sales people, avatars, or shills.

Commercialization of the net beyond a certain point will require the continued broadening of net demographics, as well as changes in the ways people navigate through the net. A fairly high percentage of net commerce is still computer related, a fact that is not much healthier commercially than using printing presses mainly to promote the sale of printing presses and related materials. This dilemma is partly a matter of demographics. Procter and Gamble, for example, does not want to be confined to selling its broad line of household goods only to "netizens."

There is currently a race between the diminishing level of skill required to navigate the web and the expansion of the group of net users. Most people are not accustomed to using the Internet, which is certainly not always a matter of their being unable to afford the proper equipment or access charges. Some persons are allergic to booleanism, and some shopping problems do not reduce well to boolean logic, perhaps owing to the lack of a standardized vocabulary. Search engines often return numerous irrelevant sites. Some persons may have incompatible tastes or principled objections to shopping on the computer. Others may believe that they lack the skills needed to use the net. Recall the surprising percentage of persons who own videocassette recorders but are unable to program them. Many commercial enterprises, however, will not want to write off prospective customers who are willing and able to pay but are not technologically adventurous.

Many sorts of commercial enterprises will want to work with and encourage those who can make web surfing easier, faster, and less intimidating. The idea is to continually lower the amount of knowledge and skill needed, or widely thought to be needed, to reach and respond to commercial web sites, for example. Voice recognition will not help if it is thought to mean simply more things to learn. Most new arrivals at the Web are not immediately interested in attempting to remember various techniques, procedures, and possibilities all at the same time. None of this contradicts the idea that the net offers the advantage of very narrowly targeted advertising to receptive audiences. As net demographics become representative of a larger cross section of the population, the average net user will be less interested in, say, buying a high-tech, net-oriented item.

Part of the difficulty of predicting the eventual degree of commercialization of the net is the possible cumulative or "snowballing" effects of prior commercial influences on the net itself. Further web commercialization, for example, can be presented as the only economically viable, or the only culturally attractive, solution to technical problems caused largely by earlier web commercialization. Commercialization thus gains ground by offering to fix problems largely of its own making. This, in turn, expands the presence and the practical influence of commercial enterprises on the web.

Consider, for example, some technical problems currently associated with the net. Dialing up may result in a busy signal. Particular sites may be overcrowded and thus not available. Audio quality does not yet match that of the other media at their best. Graphic displays, in particular, may be painfully slow, and disconnections and other glitches occur at random. Standards have not yet been established where they seem to be needed, and confidentiality and security are still shaky. Wireless is in its infancy.

More important, commercial communications cannot flourish in an uncertain environment. Either the net must be technically improved, or it will be bypassed and perhaps left to atrophy. It is in the interest of commercial enterprises to resolve the technical problems, and it may be cost effective for them to devise, or at least pay for, the necessary solutions. There is admittedly something of a collective goods problem here. Fixing a problem may be expensive, and it may be difficult for the fixer to charge all those who use or benefit from the inventions and improvements in infrastructure. Still, it is reasonable to suppose that individual firms, joint venturers and consortia, or various combinations of commercial, university research, and federal government cooperative efforts could make the necessary improvements. Ironically, the proliferation of commerce on the net has aggravated some of the most familiar technical problems. Think of the recent increases in the number of entities taking up residence on the net. Some of the new addresses are for educational institutions and for governmental entities, but by far the fastest-growing sector is that of commercial enterprises. Some of the most obvious net technical problems stem precisely from this commercial overload, or from the mismatch between current net capabilities and the increased volume of net traffic.

We may expect that the interests driving the net's commercialization will, despite the collective goods problems, offer to resolve those technical problems. It is also likely that those solutions will lead to further commercialization of the net. Although it is premature to try to envision how all the problems will be addressed, consider one possible theme and variations.

When middle-class persons perceive the physical security of their way of living to be at risk, they react in different ways. They may simply move, leaving others to cope with the problem. They may seek a collective, political solution, perhaps through increased police protection for all. Or they may arrange for private security, thereby creating a two-tiered security system of private security for the well-off and underfunded police for the less affluent.

Commercial enterprise may respond to the net's technical problems in similar ways. We might expect, analogous to the private security arrangements, the development of special, paid, "fast lanes" on the infobahn. Or in exchange for a premium payment, one could travel "first class," as opposed to "coach," on the Internet. Instead of more legroom and less punitive snacks, the extra fees would guarantee quicker and more reliable Internet transactions. The less fortunate would be consigned to second-class net service.

What is interesting, though, is that it is probably not in the broader interests of commerce as a whole to let the facilities available to the unwashed masses fall below a certain level of efficiency. That is, it is not in the interest of the Fortune 500 for their retail customers to be disconnected too many times. Commerce can hardly dazzle masses of teenagers with sophisticated graphics and audio if most of them are unable to access such displays. The business enterprise may lose a sale, if not a customer, if the customer cannot locate or reach the proper web site. If too many potential customers are paying for their net access by the hour, they may not be willing to explore a commercial site or to stay long enough to become interested in buying something. Clearly, most commercial enterprises would benefit from broadening the base of Internet users and so have an incentive to subsidize the technical upgrading of the net capabilities and the access of potential customers who might be unwilling or even unable to pay for such upgrading themselves. Profitable customers need not be affluent customers.

It may be possible to narrow the commercial subsidies of customer net technology, perhaps by offering free access to some or all distinctively commercial web sites. It may be difficult, however, to provide access to or to improve the technical quality of customer visits to commercial sites without also improving access to or the quality of visits to noncommercial sites. Even if it were technically possible, for example, to allow customers to process color graphics and high-quality audio at some or all commercial sites, but not at noncommercial sites, such discrimination may appear mean-spirited, thus destroying the public relations value of any consumer subsidy.

Surely, commercial enterprises can collectively afford to offer such subsidies if they see it as being in their interest to do so, and they can derive something of real commercial value in exchange for the partial subsidy. Perhaps the beneficiary will have to complete and regularly update detailed marketing surveys, accept unsolicited commercial e-mail, or regularly click through a gauntlet of personalized on-line advertising.

Eventually, perhaps, every cable or even every long distance customer will have free and unlimited access to the Internet, as well as all the necessary hardware and software. Even now, the cost of Internet access is dropping. But some commercial subsidies may still be necessary, and many of the most interesting web sites may be the most expensive to operate and maintain. Often, though, commercial enterprises will want to have someone else pay the subsidy, even if they have to sacrifice some of their control. In such cases, the idea will be to convince the federal government, perhaps in concert with consumers and education groups, that the taxpayers really should be paying for much of this upgrading process. The argument certainly need not be that what's good for the General Motors web site is good for the country. Surely it is in the national interest for American citizens generally to be well positioned to use the emerging technologies of the information era. Economic competition is global and requires access to information. There is, as the U.S. Supreme Court observed, a strong public interest in hearing what the voices of commerce wish to tell us.

Government subsidies can be sought not only on these grounds but also to make the net more democratic. Net technologies are still available mainly to the economically affluent, despite their diminishing cost and the increasing number of terminals in public schools and libraries. To deny access to the Internet is to deny the development of important skills, as well as access to one kind of general education. The commercialization of the Internet thus can, up to a point, rest on a broader egalitarian argument.

As commerce becomes a more pervasive part of the Internet's and the World Wide Web's economics and subsidization, its influence will also increase. This is not to say that we will ever do most of our business on the web or that the largest retailers will be purely web operations. Sometimes, however, the most interesting sites will, for reasons of cost, be either commercially sponsored sites or those heavily supported by advertising. Flashiness and technical innovation may be expensive, which will require commercial enterprise to pay for it.

The users' preferences regarding commercialization of the net will vary, just as viewers differ in their willingness to pay for more choices of cable programming. Whereas some net users may be willing to pay to avoid all advertising on the net, many will not. Therefore, the integration of commercial advertising into one's electronic trip to the Louvre may not seem much different from how commercial network television works now.

The awareness that in order to avoid advertising, one is paying, view by view, or time unit by time unit, for every "premium" site one visits surely takes some of the enjoyment out of the process. This is not to deny the appeal of pay per view television specials. But pay per view television is different because one's costs are fixed. One can plan one's evening around, say, a group or individual viewing of a particular special event. But the net is used differently. Often, one wishes to explore spontaneously—to "surf the net"— going and coming as one pleases, making serendipitous discoveries. Pay per view, or pay per access, simply does not fit that model. Uninhibited exploration is spoiled by a sense that the meter is running and so is surely more compatible with flat fees and an advertising-supported environment.

Some commercial enterprises may fear that if net usage has no budget constraints, some users may wander off the advertised commercial paths and be forever lost for commercial purposes. But most net users do have consumer interests, and advertising may eventually be more widespread and more intelligently designed than it is now. Commercially supported sites may well be the most technically advanced. Not everyone will sit still for web equivalents of television infomercials, but most people will venture out of the more purely noncommercial sites from time to time, especially when they need to buy something.

What, then, is wrong with this overall picture? Our main concern is that the cyberworld will come to reflect and reinforce the proliferation of commercial values. This concern is not based primarily on the commercial control of noncommercial speech, although that is possible. Imagine an expensive technology by which museum sculptures can be displayed on the net in high resolution, from all angles, or in three dimensions. It is easy to imagine museums' accepting the loan of this technology in return for more or less conspicuous corporate sponsorship. Should we, then, expect the museums to display skepticism or even a detached, neutral attitude toward commercial values?

We could argue that many real-world museums are already compromised by commercial values and even commercial sponsorships, but this should not make us indifferent to further developments in this process. We should not believe that because many museums are already less than pristine, it does not matter what further commercial arrangements they make. That is like saying that once the air is polluted, it is of little consequence how much more it is polluted.

Nonetheless, there are grounds for pessimism regarding the commercialization of cyberspace. Corporate interests, through the deployment of corporate resources, are likely to shape, quite substantially, the cyberenvironment. But there are no signs yet that this will lead to a monumental backlash in which we decide that it is better to spend our evenings chatting amiably, face to face, with our neighbors.

In the meantime, let us remember the stakes. American television advertising is influential but does not set the tone for, say, British or French television advertising. A trend in American television advertising does not necessarily send dominos toppling throughout the world, but cyberspace may be somewhat different. Many languages will be spoken in cyberspace. The most popular sites in the United States may not be the most popular sites in Saudi Arabia or Japan. It seems unlikely, however, that commercial influence on the net in the United States could be dominant without significantly affecting net sites, net fashions, and net experiences elsewhere.

Consider the options available to citizens of less affluent countries when the net becomes available to them. For them, the choice between paying a monthly fee for the privilege of not having to endure commercials and getting free access larded with commercials may be between an affordable net or no net at all. They will have to set aside their ambivalences about Western commercial advertising and commercial values more generally if they wish to be wired in at all.

Let us conclude with more general, and more speculative, points about the net and commercial values. Net enthusiasts commonly tout the democratic, nonauthoritarian, decentralized, nonhierarchical character of the net environment. Stephen Hawking and Roger Penrose may debate the nature of black holes right next door to the ruminations on the same subject by a mathematical illiterate. There may, of course, be a certain amount of hypocrisy in publicly delighting in this absence of hierarchy. If one is looking for medical advice to help a friend, one may well be tempted to retreat to the comforting authority of the American Medical Association or the Ivy League medical schools and skip the high school term papers on the subject.

We should not, of course, belittle the value of expressive democracy and equality. Indeed, the thesis of this chapter is that we should not expect genuine democracy or egalitarianism to become the net's dominant ethos. In some respects, the openness of the net will remain, which is good. But hierarchy and inequality will be present as well, reflecting in some measure the influence of the net's funding sources. And that influence is likely to be disproportionately commercial. The idea of history itself may eventually, in cyberspace, become disjointed or may come to refer mainly to the chronological order of the discussions at hand. All this may be delightful, but it is hardly subversive of commercial values, though it may be tempting to think so if we think only of advertising that refers to history, trust, or authority. Indeed, some classic advertising is of this kind: A trusted friend of the family. In business at this location over fifty years. Three out of four doctors recommend. But these sorts of commercial pitches are not essential to all contemporary advertising; authority-based advertising has lost ground over the last half-century or so. In all of this, commercial communication coheres with even the most allegedly anarchic sectors of the Internet. The untamed Internet ethos thus subverts some commercial values only to the extent that the Internet ethos subverts its own values: only when we doubt that all net speech is equally valuable can we see the special cultural disvalue of commercial speech's preeminence on the net. The typical commercial assumption that value is relative, subjective, or arbitrary fits quite well, in the meantime, with the currently celebrated net ethos.

Much of the commercialization of the Internet will rely on persons who want to visit commercial sites. If we stop responding to the ads, the Internet itself may stagnate, along with commercial interest. If access to the Internet for the poor or for the public in general is commercially subsidized, software blocking commercial sites or advertising is unlikely to be built into the terminals. Ways to block or bypass the blocking software itself may be developed, as in an arms race. Eventually, one may have to fool the advertisers into thinking that one has clicked on and luxuriated for some time over their ads in order to obtain what one was seeking on the net in the first place.

In response, ads for the Internet might be designed that do not use brand names or that use them in ways that the hostile software does not recognize.

Experience with television and even with the Internet may be encouraging in this regard. After all, television advertisers have generally not tried to override the various sorts of zapping technology. One could argue that some advertisers have reacted by making their commercials more entertaining. We already have experience with site access-blocking software on the Internet. How much effort have the producers of sexually oriented web sites devoted to devising ways of technically beating the voluntary blocking technology?

These analogies, however, cannot provide much reassurance. Ultimately, net users are unlikely to be able to choose between a heavily commercial and commercially subsidized Internet, on the one hand, and a more expensive noncommercialized but otherwise quite similar Internet, on the other.

The problem is, after all, both partly technical and partly conceptual. The technical question is how advertisers can develop new ways to incorporate their advertising messages as closely and inextricably as possible into the material that the user wishes to access. Internet ads need not be jarring or incongruous. In the future, one will either cybernetically tour the Louvre with the conspicuous assistance of a seller of bottled water or not tour it at all.

The deeper, conceptual problem is the dividing line between the zap worthy and the non-zap worthy. The underlying problem is not really the presence of commercial advertisements but the eventual pervasiveness of commercial influences and commercial values. To avoid the commercialization of the net in this sense may not be realistic; it certainly cannot be achieved through a clever software package.

Finally, let us speculate a bit about the ability of net users to adapt, over time, to at least some of the features of net commercialization.

People, after all, read newspapers in entirely different ways. Some persons do not even see the most prominent ads, or at least remember them, whereas others consciously seek them out. Could something similar develop on the Internet? Those who do not care for the ads could gradually "train" themselves to ignore them.

The problem here is partly one of physical layout and accessibility. If we like, we can flip through our newspaper to find the sports scores, the obits, or the horoscope, without reading any of the intervening ads. Even the ad material wrapping the Sunday comics can be largely ignored. But given the size and display capabilities of most current video monitors, the control exercised by operators of home pages, and the click-through technology, it may be difficult, if not impossible, to bypass, visually or psychologically, ads in cyberspace.

This presents a final risk. We may find ourselves voluntarily exiting an already commercialized museum site based on the alluring representation that if we will but click on a particular item, we will be transported to a more interesting, albeit more heavily commercialized, site, perhaps even complete with downloadable coupons or term papers. We thus may have to decide whether the better metaphors for such a process are nonlinearity and serendipity or distraction and malnutrition.

What Are
Controversial
Ads For?

I believe in using poetry and humor and all
that junk when it turns the trick.

Some ads are controversial and shocking ads, though this is not
intended as a judgmental or metaphysically ambitious claim. The
focus of this chapter is on the predictable and even intended reactions to ads, justified or not, of a significant portion of the viewing
public. For the most part, we ignore ads that are offensive or shocking to some segment of the audience but that the ads' sponsors did
not intend or predict to be so. We also ignore ads for controversial
products, such as tobacco. Finally we do not simply assume that any
ad that is controversial or shocking to anyone must be progressive;
instead, we explore this question with some care.

The crucial question is whether most controversial or shocking ads have a redeeming cultural value. Even if the underlying messages, intended or unintended, of commercial advertising are not culturally beneficial, aren't most controversial ads at least culturally progressive because of, for example, their themes of diversity, playfulness, novelty, inclusiveness, tolerance, compassion and sympathy, freedom, individuality, solidarity, disinhibition, engagement, and equality? Don't most controversial ads challenge obsolete, narrow, and repressive standards? Don't the transgressiveness and iconoclasm of controversial ads offer a liberating message? Doesn't the underlying relativism that such ads may validate also have progressive implications?

We might think so, based on creatively argued cultural commentary and the typical remarks of the ad's producers, if not also of the product's manufacturers. A closer look at the dynamics of controversial advertising, however, leads to caution and skepticism in this regard. At bottom, there are no convincing reasons to trust the progressivity of commercial advertisers in general, or of the suppliers of socially controversial advertising in particular, even if we can find some interesting and well-known exceptions.

Let us begin with some examples. Worldwide, probably the best-known self-consciously controversial ads are those for the Benetton Group, a clothing manufacturer that has for years conducted an advertising campaign termed the "United Colors of Benetton." Several of its advertisements and commercials contain visual images perceived by some persons or groups as shocking, offensive, or otherwise socially controversial.

Over the years, for instance, Benetton's advertising has featured war cemeteries, a roll of unraveling toilet paper, brightly colored condoms, waterfowl stuck in an oil slick, a black woman breast-feeding a white baby, child laborers, a human body stamped HIV positive, a blood-covered neonate still attached to its umbilical cord, two kissing teenagers dressed as a priest and a nun, a black girl with her hair made up into apparent horns, and a juxtaposition of 1936 Olympic Nazi salutes with 1968 Olympic Black Power salutes. Text, or language, is insignificant.

We should mention, however, that for many persons, the name Benetton summons up none of these images but, instead, Benetton's Formula One racing team sponsorships, whose social progressivity one may be excused for finding elusive. After all, tobacco firms also sponsor race cars. But what about controversial advertising images? What can be said about their social value?

First, let us set aside the issue of legal censorship. The images just described, however ambiguous and inarticulate, clearly transcend narrowly commercial speech. Instead, they raise—however vaguely and equivocally—significant and broad social issues. No one can pretend that the Benetton ads are in the same category as the announcement that tetracycline or pork and beans is available at a specified price.

At least insofar as such ads address recognizable social ideas and issues, they deserve constitutional protection beyond that merited by commercial speech, although not all legal systems would agree. At least one German appellate court, for example, ruled against several of the aforementioned advertisements.[1] The court's reasoning was that the ads constituted a form of unfair competition under German law.

The German court ruled that through its depiction of intense suffering, Benetton was attempting to evoke compassion, to associate Benetton with sympathy and compassion for suffering, and thus to enhance its corporate image in the consumer's mind. But the court rejected such tactics as emotionalistic, exploitive, and immoral. In particular, it concluded that the image of an HIV-stamped person strips such people of their dignity. All of this amounts, the court held, to unfair competition.

The logic of the German court is not entirely unreasonable. For those steeped in American free speech traditions, however, it should not be persuasive. Unelected courts should not be in the business of imputing one particular interpretation to ambiguous but consciously intended social messages and then legally condemning them on grounds of their alleged immorality as so interpreted. Reasonable persons can disagree over whether an image of a person stamped HIV positive is degrading or instead challenges such degradation. Surely the intention of the corporation, or of the ad's creative producers, was not to degrade such persons.

As a matter of constitutional law, we cannot allow courts, independently of democratically elected governments, to impose subjective judicial standards of immorality, or of excessive and permissible levels of emotionalism, in striking down social and political messages. This must hold even when the speaker's intent is vague, as long as such an intent in speaking is present. It does not matter whether Benetton is a natural or a corporate speaker or a mixture of the two. Nor does it make any constitutional difference whether Benetton's most important reason for formulating such an intent and for so speaking was to move its products. Finally, it does not matter whether Benetton's failure to speak—at all or, far less plausibly, in just this way—would have, objectively, jeopardized its profitability.

There are, after all, few insurgent political movements that an established order would be unwilling to consider immoral. We should have no more confidence in the ability of courts or governments to regulate any sort of commercial or political speech on the basis of its alleged moral or political errors than we would when the allegedly morally defective speech is not commercial and not sponsored by a corporation. One can easily imagine judicial tribunals pronouncing as immoral the speech of Socrates, Galileo, Thoreau, Gandhi, and King. Nor should the emotionalism or imagery of some such speakers disqualify them. Truth in political matters is often spoken, quite naturally, with great passion. Truth and passion are clearly not antitheses.

We should point out, however, that this familiar view does not invalidate our earlier conclusion that commercial speech can and should be regulated, generally, on the basis of reasonableness. Most commercial speech has no specifically intended broader social import. When ads do mix merchandising and social commentary, the courts may well be able to separate the two, and then the free speech clause should protect the latter more stringently than the former.

Our question, therefore, should not be one of legally restricting Benetton's expression of controversial social issues. Rather, our concern should be limited to the progressivity or other distinctive political value of controversial ads containing some mixture of commercial and noncommercial, express and implied, intended and unintended elements. The progressive contribution of Benetton's ads is, at best, not very clear.

We have seen how at least one German appellate court construed one of Benetton's ads in ways not intended by the ad's producer. But several of the ads implicating race are, individually and as a whole, arguably equivocal in their implications. Images of a black girl with her hair arranged to resemble horns and of a black woman breastfeeding a white child, or juxtaposing the Nazi Olympic salute with the Mexico City Olympic Black Power salute are, it seems fair to say, open to less than progressive—even if unintended—interpretations.

An ad, however artistically interesting, is not progressive insofar as it invites nonprogressive interpretations, depending on the political predispositions of individual viewers. Allowing persons across the political spectrum to read an ad as sympathetic to their own particular view is not progressive so much as opportunistic, however desirable this effect may be in a competitive market context.

Again, we are not accusing Benetton of racism. But it is not cynical to suggest that Benetton as an organization must either make money by selling clothing or go out of business. A tinge of cynicism might lead us to suspect that ambiguous or equivocal visual images that allow viewers to interpret them as they prefer could be a commercially ideal way of presenting social issues. Viewers with conflicting beliefs could all count Benetton as sympathetic. A further tinge of cynicism might suggest that whatever Benetton's real social beliefs, its first advertising goal is not to unequivocally promote any consistent set of social ideas—let alone consistently progressive social ideas—but to generate publicity and sales through repeated controversy. But this goal may or may not call for progressive statements. Why, then, are Benetton and other manufacturers attracted to a strategy of controversy?

Experimental evidence indicates that some Benetton ads in Europe are interpreted in ways other than those purportedly intended by the ads' creators. That is, if the officially intended messages are the baseline, Benetton ads are often misinterpreted. We may set aside the problem of whether there is always a clear, accurately reported intent underlying every such ad. The arguable breakdown in communication between Benetton and the buying public, however, may be of little concern to Benetton as a commercial enterprise. Happily for Benetton, the messages perceived by the European viewers of selected Benetton ads elicited favorable reactions. That is, viewers reacted positively to the ads, despite interpreting them differently from the meanings intended by the ads' producer.[2] What viewers perceive and like in an ad may or may not be a socially progressive theme. Again, at the risk of being cynical, we might wonder how eager a corporate speaker would be to clarify its message if the currently perceived message drew a favorable response.

Whether the more controversial Benetton ads actually led to a loss of sales is unclear. Although some German store owners have complained of adverse sales effects from some Benetton advertising, even they also cite other, unrelated Benetton policies and the general economy as possible causes as well. More generally, it is surprisingly difficult to link sales levels to the magnitude, mix, or controversiality of a company's advertising. Certainly, Benetton's recognizability and public profile have become more prominent over the past few years.

It is likely that the social stands taken by Benetton in its advertising would never have received either the initial exposure or the resulting media coverage if they had been taken by an interest group with a more direct stake in the subject. The image of an oil-mired bird, for example, could not have been disseminated as widely by an environmental group, and such a group's taking up this theme would probably not have been deemed newsworthy. The very fact that the speaker is the Formula One sponsor Benetton, and not one of the very few commercial enterprises that consistently seeks to downplay its commercial or profit-making status, may also add to the impact and interest of Benetton's social messages.

For now, let us merely note that Benetton is not the only commercial enterprise that employs controversial ad campaigns; a pattern is beginning to emerge with regard to all controversial ads. Controversial advertisements are generally defended by their sponsor in rather politically neutral and, beyond a certain point, not very progressive terms. The basic theme is a positive message about the spiritedness, savviness, spunkiness, independence, and self-esteem or inner worth of today's young people.

The messages of other controversial ads might be less bland, such as the general desirability of envelope pushing, freedom and openness, and the relativity and subjectivity of matters of taste and propriety. It is common, after all, for even uncontroversial ads to advocate following one's basic impulses and defying the rules. Nike, Burger King, and many automobile ads do this.

Less attractively, a number of controversial ads are occasionally defended on the reductivist basis of age. Hip, young people get and approve of the ads; nonhip, out-of-touch old people, who lack the media savvy, edginess-appreciation, or the visual image-processing skills of the young, do not. But probably neither hipness nor progressivism can be closely correlated, inversely, with age. Baby boomers, especially, are notoriously unlikely to concede such a claim. And if hipness is defined broadly enough to encompass all those who understand or appreciate the controversial ads, there is no reason for them to do so. According to this view, hipness is remarkably easy to acquire and surprisingly commercialized. To retain its cachet, however, it must be, or at least seem to be, a narrow, somehow exclusionary, esoteric quality. To perform its marketing function, on the other hand, hipness must be a much less selective phenomenon, open to the buyers of the product. The hip thus includes (many) young people and nearly anyone else favorably disposed toward the product. Given this paradox, the shoals of commercial hipness are not easy to navigate.

It is difficult to believe that progressivity is largely either a function of youth or of one's reaction to a series of commercial advertisements for a line of clothing. Commercial stylishness is not yet synonymous with progressivity. There is more to progressive social transformation than understanding, approving of, or even buying the products touted by culturally sophisticated or artistic commercials.

Advertising can in principle convey progressive messages, despite the objective function of commercial advertising to inspire overall consumer demand or to encourage brand loyalty or switching. As we have seen, commercial advertising by its very nature sends—at least by implication—basic messages about the normalcy, effectiveness, and propriety of consumption-oriented ways of living. This message is conveyed even if the hippest ads depreciate commercialism or insist that we not buy their products. In fact, ads that tout nonconsumption can survive the Darwinism fitness struggle only if they, paradoxically, encourage consumption or if the ad producers are willing and able to subsidize them. Anticonsumption ads that do not "work" by inspiring consumption through some sort of ironic reversal simply cannot survive.

In principle, then, there is room for ads that carry progressive messages, as the constraints of the market do not always rule out such messages. The amount of room for progressive messages depends on the producer's market-ecological niche, the degree of ad saturation, the nature of the product, the intended audience, the spirit or mood of the times, and the desired market share. The market in general does not impose a uniform political slant, any deviation from which is punished. But this discretionary room may also run in the direction of antiprogressive messages as well.

More specifically, what can be said about recent controversial advertising? The typical vagueness, largely visual nature, and atmospheric quality of these ads in some respects limit any intended progressive messages. Worse, some of the supposedly progressive ads are open to less progressive interpretations. It is possible to read progressive social messages into a number of controversial ads, but it also is possible to read some controversial ads as, for example, legitimizing commodified attitudes toward sex, distracting attention away from more useful approaches to serious issues, or encouraging passivity. It is hard, therefore, to see them as progressive.

What about the commonly implied broader message that taste and propriety are somehow relative, or merely subjective? Some of the controversial ads encourage us to set our own standards or to follow some group's standards, without worrying about whether those standards are flawed by any other measure. Doesn't that sort of message have progressive implications? Historically, haven't repressive groups always denied the relativity or subjectivity of all sorts of standards? Isn't there a clear association, then, between the relativism of standards and freedom? Doesn't relativism increase tolerance and reduce conflict?

These are important questions to which there are no quick, satisfying answers. They have been addressed elsewhere[3] and cannot be addressed here in detail. Suffice it to say that although opposition to moral relativism has been an element of oppressive ideologies, such opposition has also been part of our most progressive, liberating ways of thinking. Relativism can just as easily take the form of exploiting or ignoring the weak and deferring to the strong as any other, more progressive form. Why not tolerate those who are stronger and take advantage of or ignore those who cannot resist effectively? No group characterizes its own morality in just these invidious terms. But why not adopt just such a group-interested morality once the fun of other forms of moral posturing begins to fade? If standards are relative or subjective, why not equate morality with the interests of whatever group one cares to associate with?

Progressivism occasionally refers to the sacrifice of a group interest, especially, if not exclusively, on the part of the powerful or the affluent. Progressivism involves the redistribution of resources. If such sacrifice is to be substantial, long term, and consistent, there must be an objectively good moral reason for the sacrifice. The poor are not better off when they depend on the groundless gestures and arbitrary posturing of subjectivism.

Relativism and subjectivism of standards are thus, in the long term, not hospitable to real progressive change. But there is, on the other hand, a central role for relativism and subjectivism in consumption-oriented lifestyles. The market itself imposes no standards of judgment, taste, or morality beyond what seems necessary to sustain itself for the moment. The fashion industry—and to some extent other industries, including some consumer durables—relies on changes of fashion that appeal more to arbitrary and subjective taste than to objective improvement. The market has no inherent preference between providing basic necessities for the poor or devoting its attentions to other pursuits. Commercial markets are, in general, nonjudgmental. There are no morally objectionable demand curves. Markets do not require or even prefer any redistribution of wealth or egalitarian social change.

In the long run, economic exchange is at its most robust when we are not subjectivists about matters such as rudeness, indolence, or complacency in regard to the production and sale of goods. On the consumption side, the market is open to any taste. Consumers can be rude, indolent, or complacent as long as they remain amenable to buying. There is thus a significant split between our ethos as producers and that as consumers, which creates tensions between modern personal and economic values. As consumers, we are encouraged to break the rules, to have it our way, to defy authority, to act on impulse, to indulge ourselves, to obey our thirst, to focus on the short term and on our own gratification. The customer is always right, even when he or she is, in some deeper sense, wrong. But we are not always consumers. Sometimes we are producers, and when we are producers, our continuing to embrace the values encouraged in us as consumers can be inefficient, if not disastrous. This conflict is more than an irony; it may over time yet prove to be a source of real instability. It is not easy to embody nearly pure hedonism as consumers and Dilbertianism at work. It seems likely that over the near term, some of this role strain can be reduced in certain respects by what might be called the "adolescentizing" of the workplace.

In any event, the lifestyle of consumption does not reject the claim that all choices are equal or that value is in the eye of the beholder. Relativism in the sphere of consumption legitimizes and supports, and is supported by, other forms of relativism, in which concern for the disenfranchised is merely a matter of taste and prudence. The arbitrariness of the choice between Coke and Pepsi is compatible with a broad relativism.

This broader cultural relativism is linked to commercialism in a number of ways. Often we assume that choice among consumer goods is a matter of arbitrary variation among persons or groups. One simply likes or does not like a given product, much as one simply does or does not like a given product ad. Consumption is also relative to time. What once may have been fashionable or shocking is no longer so. On the other hand, some of what is currently shocking may once have been less so. Finally, consumption is relative to place. Different countries and different regions within the same country have somewhat different tastes in products, brands, or ads. We are not yet an homogenized global village.

This sort of commercially enshrined relativism has, as we have seen, an antiprogressive side. Let us conclude by asking whether we are satisfied with what commercial relativism can offer us. Think of a more or less overtly racist commercial advertising theme or image drawn from any point in American history. Such an image probably appealed to some people in its time and place, because ads that offend most of their actual customers cannot survive.

But we would also want to condemn such ads as racist. The crucial point is that we would—or at least should, and for very practical reasons—want to condemn the ads as universally racist, and not merely as racist by our own, perhaps anachronistic, standards. The fact that an ad has a broad popular constituency should not mean that it is not racist, even if no one objects to it when it first appears. We do not want to say of some ads merely that they are racist by our standards, if not by the dominant standards of their day. Rather, we want to say that the ads were racist, and wrong, even if no one at the time thought so and even if the culture at the time lacked the resources to see the ads as wrong—which in any event is unlikely. We need standards higher than sales growth or contemporary popularity with a target market.

The dominant culture of the times may be invoked if someone seeks to mitigate the moral blame we might otherwise impute to the racist ad's sponsors. But the degree of moral blame imputed and the wrongness of the ads are separate issues. We should not be content with the relativist response that the allegedly racist ad might be deemed worthy of condemnation by us but not by those of an earlier day, with no overarching cultural standards to appeal to. With regard to such cases, we cannot be willing to settle for a draw between the racial judgments of two allegedly incommensurable cultural eras. Sometimes an idea is not just earlier or later, but better or worse, on grounds transcending narrow, particular cultural standards. At least, this should be the standard set by progressive thought. If not, progressivism has given up on genuine progress, and on much else besides.

Most controversial ad campaigns are too equivocal to count as progressive. Youth is not hipper than middle age. Nor is the opposite true, as those of us who seek youth in any of its artificial forms and guises must concede. Spiritedness and independence do not take their highest or most progressive forms in particular choices among consumer goods, let alone in a particular designer label. Inner worth, a subject on which Immanuel Kant had as much to say as any commercial advertiser does, is not associated with an interest in fashion or in a particular line of expensive clothing. Progressivity and glamour are not inseparable.

None of this discussion attempts to evaluate the subjective intent of any controversial advertisement or of their creative ad producers.

But we should point out that there is no law of nature holding that controversial or shocking ads must even pretend to be progressive. Indeed, the opposite is possible. We can envision intentionally controversial or shocking ads that, in contrast, have antiprogressive implications. We can even imagine such ads, targeted at carefully chosen niche markets, being commercially successful, despite or because of the adverse journalistic and broader public response. It also is not plausible to say that progressive commercial ads actually shape their viewers' attitudes, beyond simply mirroring them, while denying that this could also be true of antiprogressive ad messages.

Commercial goods, after all, are generally produced by persons sympathetic to the idea of making a profit and are sold to persons sufficiently affluent to pay for them. Small, politically weak minorities may not have much relevant market punch. Or the producer may—in an increasingly diverse, fragmented, heterogeneous market—be seeking a profitable niche, a sufficient sliver of a market share, rather than broad market dominance. Perhaps it can afford to alienate some groups precisely in order to attract a stable, enthusiastic, if narrow, following. Not all social groups use all products and brands at equal rates, now or in the foreseeable future. If we can afford to alienate some potential customers, it is better for us to alienate those unlikely to buy our product under any circumstances.

A strategy involving the intentional alienation of potential customers may seem nontraditional, if not irrational. That is, the traditional assumption is that controversial ads do not "work," that one should not, in effect, turn away paying customers.

Most marketers are not interested in alienating some potential customers to attract others. Broad-based, multiple-product, household-oriented companies such as Procter and Gamble and Kraft Foods fall into this category. But other sorts of enterprises may not feel this way. Some companies may assume that they should not aspire to a dominant market share of a very broad audience, in the way that Coke and Pepsi do. Perhaps a modest, distinctive niche is the best survival strategy for some firms.

The problem here reflects the dominance of the commercial culture. Commercial advertising is threatening to reach the saturation point. Even though we miss most ads, we are bored or annoyed by our repeated exposure to a few. New media for advertising are constantly cultivated. Ads are both numerous and ubiquitous. But as the number of ads and ad venues proliferates, the amount of attention paid to any given ad or campaign tends to diminish, even assuming that the ad is noticed at all. In Britain from 1985 to 1995, the number of different television commercials aired daily increased from 200 to 4,500.

This is the problem of inaudibility or inconspicuousness. Our own ads are in danger of being overlooked or drowned out because the competition for the viewers' attention is today more intense. Our ads must therefore stand out. In theory, we could try to attract attention by using superior ads. Or we might envision a way of producing novel, more entertaining, less demanding, or attention-grabbing but not controversial ads. Continual qualitative excellence, or even continual technical or thematic novelty is not, however, easy to achieve. We could therefore seek controversy, the rough equivalent of shouting in order to be heard above competing voices. Likewise, if a student desperately craves attention, he might pursue excellence or let loose a frog in the back of the classroom. If we capture viewers' attention through controversial ads, others may be forced, perhaps against their better judgment, to embrace similar strategies. The penalty for letting loose a frog in the marketplace may be low, and the penalty for not doing so may be high. The degree of controversiality needed to get attention may thus be gradually ratcheted up, in an eventually self-defeating manner. If too many people are shouting for attention, only those with the loudest voices will have an advantage.

Increasingly, therefore, the task for many advertisers is simply to be noticed and remembered in a sufficiently favorable way by some fraction of an audience. Audience-recall rates for typical ads, for those who believe in the significance of such numbers, have over time dropped alarmingly as the numbers of ads, venues, and advertising media have expanded. The task of staving off diminishing ad recall must be solved by some legally, financially, and culturally acceptable means, for some market of acceptable size and composition.

Perhaps, then, sellers can find an increasingly powerful market logic in favor of controversial ads, especially those sellers who cannot expect to draw broadly from our segmented, diverse, heterogeneous market. They could try to startle their audience, even if it seems more difficult to startle. But why can't the controversial ads be controversial in ways that promote progressive thought and progressive movements?

We already have part of an answer to that. Most commercial enterprises themselves and, in many cases, their most valued customers have no consistent stake in progressivism. Creative advertising executives or their employees might be more sympathetic, but the autonomy that clients can or will grant to the advertising firms receiving their commissions is limited. At some point, economic results matter to the client. Indeed, some of the major advertising agencies often talk a better game of progressivism than they practice; the percentage of women and minority decision makers at some of the major ad agencies is often the same as that at many commercial enterprises not especially noted for their progressive outlook.

In any event, there is a more systemic reason that we should not expect controversial ads to be consistently progressive. If they work at all, controversial ads work in part based on their distinctiveness or their unfamiliarity. If most controversial ads were also progressive ads, they would bear the seeds of their own destruction, obviously an unstable state of affairs. A more stable equilibrium would reassert itself. If too many controversial ads were also progressive ads, the edge of novelty, shock value, and cutting-edge controversiality would be eroded. Many people would note the link between controversiality and progressivity. The progressively controversial ad would itself become predictable and familiar. When it became familiar or predictable, its rationale would be lost. At that point, there would then be greater controversy, shock value, and new customers to be wooed with unfamiliar, antiprogressive, or at least nonprogressive, controversial ads. Whatever the overall level of controversial ads, some variable or stable mixture of progressive, antiprogressive, and nonprogressive controversial ads will always be in play. Remember that in the noncommercial realm, controversial bumper stickers and T-shirts do not invariably bear progressive messages.

The threshold level of shock value varies over time and from subject to subject. It is difficult in some contexts to say much that is widely considered shocking about, for example, the sitting president of the United States. Other subjects still have some potential for shock value merely by being mentioned publicly or in a commercial context. None of these tendencies, however, seems to advantage progressive commercial speech. In fact, a case to the contrary could be made.

Consider that our broader culture has struggled for decades to subdue the blatant negative racial and ethnic stereotypes in commercial advertising, including product logos. This social task is not, of course, yet complete, and it is possible that a gradual ratcheting up of the level of shock value needed to gain public attention may eventually work against the fulfillment of this task.

For example, if and when advertisers conclude that the level of controversy in advertising has risen so high that controversial ads must now be intensely controversial, the general rule against negative group stereotyping may be threatened. An advertiser might attract attention by, for instance, ambiguously unflattering depictions of undocumented aliens. That might generate media attention and adverse reaction in some quarters. But some enterprises might be inclined to sacrifice those potential market segments if the ad played well elsewhere. Presumably, such ads would be designed as purportedly humorous, so that those objecting to them could be accused of having no sense of humor.

Undocumented aliens would be almost too easy. Welfare recipients of one sort or another might also be targeted, with no great marketing loss if the ad campaign were executed cleverly. Some forms of mental illness might also be targeted. Some groups are not in a position to boycott or otherwise effectively fight back. If this antiprogressivism sounds too malicious to be plausible, remember that the underlying logic is not to attack the weak or disadvantaged as such but to seize the most inviting way to respond to a marketplace imperative to generate controversy and attention.

At some level, we may still believe that ads undermining particular groups cannot be good business. But let us consider some persistent patterns in advertising. It would be gratifying to say, for example, that advertisers had outgrown blatant sexism in advertising or that sexist advertising creates such a backlash that it simply does not pay. That would be gratifying but false.

If the advertiser is targeting only a particular demographic segment and the ad has a light, comedic touch, blatantly sexist ads can still pay, despite or because of whatever controversy ensues. The advertiser gets the benefit of the increased publicity and public discussion of its brand name. The ads may be replayed, for free, in news and info-tainment programs or other unusual venues. As the controversy and the free publicity peak, the advertiser then can vigorously disclaim any sexist intentions, donate a relative pittance to some related charity, and pull the ads as a gesture of good faith. Many viewers, after all, were not offended but amused. Aren't tastes in these matters subjective, anyway?

The environment for sexist ads is still, in some respects, supportive. Appeals to sex in advertising are increasingly direct, and if this trend is less popular with women than with men, this is, from some perspectives, merely unfortunate. Sexist behavior in television programming itself is common and is commonly validated by the program itself. One survey, for example, of a number of prime-time network programs found that 40 percent of the sexual behavior depicted fit commonly used definitions of sexual harassment.[4] This sort of depiction in network programming in itself tends to validate the behavior. But consider, as well, that there is a laugh track accompanying some of this programming. Presumably, one use of the laugh track is to tell us when laughter is an appropriate reaction. The issue for us, again, is not whether sitcoms and their laugh tracks are by themselves an irresistible or even a powerful influence on the behavior of the viewers. Our main focus is instead on issues of progressivity in advertising, or the lack thereof.

One of the principal obstacles to discouraging sexist advertising is related to the underlying problems of relativism and subjectivism. One person's restriction on sexist advertising will inevitably conflict with another person's loosely bridled hedonism. For many of the targeted audience members, blatantly sexist ads are enjoyable. At some point in our cultural history, we could not have pleaded our own personal enjoyment as a sufficient defense against disturbing others, let alone undermining their basic interests. Today, however, the fact that many persons enjoy such ads in the privacy of their own home is often thought to be the moral beginning and end of the issue. The ads' offensiveness to others is a matter of their own sensitivity. If one doesn't care for sexist or racist ads, one can simply not watch them or try to organize a boycott.

The ad producers can try to rationalize the whole business by claiming that sexist ads do not validate or reinforce sexist behavior; they merely reflect the sexism of society as a whole. Few persons really believe, however, that the number and content of such ads will not, over time, have an effect on social attitudes, however difficult such effects may be to trace. We learn attitudes from many sources, and there is little reason to believe that all of us rigorously filter, compartmentalize, domesticate, or discount all advertising, or even all invidious advertising. Why should sexism be different in this respect from, say, televised violence? There is something odd about well-compensated ad agencies asserting that they cannot change or reinforce social attitudes over time while at the same time claiming that they can increase sales or market share for their client.

There is thus no reason to assume that controversial or shocking ads usually are progressive, as opposed to being nonprogressive or even antiprogressive. No one should expect controversial ads to undermine the broader commercial messages implicitly touting consumption as a way of life. Controversial ads are not meant to promote progressive politics at any level but are meant, instead, to make their corporation more visible and to move particular goods and services.

Let us conclude with brief examples of mildly controversial British ads. One, for a beer company, involves two men discussing the history of an old oak tree. They then proceed to cut down the tree for use as a beer table. This ad, targeted, one would imagine, at male beer drinkers, establishes that at least when approached in a lighthearted manner, environmental concerns need not be treated with reverence. It is difficult to see this controversial ad as a blow for progressivism. Of course, any ad can be read in any way one wishes. Maybe remarkably crude antienvironmentalism is thought to be alienating or able to provoke a backlash. But it is difficult to see such an interpretation as necessarily progressive.

Or consider a pair of multiple award-winning British ads for a motorcycle manufacturer. One features a son buying a motorcycle for himself rather than an electric wheelchair for his elderly father. The other has a divorced mother receiving no alimony check because her ex-husband has instead bought a motorcycle. Both these ads, again, are meant to be humorous, and many viewers find them inoffensive. Indeed, any offensiveness may be unintended and subjective at best, if not a matter of the peculiar perspective of advanced age. More to the point, the ad may play well with its primary market, presumably young males. There is no rule that humor must be subtle or refined.

The creative advertising personnel who produce such ads are, statistically, unlikely to be either elderly and immobile or financially dependent on an alimony check. Even if they are controversial, such ads are at best devoid of progressive content, a fact that may be of little concern to the advertising personnel. Some ad makers even redefine offensiveness so that it is less a matter of insensitivity to the relatively powerless and more a matter of cowardly or unimaginative adherence to formula and convention. The offensive becomes the boring. No boredom, no offense.

At some point, the otherwise unprincipled rejection of formula and convention itself may come to be recognized as a standard, conventional, formulaic approach to advertising. Even then, new formulas will be devised, or discarded formulas will be recycled. We should probably expect offensiveness in advertising, however politically pointless or regressive, to persist. In our culture, offensiveness sells in some circumstances, especially when the offended parties do not matter much economically.

For politically pointless controversial ads by mainstream advertisers to disappear, we, the public, would have to exercise a degree of hypocrisy and self-restraint. We would have to pretend that we never enjoy what is predictably offensive to others. And we would have to act, in a manner expressing self-restraint, on this hypocritical theme, pretending to be better than we are. As a culture, though, we do not seem comfortable with either hypocrisy for a good cause or self-restraint for the benefit of those less influential than ourselves.

How Do Ads
Describe Us?

One of Mrs. Babbitt's virtues was that, except during dinner parties, when she was transformed into a raging hostess, she took care of the house and didn't bother the males by thinking.

c h a p t e r   f i v e

Commercial advertising addresses different groups of people with mixtures of insult and flattery, but also with some broad recurring themes. Many groups—teenagers, women, young adults, even baby boomers—are encouraged to think of themselves as independent minded and sometimes even as defiant of authority, and these themes of rebellion and independent mindedness are interpreted in different ways for different groups. Ultimately, though, rebellion is supposed to take the form of market-based consumption. Rebellion is against those who would deprive one of consumption or who would presume to dictate one's consumption choices. Rebellion typically aligns the rebel with one product against its similar competitors.

Rebellion as rebellious consumption begins in childhood. Commercial speech does not wait for the maturation of its audience's faculties. At remarkably early ages, children recognize some commercial logos, including that of Joe Camel. Early on, many children trust Fred Flintstone and Barney Rubble for sound and disinterested advice on which breakfast cereals are best. In addition, children may watch an hour of narrowly defined commercials each day, not counting television programs that are based on commercial products or that amount to full-length commercials themselves.

Children have been exposed to television commercials for decades, but the balance of power in socialization has shifted a bit. The number of television commercials seen annually by children, according to one estimate, increased from 20,000 in the late 1970s to about double that figure in 1987.[1] At the same time, whatever potential countervailing influence parents might have had has gradually been reduced.

According to the Carnegie Council on Adolescent Development, the time that children spend with their parents has, over the past thirty years, decreased by at least one-third while at the same time, the substance and content of the interaction have remained the same. Thus even if parents disapprove of the implicit messages of television advertising for children, they have many fewer hours than they once did to counteract this greater volume of more sophisticated commercial messages. Parents thus have substantially fewer resources—time and energy being the crucial ones—to contest a potential adversary with greater resources.

Interestingly, those who doubt the wisdom of commercialized lifestyles face a dilemma with regard to children. Even if pacifism is a moral ideal, it is not clear that it is best to inculcate pacifism in a child who will grow up in a violent, predatory environment. A similar, albeit less dramatic, choice must be made regarding children's exposure to commercial values. At a minimum, children must understand the power of commercial values. Thus, reducing children's exposure to commercialism or its effects means risking their isolation by their peers, at a real psychological cost.

Children do not watch commercial television all the time. Competing activities, including the increasingly commercialized Internet, may be becoming more popular among the young. Children may play with other children, which may either undercut or, sadly, reinforce commercial values. Or they may play computer games, which in many cases should be counted as neutral in the struggle between more and less commercial values. On the one hand, computer games are a commercial product, but one that may encourage the players to think in noncommercial, albeit rather antisocial, terms. More realistically, it may reward hand-eye coordination in a noncommercial if ultimately harmful or pointless way. Children may claim to know that computer game violence should not be carried over to the real world. But do they ever claim any analogous distancing from commercial consumption itself, as opposed to particular commercials?

The preceding discussion assumes some degree of parental hostility to their children's absorbing excessively commercial values. Many parents, including many business people, object to their children's being exposed to excessive, or excessively early, commercialism. Others, however, do not do so, at least not consistently. Many parents themselves have embraced commercial values and may not be aware that their children are doing so as well. Some parents may see their children's adoption of commercial values as reflecting realism, maturity, their freedom of choice, or their developing autonomy and so respect their choice as a matter of principle.

Other parents might prefer that their children be exposed to less commercialization but, for more pragmatic reasons, do not commonly act on that preference. Parents may be ambivalent about commerce, consumption, and culture, and society ordinarily points children in commercialized directions. A great part of the public world is commerce, and in that sense, television advertising itself may be regarded as educational television.

If time and energy are increasingly scarce resources against a nearly ubiquitous antagonist, perhaps more discretion is necessary. Under such circumstances, is it desirable or even possible to argue frequently about watching commercial television, for example, or to supervise or participate in alternative, noncommercial activities? Trying to limit the influence of commercial values on children may produce only conflict. Surely there are higher priorities, including the child's safety, general education, avoidance of directly immoral or illegal acts such as cheating or stealing, and even undisturbed play.

Some children find that consumptionist values are ratified at school. This may be done through conversations with their friends and even through designer labels on jackets, shoes, or sunglasses, the possession of which occasionally inspires crime. The ratification of consumption at school may also be an officially sponsored twelve minutes of award-winning television programming in the classroom, including two minutes of commercials and, occasionally, commercially developed lesson plans.

It is easy to understand the popularity of such a program in the classroom. Given a choice between watching a Pepsi commercial or working for an equal amount of time on sines and cosines, most of us would opt for the former. Nor should we be startled if even the classroom teacher prefers the twelve minutes of respite, whether or not they must then be followed up by a classroom discussion.

The producers of these classroom programs are willing to argue for the educational value of a wider and wider range of programs.

Almost anything can be said to contribute to one's social skills, for example. It is, as usual, the implied underlying message that is disturbing, in this case that commercial pitches are nearly ubiquitous. We may begin to wonder whether the commercial establishment is suggesting that many children cannot be trusted to watch a sufficient amount of commercial television on their own, hence the classroom supplement. The message need not be that the programming made financially possible by the commercials is always less important than the commercials but that commercial messages should be expected in, and belong in, nearly every possible venue. Commercialism, it seems, neither is nor should be limited in this sense.

Children's commercial television conveys a sense of inevitability. After all, even most adults do not always prefer to watch dramatizations of *Antigone*. For producers of children's programming, cost effectiveness often means formulaic animations closely tied to commercial products. In the extreme, the cartoon is essentially an infomercial. The program, in effect, coincides with the commercial, with the complication that the hybrid program-commercial itself is interrupted for commercials.

The current Federal Communications Commission (FCC) rule clearly limits commercials during children's programming to ten and one-half minutes per hour on weekends and twelve and one-half minutes per hour on weekdays. Interestingly, the regulation defines commercial matter as "air time sold for purposes of selling a product or service."[2] In a sense, of course, all airtime on commercial television is sold for this purpose. A more traditional analysis would be that programming is the inducement to watch discrete commercials. The network or station pays for the programming but not for the commercials. By the way, the FCC rules are not always followed.

Equally interesting is the attempt to deconstruct from the other direction the distinction between programs and commercials. The

FCC regulations praise educational and informational programming for children. Included is "any television programming which furthers the positive development of children 16 years of age and under in any respect, including the child's intellectual/cognitive or social/emotional needs." This is a broad but, no doubt, reasonable definition.

One problem is that a case can be made for including some percentage of, if not all, purely commercial advertising within the scope of this definition. The distinction between advertising and programming conducive to developing useful life skills is not clear. Can we say that teenagers need to have an informed opinion about trade policy with China more than about the merits of competing cars, credit cards, or long-distance phone companies? Consider the occasionally annoying comparative ads run by AT&T, MCI, and Sprint. One can say with a straight face that exposure to these ads helps young people develop useful and important skills in spotting noncomparable claims; appreciating restrictions, disclaimers, and the proverbial fine print; recognizing hyperbole; checking for the assumed baseline of discounts; calculating actual costs and actual benefits over the short and long term, including rebates; and so on.

These skills are important, and viewing commercials is arguably part of developing them. Accordingly, to some degree, ads may intend to promote them, even though no one ad may intend to promote overall skepticism on the part of the viewer. In general, such ads can teach useful comparative shopping skills in important markets, or consumer savvy, even if they are not advocating any recognizable social idea or contributing to a discussion of social policy.

Drawing a useful line between educational programming and noneducational commercial programming is no less problematic. No one can quantify the effects of an afternoon special about self-esteem, although such a special could easily be classed as educational. Portraying ways of living that are noncommercial—that emphasize honor, loyalty, and concern for family reputation, as among the more respectable Klingons—may, on the other hand, be categorized as noneducational. Watching Lieutenant Worf sacrifice worldly success for the sake of honor is not deemed educational in a commercialized, more Ferengi-like society. Of course, if there were a televised reading of the portions of Plato's *Republic* discussing the rule of the honorable, or timocracy, that hypothetical, unwatched program would count as educational.

The lesson is that the government has no politically feasible and readily enforceable system of regulating the commercial market's television programming for children in such a way that conscientious parents can assume that their own intervention is unnecessary. In our culture, it is unrealistic to imagine that the main sorts of programming actually watched by most children after a certain age do not, both conspicuously and subtly, convey consumptionist themes. A C-chip to block commercialism is, for our society, unimaginable.

Now we shall broaden our demographic focus. Teenagers and young adults present interesting commercial paradoxes; they resist categorization and easy summary. But in this, they may resemble their predecessors. Indeed, because there are so many common themes, it is easy to overstate the differences between today's teenagers and young adults and their predecessors regarding consumption. To see the generations as internally similar but widely divergent from their predecessors quickly outruns the evidence. We could just as easily emphasize differences within a cohort and continuities between generations.

Given the fun of labeling and stereotyping, it is widely believed that teenagers and young adults nowadays are sophisticated but skeptical about advertising, without having abandoned consumption as a lifestyle. They are said to be much alike across the globe, largely because of American television. Young people do not enjoy being told who or what they are, what to buy, or how to live. Perhaps they are more sensitive about such matters than previous generations were, although one might remember the 1960s in similar ways.

The irony is that even though young persons stress that they do not want to be told how to live, in some respects they perceive fewer available and attractive options or deep reasons for pursuing them. Disturbing questions remain unresolved. Even if one could avoid a consumptionist lifestyle, why should one bother to resist? Isn't distrust and suspicion of commercial or political authority pointless if there are no good reasons not to go with the flow? Resistance is likely to be either futile or arbitrary. The lifestyle rebellions of the 1960s had mixed success and unexpected costs. In any event, lifestyle rebellions against commercialization may be less appealing under the current circumstances, in which job security, financial comfort, and physical health and safety cannot be taken for granted.

For whatever reason, teenagers and young adults today do not seem inclined to embrace alternatives to consumptionist lifestyles. This does not suggest that they have no interest in particular social causes and issues. It is merely that whatever social activism they do display does not generally take anticonsumptionist forms. No doubt there are elements of anticonsumptionism in, for example, some forms of environmental activism. But most young persons seem more inclined to recycle than to refuse to buy a consumer good, recyclable or not, in the first place.

About their elders, the baby boom generation, not much need be said. For advertisers, of course, ignoring the baby boom generation has rarely been conducive to financial health. Because of its sheer size and attitudes toward consumption, the baby boom generation has always had, and will likely retain, the power to redefine standard marketing techniques. Even denying them a gradually redefined sense of perpetual hipness may be risky. Marketers may have to devise a delicate and subtle, continuously adjusted mix of realism, accommodation, flattery, nostalgia, humor, and creativity.

One way of looking at the numbers is that for the next sixteen years, ten thousand people every day will celebrate their fiftieth birthday. By 2005, baby boomers will form the majority of Americans between the ages of fifty and seventy-four. By that time, the roughly 70 million to 75 million baby boomers will probably control three-quarters of the nation's wealth. This is not a group to be trifled with.

Nor is it clear that aging boomers can be dismissed by advertisers as set in their ways, unconvertible, or not worth bothering with as long-term investments. In a number of markets, a fifty-year-old boomer may have several decades of consumption decisions yet to make. Boomers may well be more open to change in their consumption patterns—both switching brands and buying new products—than their predecessors were.

For some marketers, the main problem may be to attract aging boomers while not alienating younger cohorts—imagine trying in earlier decades to persuade boomers to join in their own parents' consumption choices. For others, the chief marketing difficulty will be recognizing boomers' changing priorities and appealing to them without appearing to mock or patronize.

One commercial features a reprise of Janis Joplin's originally satiric wish for a Mercedes Benz, but this time played relatively straight. The irony here is, for some boomers, a bit awkward. There is a risk that some will be confronted too abruptly with their former, sometimes more idealistic, less materialist selves. Surely the desired response to this Mercedes ad is not that one once was young and disdained status seeking but has now been ground down, has lost one's fervor, or is even simply more pragmatic about such things. Instead, the idea must surely be one of associating youth, playfulness, and a certain form of hipness with Mercedes.

Somewhat less risky are a series of quirkily photographed commercials for "relaxed fit" or "loose fitting" jeans, clearly targeted at boomers whose devotion to diet and exercise has been only intermittent. The jump cuts, disjointedness, and odd camera angles suggest a sense of hipness, playfulness, and unconventionality. Just as important is the underlying theme of comfort. The physical comfort of one's attire is a selling point not lost on the older boomer cohort.

In the abstract, it is unclear whether references to the 1960s and 1970s in advertising help or hurt in appealing to boomers. Some might remember those decades as times of conflict, struggle, war, assassination, scandal, or disillusionment. But others think of those decades as a more innocent, in some ways less threatening, era. Ads that convey a 1960s or 1970s mentality may be nostalgic to some boomers and portray a certain enviable simplicity or innocence to some members of younger cohorts.

Mainly, though, these are issues of marketing strategy. We need not doubt the baby boomers' commitment to consumptionist lifestyles. It is not plausible to imagine that as boomers turn fifty or sixty, they will repudiate ways of living that they have chosen over the past twenty or thirty years and resurrect in some form a nonconsumptionist lifestyle that only a few consistently embraced in their youth, and many not at all.

Certainly, the consumption patterns of boomers in their fifties and sixties will not exactly parallel those of their parents. Some will sail off into cyberspace, if not to Tahiti. Others may become more active in their communities or spend more time on social causes. Some will want to retire earlier, or later, than their parents did. Some may want to return to classrooms or at least to a college town atmosphere. Inadequate retirement funding will play important roles over time.

We should be realistic, though, about boomers' consumption after they retire. In many cases, boomers have saved relatively little for retirement, especially in light of their anxieties over social security and the future cost of medical care. They have done so not because they have, in general, turned their backs on available larger incomes or have donated higher percentages of their incomes to charity than earlier generations did. If many boomers have not yet saved enough for their retirement, this reflects what they take to be large current expenses, mainly for individual or family consumption.

The generation that popularized bottled spring water and aspired to own a BMW is not a likely candidate for mass conversion to some form of asceticism. Again, far from all boomers were at any time serious about countercultural values. And even those who emphasized the importance of not judging persons based on their appearance may at the time have assumed the superiority of youth over age. Whatever conscientious objection against cosmetic surgery boomers may summon may be no greater than that of their predecessors or successors.

In sum, it is impossible to predict precisely the boomers' consumption behavior over the next two decades. It is difficult, however, to see the major theme as a significant, voluntary de-emphasis on consumption, whatever their retirement prospects. At this point, consumption is part of the boomers' identity.

Let us again shift our focus, this time to a brief look at the issue of gender in advertising, in particular, at women as targeted consumers. If we wonder what commercial advertising says to women, the answer is clear: advertising will say to women whatever it takes to encourage their commercial consumption. The history of twentieth-century American advertisements either depicting or pitched primarily at women is complex and subtle. Almost any claim about the techniques of depicting or targeting women can be supported.

Advertising trends regarding women are not uniform. No particular form of sexism in ads, for example, is confined to a narrow time frame. A few ads from well over half a century ago portray women consumers as knowledgeable, independent minded, and publicly assertive, if in some cases only about her consumption choices. Not all the most recent ads go even this far. A few relatively old ads— long antedating the pseudoprogressive ads for Virginia Slims cigarettes—manage to mention, and then trivially link, women's political movements to the consumption of this or that product. Car commercials satirize sales pitches to women that focus on the vanity mirror, but other car commercials continue to trivialize women's real concerns.

Some recent ads, including one for Nike on the chance for women to play sports, are arresting and, in some respects, relatively progressive. But on the other hand, a recent ad for a major producer of diamonds asserts, in distinctive orange print against a generally black-and-white background, that "to know diamonds is to know her." This is a striking claim. Let us grant that both diamonds and humans are carbon based or that in our society, diamonds are in some sense a social construct. Still, it would be hard to beat the literal reductivism of equating diamonds and women, at any time in the history of American advertising.

This is not to suggest that even the Nike "If You Let Me Play Sports" commercial is unambiguously progressive. Some of the touted benefits of sports do not seem to require that the sports be funded by a school or even organized. So there is, in part, a sense in the commercial of waiting for permission to engage in cardiovascular exercise and competition as a group, even though this should not require official sanction. Nike, it is true, does not suggest that expensive personal apparel is necessary for any of the cited benefits of sports. In fact, viewers may infer that given the minimal differences among footwear brands, they can reasonably choose their shoes on the basis of the ads' progressivity. But also note that for years, promotions for the NCAA have extolled the virtues of athletics, at least for men. And remember what selectively progressive commercials tend to obscure, that there is more than one dimension of progressivity on which to judge corporations, not all of which are likely to be mentioned in the ads. Hiring and employment practices are one example.

Our focus, then, cannot be on establishing distinctive trends in the depiction of or marketing strategies for women over time. Instead, let us reflect a bit longer on some of the ways in which commercial advertising undercuts the interests of women, commonly by directing their personal and social concerns toward unproductive commercial channels.

How, for example, does the commercial culture encourage women's independence and creativity? At a general level, some recent commercials encourage independent-mindedness on the part of women, albeit reduced to something like mere spiritedness, spunkiness, feistiness, sassiness, or some similarly adolescent state of being. These qualities, whatever their value, are to be displayed through commercial consumption, that is, the consumption of particular commercial products. At its lowest point, women's self-assertiveness takes the form of consuming a certain brand of women-friendly cigarettes.

Alternatively, creativity is expressed through women's choices of clothing styles or of what to buy and wear on a given occasion. Choices of makeup, too, express one's creativity, indeed, one's individuality. Consumption thus becomes self-expression. The paradox of expressing one's independence and individuality by following a well-budgeted ad campaign's suggestions, along with thousands or millions of other women, is not deeply explored. One is left to wonder how the creativity of Michelangelo or Leonardo might have been expressed if similar vehicles for the expression of creativity had been available in Renaissance Florence.

The heart of the problem is not that women's choices among, say, clothing items are limited. Often, the commercial market is criticized for promoting uniformity or conformity to one or a few standard models. One size fits all, though, is hardly the essence of today's commercial market. Markets can offer a varied array of choices. The age of mass production for a mass market has faded. The technology is now available for men and women to participate in designing their own fashions via the Internet.

At this level, the problem is thus not of product uniformity. Rather, it is that all the proposed options are commercial responses. The virtues—and the deficiencies—of the various options are largely shared. Beyond a certain point, adding more shades of nail polish or lip gloss as vehicles for expressing creativity and individual personality has only limited value. Encouraging creativity and individual expression in less commercialized ways, on the other hand, might have greater value.

Some recent commercials, nevertheless, show women asserting themselves in noncommercial ways, sometimes at the expense of some boorish, or merely hapless, male. These sorts of commercials exemplify what might be called Rorschach feminism. Several commercials feature a spiritedly assertive response by a woman to off-camera male behavior. The male provocation is sufficiently hazy so that a wide range of viewers can feel validated by, or at least neutral toward, the commercial. These Rorschach feminist commercials also accept, if not encourage, nonfeminist interpretations.

If one is so inclined, one can see the male as either a victim or a scapegoat. Or one can read the commercial entirely differently, perhaps reading in, as provocation, whatever one happens to have personally experienced or conceives of as sufficient to justify the woman's response. Either the man in the commercial is at fault in some way supplied by the viewer, or the woman is merely reacting to the conflicting and burdensome obligations that women commonly must bear. The ideal such commercial would be read as feminist by all and only feminists and by nonfeminists as validating their own stereotypes and worldviews. Surely the most effective commercials are those that in some sense are produced by each prospective customer.

Whether this sort of ambiguous commercial presentation advances women's interests is doubtful. It is not clear that nonfeminist viewers are even aware of the feminist readings. But the ambiguities, the openness, and the undeniable spiritedness of the female protagonist allow the ad's producers to assert the contrary if and when they are so inclined. Feminist viewers may feel reinforced—at least until they see the ad's duplicity. The perfect ad would allow every sort of viewer to feel vindication, leading to identification with the ad's producer and purchase of the product. This commercially ideal outcome seems unlikely, though. For a time, feminists may be willing to identify with ads they come to recognize as only equivocally feminist. For the moment, anything is better than nothing. But this sort of equivocal commercial feminism may quickly fade.

The overall message of most contemporary advertisers for women is not likely to be one of reasonably consistent feminism. In crucial respects, the overall effect of contemporary advertising is to place many women under contradictory strains. It is important to appreciate the currently incompatible demands to which women in particular are subjected. If women are no longer badgered so intensively about rings around shirt collars, they are now subjected to new sorts of double binds.

Consider, for example, the occasional use in commercial advertising of women models who appear to many viewers to be underweight. No doubt one can conceive of some sort of progressive account of this, but some viewers have argued that such ads increase the societal pressures on women to be healthfully or unhealthfully thin. No one supposes that any particular ad campaign, or even advertising in general, dictates ideal body weights for women. But it is difficult to argue that advertising has no effect on public and private behavior, especially in matters loosely related to fashion.

In an ideal world, women of all ages would be largely indifferent to body image, beyond reasonable health concerns. For the moment, however, we live in a world in which young women, especially, are not invariably assigned their status on grounds independent of their physical appearance. An important point is that it does not necessarily help women to be presented with alternative, nonemaciated, but practically unattainable models of attractiveness. Nor does it help them to recognize that much of contemporary American commercial culture does not itself care whether women are thin.

Although generally, the commercial culture does not idealize being overweight, a moment's reflection and a calorie counter can establish that important, well-funded elements of the commercial culture do want women, along with children and men, to be overweight. They want this at least in effect if not by subjective, conscious intent. In some sense, we are a diet- and exercise-conscious society. We tend to talk much better about it than we practice it, however. In this regard, many of the leading and most publicized items at various major fast-food chain restaurants are of little help, and the leading fast-food chains are typically among our leading commercial television presences.

The fast food restaurants may be able to claim that they do not affect public tastes but only reflect tastes that were established independently. As usual, there is some truth in such claims, which vary depending on the industry. For decades, our fast-food tastes have been heavily reinforced by commercial advertising. It may be too much to claim that slightly healthier versions of a range of fast-food items could not be sustained.

Admittedly, the relatively low fat McLean Deluxe sandwich did not draw an immense following. This may, however, reflect the incongruity of having to make a separate choice for relative healthiness in a commercial environment that does not celebrate rigorous nutritional standards. More likely, its failure may have been the result of previous advertising. Similarly, some McDonalds salad items have not been popular, and other chains have experimented with lighter items, with only mixed success. Several chains have gone in the other direction, by emphasizing the presence of bacon. Ultimately, whether the fast-food chains themselves can do much about this less-than-ideal state of nutritional affairs is not important to our purposes. A bit of arithmetic suggests that the more seriously one takes the fast-food chains' advertisements, the less likely one is to avoid getting fat.

Fast-food advertising is not irresistible; it does not completely bypass rational reflection and deliberation. But such advertising is, at least, a persistent theme heard by men, women, and children. Repetition, in respectable contexts, tends to normalize what is repeated. Again, the fast-food chains do not consciously wish anyone to be overweight, but the arithmetic is simple for those who overindulge.

Both the messages that promote obesity and those that promote extreme thinness have persisted. They both exert an influence, often on the same persons. The main point, especially for some young women, is that such incompatible messages do not necessarily cancel themselves out or counteract each other. If they did, they might create a measure of freedom. One could then use the undue thinness ads against the high fat ads, and vice versa, creating an overall condition of neutrality.

Unfortunately, the result of the conflicting messages about weight is not one of mutual negation and liberation. The commercial culture does not say, in effect, "Be either thin or fat, or in between, entirely at your informed discretion." Instead, young women's arms are pulled simultaneously in opposite directions, and to be thus pulled is not to be free of cultural constraint. Of course, many women at even the most vulnerable ages have the resources, the alternatives, and the social support to steer a course between incompatible harms without any sense of inadequacy or deprivation. But there is little progressive value in subjecting young women to this otherwise pointless commercial tug-of-war.

This is not to argue that all, or even the strongest, influences on women's beliefs about how they should look are commercial. Women have been pushed, prodded, distorted, and injured in many cultures by noncommercial institutions. Our point is simply that in our culture and in various media, commercial messages constitute part of the problem. It seems unlikely that women will attain even the modest dispensation from preoccupation with appearance enjoyed by men as long as the commercial badgering of women based on appearance continues. Even noncommercial pressures on women to meet particular standards of appearance may, in some cases, be influenced by commercial forces.

To summarize this brief look at advertising and the interests of women, let us say that commercial speech seems to be generally unprincipled or agnostic regarding the interests of women, but there remains an obvious bottom line: Women who are not pulled in opposing directions may take one of a number of different paths, perhaps at some cost, but each of those paths should lead to commercial consumption. Women should think carefully about which products and services promote their interests, or best help them express themselves, and tailor their buying accordingly. Women's interests beyond commercial expression are largely off the screen, except insofar as the very idea of noncommercialism can be used as a commercial selling point.

The relationship between mainstream advertising and American racial and ethnic minorities has been equally complex. This is again a large story, about which we can say little here. At its worst, American marketing and commercial speech history is replete with what are now widely recognized as racist messages and images. In great part, they reflect the norms of the broader society, but we should remember that the record of advertising agencies themselves has not always been exemplary. Even today, the percentages of African Americans and Latinos working in advertising are about 5 and 7 percent, respectively.

Ethnically stereotypical logos, trademarks, and other visual commercial images have largely been abandoned over time, with some traditional icons having taken on a slightly broader ethnic character. For example, the General Mills construct known as Betty Crocker has frequently been updated to reflect fashion and age demographic concerns, and recently she has been democratized as well, her features modified to suggest American ethnic heterogeneity. It has been suggested that different consumers can now see Betty simultaneously as Caucasian, Asian, Latina, or Native American. General Mills representatives hold out for even more inclusiveness.

The point is not to encourage Latinos to see Betty as Asian or to encourage Caucasians to see Betty as Latina. Those sorts of readings would be commercially pointless at best. Instead, the idea is to encourage what might be called noncompeting diverse identifications with Betty. Ideally, we each should identify with Betty on the basis of our own ethnic group. Betty is one of us, and we therefore feel comfortable with her and accordingly will want to buy Betty Crocker products. General Mills apparently notices or cares about our group in particular, so all other things being equal, it presumably deserves our gratitude.

This Rorschachian process still has pragmatic or cultural limits. If one wants to sell a specific ethnic cuisine to a heterogeneous society, one might just as well depict an ethnically identifiable chef, for the sake of recognizability if not of authenticity. In general, though, advertisers have learned that it is in the overall interests of commerce if their ads invite the previously uninvited, along with their credit cards, into the big tent.

As long as the only issue is who is to be depicted in the advertising, most commercial speakers can live with any set of cultural rules. This is not to deny the importance of such issues; they are a part of some of this century's most significant debates. But as long as our attention is devoted exclusively to which faces are welcomed into the ads, we are not yet asking whether it is in anyone's interest to be buying the implied commercial logic. One should object on principle to being invidiously and arbitrarily excluded from, say, a social club. But it does not follow that one would be better off as a member of that club. Being excluded from the face of mainstream advertising is objectionable, but it does not mean that one should not only resist exclusion but also lead a commercialized life.

Overall, commercial advertising's attitudes toward ethnic minorities is probably only slightly less complicated than those of the society as a whole. Advertisers know now that the stereotypical Frito Bandito or the historical servile kitchen worker are unacceptable, but they may still not take the trouble to learn all they should about minority customers. One large phone company, for example, ran a Spanish-language version of an ad encouraging customers to call their presumably telephonically neglected mothers. Apparently, the ad's creators were familiar with the tendency not to bother to stay in contact with one's mother and sensed the possibility of playing on the resulting sense of guilt.

The problem, however, is that resisting cultural stereotyping does not mean that a group's experiences can always be universalized. Not all ethnic communities equally emphasize remoteness from one's mother. As it turned out, Latinos' response to the ad was less than uniformly appreciative. The implication that one needed to be reminded to call one's own mother was perceived by some as inappropriate or even insulting.

Nor do all advertisers obsess over the cultural healthiness of their use of minority images in their advertising. There obviously are more African American doctors, lawyers, police, and accountants than athletic stars or music celebrities, but mainstream advertisers have continued to insist on what might be called standard formulas of atypicality. The reader may wish to compare the number and media prominence of African Americans in current ads whose function is to convey authority with those who are there to trade on their reputation for phenomenal athletic skills or just to bestow an aura of hipness.

There are, one supposes, worse messages about African Americans that advertisers could send than that of athletic prowess or generalized hipness. Worse messages have been sent in the past. But a moment's reflection suggests that messages at this level may be socially counter-productive, however effective such ads may be in creating broad consumer demand. Unfortunately, there is no reason to expect commercial advertising to depart from allegedly winning formulas for the sake of contributing, over the long term, to societal health.

This is not to suggest that there is some imperative that drives advertisers to stereotype African Americans, other minorities, or women, either in their advertising itself or as consumers. Such strategies may occasionally pay off, just as ideologically progressive advertising may. But it is neither the stereotyping nor the progressivism that must drive successful advertisers. Both strategies may be deemed appropriate if they pay off, and they pay off when viewers are converted to consumers.

To put the matter in vaguely Kantian terms, by its nature, commercial advertising does not treat the members of its audience as ends in themselves or as repositories of absolute, unconditioned worth. To do so, an ad would have to hold open the possibility of countermanding its own selling message, if necessary, for the sake of the audience. Simply relying on the consumer to recognize and promote her own interests does not mean that the seller has met Kant's standards. This is not a matter of treating adult customers as children. Instead, commercial advertising treats its audience as a consensually available means to corporate ends. Generally, advertising does not emphasize that one should buy only if it is in one's interest to do so. Warning labels and drug counterindication messages go some distance in this direction, but not far enough. Undoubtedly, many sellers think of their products as more worth buying than those of their competitors. But commercial advertising does not depend on such corporate beliefs.

Commercial advertising also does not depend on the seller's belief that the buyer would be better off buying the product rather than keeping the money needed for the purchase. Here we are continuing to assume free and voluntary, nondeceptive transactions. We may assume that over time, shoddy or disappointing goods do not pay. Would commercial advertising cease if sellers knew that buyers would come to regret their voluntary purchase or would be better off buying something else instead? One would imagine not. Advertisers may, but need not, care about the real interests of their customers beyond the substitute for care dictated by the market. To a commercial advertiser, a potential buyer need not be thought of as anything but a complex, voluntarily motivated, or self-programmed machine, with some built-in capacity for retaliation when disappointed. This is the bottom-line logic of commercial speech.

The Current
Status of
Commercial
Culture and
Some Political
Responses

Do you know the fellow who's really *the*
American genius? Why, the fellow that writes
the Prince Albert Tobacco ads!

c h a p t e r   s i x

Some time ago, the Swedish Space Corporation considered placing
giant illuminated commercial billboards in space, but it noted that
"astronomers are against the idea because they would mix up billboards with stars."

This problem is not confined to astronomers, and let us hope that
we all continue to see some distinction between the celestial and the
commercial. Eventually, however, astronomers may not be more able
to prevent the commercial blighting of the heavens than computer
scientists can prevent the commercialization of the Internet. In the
meantime, perhaps our short attention span will save us; that is, we

may quickly lose interest in even a reprogrammable celestial billboard, thereby making it commercially unattractive.

Unfortunately, our capacity for disbelief—which may also have saved us from stratospheric billboards—can be made irrelevant over time through desensitization. For the present, we may be surprised by the commercialization of public schools, the renaming of public streets for commercial sponsors, Janis Joplin's Mercedes pitch, restroom advertising, the Shaker hymn "Simple Gifts" in the service of materialism, an official commercial bottled water of a papal visit, the corporate sponsorship of the computerized age progression of the images of missing children, the commercial transformation of the Olympics or of sports in general, commercials during subsidized long-distance phone calls, the commercialization of public parks in exchange for modest contributions to city budgets, or the projection of a particular Cadbury brand logo onto the dome of St. Paul's Cathedral.

In fact, our initial astonishment may sometimes stick. The use of St. Paul's, for example, was based on a misunderstanding and was not repeated. And there are, for the moment, no celestial billboards. One pleased shopper found in a $3 bin at a discount store a pair of designer sunglasses that had sold for $275 the previous year. On the whole, though, betting against the gradual proliferation of commercial values is not advised.

Many factors seem relevant to explaining why commercialism has become pervasive. Some ads are entertaining and qualify as an art form. More important, much commercial speech offers useful information about useful products.

Increasingly, commercialism tries to enter our airspace under our radar by seeking to undermine the conventional distinction between commercial advertising and entertainment programming, or even real life itself. Some commercials even have commercials nested within them. The aim is not just to stave off ad saturation but also to delay jadedness, boredom, and defensiveness as well. Perhaps the need for advertisers to go to such lengths provides some grounds for optimism.

Recently, some advertising has been thought to add to the value of the product or, in a metaphorical sense, to be actually what the consumer is buying. That is, we might buy an item less for itself than to associate ourselves with the perceived merits of the commercial or with some aura or message that the commercial is thought to impart. In such cases, advertising involves little "waste" or "inefficiency," contrary to what is commonly argued.

After all, one pair of athletic shoes may not seem much better than another, apart from the commercial's theme, imagery, mood, technical sophistication, or celebrity endorser. Accordingly, one possible commercial theme is that some of us are too sophisticated to buy shoes on the basis of crass commercialism. Instead, we buy them because the maker recognizes our resistance to hucksterism. Many of us resent the excesses of commercialism and materialism, but just not seriously or consistently.

In a sense, it is even a bit misleading to say that we have come to endorse commercial values. We do not revel in commercial values. Rather, our commercialism has led us to lose interest in, or the skills and time for, alternative ways of living. For example, pollsters who ask people what the word *democracy* means to them are sometimes amazed by the extent to which young persons, in particular, refer to the freedom to buy and consume whatever they wish, without government restriction. These definitions of democracy, by the way, usually do not center on the needs of the poor; a consumptionist democracy is one of incommensurable and unrestrained tastes backed by the ability to pay, rather than the redistribution of purchasing power. Playing on this conception of democracy, advertising itself often takes up the theme of individual consumer choice and personal entitlement.

In some measure, commercialization has taken the place of a now lost faith in the competence and authority of public institutions and collective decision making. For many persons, for example, personal security is not ensured by government at any level. All politicians, of course, support reduction of crime rates. But for some persons, the solution has taken commercial, individualized forms: handguns, removable car radio faceplates, sprays, antitheft devices for cars, locks, alarm systems, or even private security guards as opposed to the mutual assistance of neighbors. These are not, however, intended as genuine solutions to the problem of crime. Indeed, to a large degree, they do not even deter crime so much as displace it onto another victim with no commercialized defense.

Commercialization more basically reflects a number of underlying societal trends. Advances in communications technology, urbanization, increasing wealth itself, the Keynesian revolution in budgeting, changes in family size, and the decline of competing institutions all have played some role. But it is surely too simple to say that commercial advertising itself has not played an independent role and only mirrors independent changes in American values.

No doubt, advertising by itself cannot reshape our values as though they were modeling clay. It is difficult to believe, though, that over time, advertising in the aggregate has had absolutely no power to legitimize, reinforce, stabilize, or gradually modify those values, even at the margins. Sometimes what we do is determined not by our failure to think of an alternative but by whether we think that alternative is normal, attractive enough, or considered embarrassing by others. This is the natural space of advertising's efficacy.

Even if persons want to repudiate consumptionist lifestyles, they may have difficulty doing so. People may feel that they have to work long hours for a variety of reasons, including the need to pay for past—as opposed to future—consumer purchases. The necessity to work long hours, for any reason, requires time, energy, and attention and thus slows the development of less consumptionist lifestyles.

In addition, we generally do not seriously and consistently wish to reduce our consumptionism. Rather, our attitudes tend to be conflicted, and however unsatisfied we may be with focusing unduly on consumption, we find it difficult to give it up. Ironically, if we cut ourselves off from consumptionism, we would be disrupting many of the familiar bases on which we relate to other people. Our lives are commonly filled with stresses and responsibilities that at best are difficult to manage, and advertising and consumption offer some sort of relief.

In recent decades, advertising has typically not been judgmental. It tells us that we deserve, and are capable of appreciating, what the commercials promise. In earlier decades, ads might have created stress and fear—and then sought to relieve them—but this technique is now less common. Today's ads tend to be less challenging. The mature adult in us might wonder why we deserve a Caribbean cruise, or even why we deserve a break today, whereas a Haitian sugarcane worker, for example, would not. Commercial advertising, however, does not always appeal to our highest powers, to dispassionate self-assessment, or to personal and social responsibility. Instead, consumption, as opposed to most forms of market production, can often accommodate an essentially adolescent state of mind.

In fact, even expensive items, such as automobiles, can be sold on the basis of adolescent rebellion, self-indulgence, and aimless defiance. One recent automobile commercial even took this regressivism a step further by depicting a car as a toy to be drooled over in an infantile fashion. Automobiles also are pitched in other, more responsible ways. Given the need to break through the clutter of ads, we sometimes see an opposite but, in a way, an equally incongruous pitch, as in the case of a well-known insurance company's ad touting, ironically, the virtue of self-reliance.

The point is not that commercial advertising does not treat us as competent, mature adults with certain limits and capacities. Instead, advertising takes whatever approach it needs to take. We do not always need or prefer to be treated as less than mature adults. On the occasions, however rare or frequent, when we would appreciate relief from the pressures of maturity and the unflattering judgments of others, commercial advertising can accommodate us. Those occasions do seem to be increasingly frequent, if we judge them by the amount and variety of judgmental and fear-inducing magazine advertising in the first half of the twentieth century.

Generally, the ability of advertising to adapt to changes in communications media, audience demographics, economic and cultural circumstances, and even the public mood is remarkable. Advertisers seem almost limitlessly resourceful in preserving their own commercial utility over time. For this reason, it is difficult to accept the thesis that consumer jadedness, the demise of broad, homogeneous markets, cynicism toward ads, ad clutter, the mass abandonment of traditional television for new media, economic depression, or any combination of factors will dilute the cultural influence of commercial advertising. Just as economic markets themselves have historically overcome or accommodated a wide range of challenges, commercial advertising has shown great adaptiveness.

Advertising has always been forced to devise new or to recycle responses to consumer boredom, for example, and boredom can set in quickly. In certain respects, the power of advertising is limited; most does not have much authority, even in those cases in which it is noticed and remembered. After all, it would be odd for us as a society to ascribe only diminished authority to most of our major social institutions but to continue to treat advertising with unquestioned deference and respect.

Some advertisers appear to be aware of these problems and respond with more expensive ads, trendy ads, highly self-conscious ads, or more juvenile-spirited ads. A number of recent British ads seem to be based on the classic juvenile strategy of attracting attention through socially pointless misbehavior. The more self-referential and explicitly self-aware that ads become and the more that they recognize their role in the commercial system, the easier it is to imagine that they may be losing their ability to fulfill their traditional commercial role.

Certain instabilities are built into the advertising system. For instance, will we always be incapable of doubting the meaningfulness of celebrity endorsements of shoes, drinks, or snacks? More broadly, will we always be powerless to decide how much we wish to pay for designer labels? How much would we be willing to pay for clothes, accessories, automobiles, and so on if we were sure that no relevant third party regarded those brands as fashionable? Isn't fashion itself subject to deconstruction?

Current patterns of commercialism may reflect fairly deep and stable ways of behaving. But our present commercial culture is also not simply the reflection of a fixed human nature. There is no guarantee that advertising and commercial speech will always be able to reconcile the tensions and conflicts arising in the broader system of producing and consuming goods.

Consider, for example, the currently expanding gulf between the ethos of successful global competition in production and the ethos of consumption. In the world's major product markets, the necessary traits are still much as Max Weber described them: successful competitors must commonly value investment, long time horizons, thrift, technical curiosity, self-discipline, planning, precision, clarity of thought, quantitative measures, deferral of gratification, and guidance by objective standards. However repressive we may find this state of affairs, it still affects much of the production process and many workers in competitive industries.

Our ethos as consumers, on the other hand, diverges from this model. As consumers, we are commonly flattered. We deserve whatever is offered, assuming that we are able to pay for it. We are told to obey our desires. We are indulged and entertained. Demands on our capacities in the sphere of consumption are kept modest. Even print ads do not ask us to read nearly as much as they did a half-century or more ago. In sum, not much is asked of us. An exception may be using a computer, but at least the ads on the computer are not challenging, and in this arena many consumers bring some expertise from their producer/workplace roles.

This contrast between the ethos of production and the ethos of consumption is probably overly simple and, in some respects, inaccurate. Many of us, for example, would prefer to read an essaylike print ad from the first half of the twentieth century, at least on the back of a breakfast cereal box, than endure repeated viewings of a television commercial essentially consisting of a single joke.

Still, we must wonder how long we can successfully compartmentalize such strikingly inconsistent treatments, forms of address, self-images, and broader ways of thinking. More is involved than a stable, recurring cycle of discipline and relaxation. Our capacity to lead double lives is large but not infinite. How can we be sure that our consumer ethos will not gradually seep into the realm of production, perhaps through our role as consumers of high school and college education, in ways that hamper the growth of productivity and the ability to compete internationally? What if it turns out that increases in productivity and success in international competition require more devotion to math, engineering, and science than we find appealing?

The problem, contrary to frequent suggestion, is not that our economic system relies on standardized mass production and sales to a mass market in an era of fragmentation. Advertisers have adapted quite well to the fact that television viewing no longer consists of a three-generation family gathered in front of the *Ed Sullivan Show*. True, we are still subjected to pitches for standardized products in the name of expressing our individuality. There is, however, no reason to suppose that the economic system, with the assistance of cybernetic technology, cannot accommodate even rather narrow, parochial, but well-funded consumer tastes. The market can offer us hundreds of shades and tints, without strain, as long as we continue to consume.

Thus even though advertising and commercial speech face unprecedented challenges, they also have shown great adaptiveness and resourcefulness. It is difficult to say, therefore, much about the prospects for eventually overcoming the general dominance of commercial values. Even on this modest basis, though, we should still resist the defeatism, the rationalizing, and the pseudotriumphalism of some elements of the postmodernist left.

Some writers have noted the pervasiveness and adaptability of commercialism and assumed that it was invincible. They then have rationalized, with less justification, this result as somehow being progressive. Of course, there are insights to be drawn from such rationalizations, but the overall conclusion is ill judged and counterproductive.

There indeed are progressive elements in the desire of much contemporary advertising to validate equally all segments of its targeted audience. If we are apparently valued and catered to as consumers, why should we accept so much less than this as a worker? If we develop a protective carapace of cynicism, irony, or jadedness as a response to commercial advertising, perhaps we can similarly distance ourselves from politicians that do not promote our real interests. Perhaps the postmodernist consumer should be most skeptical of the idea that links consumption with human fulfillment.

We cannot achieve our greater goals in life by accommodating ourselves, however ironically and sophisticatedly, to the culture of consumption. Nor is freedom just one more arbitrary construct. As we have seen, the liberation that can be achieved through commercial consumption is, for most of us, rather modest and trivial. Liberation in this limited sense still consists mainly of changing the mix of goods that we consume, perhaps while thumbing our nose at some real or supposed authority figure.

The postmodernist impulse is to absorb all the progressivity it can from its underlying relativism and moral pragmatism. Such an impulse is thought to promote the interests of the subordinated if such groups become suspicious of commercialism's claims. Unfortunately, the theory is extended well beyond skepticism toward the ideological distortions of dominant groups. Instead of unmasking distortions of truth by those with power, the idea of pursuing any objective truth, however fallibly, is itself often jettisoned. Truth is reduced to a vaguely defined group's perspective or convention. Anything more is said to be something dismissively called foundationalism.

Whether this postmodernist downsizing of the idea of truth really promotes the interests of the least affluent is an important question but not a difficult one. We have seen that with the abandonment of any possible objective right or wrong, the moral logic of redistributive sacrifice in favor of the least affluent evaporates. Indeed, why should a powerful group permanently abandon its valuable privileges beyond the extent dictated by prudence, in the absence of an objective reason to do so?

Such a sacrifice seems especially incongruous and absurd once we accept the logic of commercial consumption. The commercial culture teaches us the value of personal acquisition and spending. To the extent that we are influenced by such values, we judge persons by what they have to spend and on what they acquire. This is a matter of spending on ourselves, our families, or our friends. Spending our own resources on strangers, and particularly on the least affluent, is a matter of charitable giving as opposed to the culture of consumption. To redistribute wealth to the poor means that the more affluent voluntarily leave themselves with fewer resources available for consumption and thus in a commercially less favorable position. For the consumption minded, this borders on paradox.

Can we say, though, that some currents of relativism and pragmatism can actually subvert advertising and the culture of commercial speech? Some elements of postmodernism tend to subvert any text, or any favored reading of that text, including advertisements. But it is difficult to see why commercial advertising could not survive the abandonment of objective truth and falsity. Consumptionism can adapt more easily than most institutions to the abandonment of epistemology. Consumption does not require depth or ambitious foundations. Is there really any great tension between relativism regarding truth, on the one hand, and the culture of advertising, on the other? If we decide that neither Coke nor Pepsi is objectively better than the other, have we thereby barred their successful advertising? Advertising can rely on truth as merely a function of group belief; the point is to increase the size of one's own consuming group.

Let us consider two distinct activities, exciting an electron and exciting a commercial customer. Generally, disdaining objective truth impairs our ability to accomplish the first task. We cannot dismiss the truths of Bohr, Pauli, and Dirac as truths only for them and arbitrarily posit some alternative truths more appealing to us. Or if we do, we will not accomplish what we set out to do. The natural world is, in this sense, recalcitrant. Truths about electrons may in some sense be socially constructed, but they cannot be constructed in any way that we want.

The realm of commercial consumption is often different. If we wish to excite customers, it may not pay to fret much about whether our brand of cola is objectively or foundationally better than its rivals. The superiority of one brand to another is at best a relative or noncognitive matter. But image may matter, even if we build our image by disclaiming an interest in it. If we cannot say that one brand is objectively better than another, the marketing process need not suffer. Instead, we can be made to feel strongly about matters of taste. The culture of consumption is compatible with subjectivism.

Denying objectivity, therefore, does not jeopardize the culture of consumption. Either it is clear that a product achieves some observable result, or it is not. If it is, as in the case of a safe and successful commercially advertised vaccine for a dreaded disease, the playfulness and deflations of postmodernism will be set aside. If it is not clear, the product can adapt or die in an atmosphere of nonobjective competing claims. In either case, commercial markets are not dissolved in an acid bath of relativism.

Relativism by itself offers us no higher values than the self- or group-interested hedonism of commercial advertising. It is sometimes argued, however, that commerce can break down barriers of prejudice and ignorance. In particular, it is argued that our culture of individual consumption creates tolerance and a reluctance to tyrannize. The claim might be that our consumerist narcissism leaves us both too self-absorbed and without a metaphysical apparatus to hate or oppress others.

There may well be something to such claims. Outsiders often find some sort of commercial niche, but relativism has no strong logical link to tolerance. Relativism might just as well take the form, conveniently, of deferring to the strong and taking advantage of the weak. The weak might object to this, according to their own moral scheme. But it is the essence of relativism that one is not bound by another group's moral scheme. One might choose to incorporate the interests and preferences of the weak into one's own moral scheme, beyond the dictates of prudence. But then, as we have seen, why bother? Note that even today in the realm of private charitable giving, there seems to be a shift toward various middle-class, albeit worthy, recipients. Charity may be increasingly staying in the donor's neighborhood and not crossing economic class lines.

To the extent that we are absorbed by commercial consumption, we may indeed become too busy or too narcissistic to hate. Bargain hunting may lead us to outsiders. Certainly, great personal wealth can take the edge off confrontation. On the other hand, we must ask whether young persons would be assaulting, and occasionally killing, people for jewelry or clothing in the absence of a culture of commercial consumption. We should look carefully before we conclude that consumptionism inoculates us against hate and divisiveness.

Let us look, for example, at recent developments in the fields of racial and ethnic relations, hate crimes, anti-immigrant sentiment, attitudes toward welfare recipients, capital punishment, sentencing reform, and the availability of habeas corpus before we conclude that our preoccupation with acquisition and spending has enhanced our tolerance of our neighbors. Those areas in which we all do get along better may be explained without appealing to consumptionism. That is, we should not be too quick to assume that our disinclination to fight bloody wars is driven by our desire to consume. For instance, did the Persian Gulf War have nothing to do with the availability and price of petroleum?

If some people on the postmodernist left have tried to rationalize the influence of the commercial culture, many on the cultural right and, of course, on the economic right have been eager to react in an at least equally accommodating fashion. We have already seen that religious groups, wherever they may stand on the political spectrum, have an incentive to mute their criticism of the commercialization process. Probably the religious institutions' best reason for downplaying any criticism of commercialism is considerateness. It is not clear how realistic it is to expect large numbers of responsible adults to abandon their commitment to commercial values. Even asking a young person to abandon consumptionism is difficult. If it is unrealistic to expect this, however much everyone involved might wish it otherwise, it is not clear that religious groups will press the issue.

On the other hand, religious groups could at least clarify the issues more than they have. Beyond some minimally necessary point, encouraging compartmentalized or inconsistent thinking about the role of material goods encourages unnecessary self indulgence. Most religious groups, for example, think of greed, vanity, covetousness, envy, and cupidity as vices. On the other hand, many of their adherents evidently distinguish between these vices and the desire for many expensive material possessions. A wish to possess expensive material goods is thought of as normal rather than vicious. Unfortunately, this distinction can become so blurred as to merely rationalize the aforementioned vices.

Some cultural conservatives have underplayed the tensions and incompatibilities within their overall social beliefs. The destructiveness of nearly ubiquitous advertising and commercial marketing on shared family activities is an example. Efficiency in advertising probably requires sending different messages, and therefore different television programs, to different family members. Commercialism contributes in this and other ways to atomization and to privatization within the family.

Those on the cultural right have generally reserved their criticism for the still small percentage of non-misleading advertising that they find objectionable on independent grounds, such as a reliance on sex and violence or an envelope-pushing vulgarity. The more typical advertisement, incorporating none of these features, passes without objection. Consumption is viewed as the necessary obverse of a healthy system of economic production.

Although some people on the cultural right offer broader critiques of commercialization, their ideas are usually dismissed as snobbish and elitist, despite their roots in the basic themes of writers such as Adam Smith. Contemporary conservatism has been increasingly divided between religious movements and market apologetics. If the voice of most major religious groups is muted on the issue of commercialization, we should expect the conservative response to commercialization to be one of overall support.

Economic conservativism joins with much of contemporary liberalism in deferring to the market's revealed preferences. On this point, the liberal justices on the U.S. Supreme Court are difficult to tell from the conservatives. Both groups see non-misleading advertisements of legal products, at least to adults, as a valuable form of free speech in which information is conveyed or a potentially mutually beneficial transaction is proposed. If anyone, including a government, for any reason, does not care for such speech, the proper remedy, even in the case of tobacco or liquor advertising, is said to be counterspeech. All else is governmental paternalism.

Another similarity between economic conservativism and much of contemporary liberalism is that neither seems much interested in what is culturally necessary to sustain market institutions, or liberal institutions, in a reasonably stable fashion over time. Too often, markets and liberal institutions are thought to require only a police force and the availability of schools, families, and other intermediary institutions. To the extent that these institutions themselves reflect voluntary choices, it might be thought that market and liberal institutions are broadly self-sustaining. Left to themselves, along with legal enforcement, markets are thought to be broadly self-perpetuating.

This assumption, however, is likely to be wrong. We have seen, for example, a dangerous gap between the qualities and skills needed by successful workers in internationally competitive markets and the lessons about ourselves as consumers imparted by commercial advertising. Consider the possible effect of a culture of consumptive indulgence on our massive public and private collective indebtedness and our neglect to maintain our infrastructure. Although these problems seem manageable now, there is something a bit unsettling about our current high levels of personal bankruptcies during a prolonged period of fairly low overall unemployment and interest rates. But we can take a range of attitudes toward the well-being of our successors. We can sacrifice on their behalf and, until recently, have done so. At the opposite extreme, we can indulge ourselves by borrowing for the sake of current consumption and then present the bill to future generations, who are not now in a position to stop us. There is nothing about market exchange that ensures that we will always sacrifice so that future generations will be better off.

Beyond some point, imposing the costs of current consumption on unconsenting parties can be socially destabilizing. Any increasing disinclination to invest in human capital, in either ourselves or future generations, is unlikely to be compatible with long-term success in a globally competitive economy. How people choose to spend their time and resources eventually affects their real productivity. Ultimately, a commercial society's success or failure requires more than, for example, allowing people individually or collectively to choose between current consumption and investment based simply on their own current preferences, however those preferences were culturally shaped.

It is thus fair to say that uncritical support and accommodation for the culture of consumption can be found at various points on the political spectrum. Thus it is not surprising that even some of the more controversial features of commercial speech receive enthusiastic protection across the ideological range of the current Supreme Court.

To challenge this consensus is certainly not to privilege hard work, production over consumption, or asceticism. Our point is not that production is nobler than consumption or that the value of production is always independent of commercial consumption. Production can, as much of the human race routinely observes, be alienating and degrading. Commercial consumption at its best can be uplifting and ennobling or, at least, fulfilling. Overall, however, the effects of an emphasis on consumption are not conducive to nobility or, for that matter, to happiness or freedom.

Let us conclude by referring briefly to a public dilemma, the link between the current ideologies of commercialization and the problem of environmental management and renewal. Assume that there is no clear and simple relationship between commercialization and the threat to the environment. It is true that noncommercial activities can threaten the environment. Certain forms of production and consumption can have widely varying effects on the environment, and there is no reason to suppose that the production and consumption of a basic necessity like paper or health care must be more environmentally friendly than would be the case with a luxury good.

Most other things being equal, we would expect increasing risk to the environment as levels of production and consumption rise. Not all else, however, need be equal. We have independent choices to make regarding antipollution technologies and investments. We should not expect to be able to predict changes in levels of air and water pollution merely from changes in consumption levels. Any level of consumption can be achieved in more and less environmentally responsible ways.

Still, there is good reason to believe that consumptionism is competing with environmental concerns. For example, think of Congress's recurring desire to sell off public land for commercial development. Or consider the activity of consumer recycling. From a psychological standpoint, recycling used goods and containers requires more of the disciplined ethos of production than of the indulgent ethos of advertising and consumption. Recycling can be tedious, unglamorous, messy, and inconvenient. It may amount to an imposition, with its own scheduling imperatives. Recycling brings little of the flattery, self-indulgence, and social display often associated with advertising and consumption.

Recycling can occasionally be linked to the ethos of consumption, as when one buys an environmentally friendly household good. Major purchases of an environmentally friendly item could even be objects of Veblenian conspicuous display. Generally, however, we must expect less enthusiasm for voluntary recycling to the extent that the ethos of consumption displaces the ethos of production. By analogy, we may be less willing collectively to pay for cleaning up Superfund sites because we see such cleanups as detracting from our current consumption.

Both conservatives and liberals have reason to be concerned about the environment. For economic conservatives, pollution is a negative externality not incorporated into the prices agreed on by willing buyers and sellers. For some cultural conservatives, pollution may involve waste or the dissipation of an inheritance. For liberals, pollution is a burden typically imposed on the politically or economically power-less. None of these approaches by itself, or even in combination, is likely to lead to an optimal level or distribution of pollution. We must also consider the gradual strengthening of the ethos of consumption, as contrasted with the ethos of production. In some respects, a clean and healthy environment is commercially marketable, as in some residential real estate contexts. But environmental purity is not as widely advertised as are other more tangible or divisible goods with which it competes. Being commercially unspoiled does not receive much reinforcing publicity. The causal relationships at work here may be subtle, difficult to show empirically, and long term, without thereby being worthy of dismissal.

Commercialization
and the Status
of the Poor

Babbit was again dreaming of the fairy
child, a dream more romantic than scarlet
pagodas by a silver sea.

c o n c l u s i o n

If commercialization is both pervasive and unfulfilling, why don't we recognize this and try to make changes for the better? We have offered a number of answers in this book. Let us emphasize again one of the most disturbing: the commercialization process changes not only what we value but also what we are capable of valuing. Thus it may hinder our very capacity for enjoying less commercial values.

For example, suppose a society undertakes what we call an arm's length contractualization of marriage. Persons enter into arm's length contractual marriages because they recognize that too often the ideal of trust, sacrifice, and long-term commitment in marriage masks inequality, vulnerability, and exploitation.

Whether the arm's length contractual or, more simply, the commercially modeled marriage can really abolish the inequality and exploitation of earlier marriage patterns is, at best, debatable. In any case, it is difficult to believe that commercialized forms of marriage amount to the summit of human fulfillment. Yet for many of us, they now may be the best of which we are capable. Can we all, through an effort of will, set aside commercialized forms of marriage in favor of long-term commitment, trust, and self-sacrifice without exploitation or inequality? Can we even imagine what this ideal might be like, let alone be capable of approaching it in practice?

Or think of the art and skill of extended social conversation. Is there any guarantee that our devotion to television, work schedules, computer games, and on-line chat rooms will not erode our ability to engage in and enjoy various kinds of extended, face-to-face social conversation? Won't we instead assume that such conversation really deserves its marginal role in our lives?

Finally, consider the possibility that the commercialization process will one day exercise a more general influence over what we think of as moral and immoral behavior. We may already be seeing an element of this in the increasing commercialization of marriage. Why shouldn't we expect notions of morality to be affected more generally by commercial norms and values? Of course, in some ways, this expectation might be progressive. But it is difficult to believe that morality should track commercial values and current patterns of commercial buying and selling.

Setting aside such broad speculations, let us return to the subject of the poor. Those concerned with poverty in our society may wonder what sort of relationship with the commercial culture it is in the interest of the poor to have. We noted the generally weak relationship between consumption and happiness but exempted the poor. We saw some of the ways in which the culture of consumption undercuts freedom. Yet the problem of poverty, almost by definition, seems to bespeak insufficient participation by the poor in just that culture. There is an obvious sense in which the poor do not fully share in the material bounties of a commercial culture. But there would be an equally obvious irony in concluding merely that the poor deserve to be as fully incorporated into the commercialization of values as everyone else does.

We are not suggesting that the poor are normally excluded from the commercialization process. Their money works just as well as anyone else's does. Although not many marketers target their efforts exclusively to the poor, there are exceptions. In particular, the poor in the United States and elsewhere form a disproportionate foundation of consumer support for the tobacco companies. We can even imagine the poor being appealed to on the Internet, if only on public terminals heavily larded with advertisements.

The poor are also directly connected with the commercial culture and its values in the form of televised advertising. Less directly and more benignly, the poor partake of whatever price reductions accrue through advertising, even if they often still pay more than richer people do. No doubt the poor benefit in some economic respects from the commercialization process.

It would be a mistake, however, to conclude that the culture of consumption is in no respects antithetical to the interests of the poor. That is, the social devaluing of the poor is not a new phenomenon. Historically, many societies have devalued those who have never been in a position to offer much in the way of economic value. Our society, though, is coming to be somewhat different in this regard.

As we have seen, in our society, commercial values and interests have ascended to dominance. This has meant, quite independent of anyone's intention, that other competing systems of value have gradually diminished in importance, in a complex, uneven process. But one clear inference is that we are increasingly judged on the basis of our ability—past, present, or future—to contribute usefully to the commercial culture. There are, of course, other ways of judging persons, or of extending and withholding honor and respect. Such ways are, however, currently fading in importance.

Increasingly, then, the poor are judged mainly on basis of their poverty, or their limited ability to sell their assets in the commercial marketplace. Most of the other possible grounds for respect are gradually becoming weaker. Although this argument cannot be linked to every cultural trend or fad, this process seems consistent, for example, with the recent bipartisan impatience with welfare and even with welfare safety nets.

Our society's aim should not, of course, be to accord dignity and respect to the poor solely in conjunction with their poverty. Surely the most important step is relieving the poverty itself. Indeed, this task is morally compelling, even if many of us find increasingly alien the idea of reducing our own levels of commercial consumption in order to enhance those of strangers.

Suppose though, for the sake of argument, that as a society we are able and inclined to make substantial inroads against involuntary poverty. Can we imagine a future in which those persons newly delivered from poverty do not enthusiastically embrace the culture of consumption, with all its eventual limitations and disappointments? This may be unrealistic. Instead, an embrace of consumptionism may be irresistible for most of those somehow brought from the margins to the center of our commercial culture.

What we can do for the poor in this regard, beyond relieving their poverty, corresponds closely to what we should be doing in our own narrow interests. We should rethink our recent exaltation of commercial speech. Permitting the reasonable regulation of commercial speech might contribute to a broader process of "denaturalizing" the currently dominant culture of consumption and of legitimizing other approaches to contemporary life.

We began this book with a brief tour of the Arrid-Mentos Junior High School, an amalgam of satire and fact. As time passes, the portion of the Arrid-Mentos story that is satire diminishes, and the portion that is fact increases. Predictably, those schools catering to relatively poor children will be especially affected by the commercialization of their education, despite the limited buying power of poor children and their families.

Many producers have little interest in addressing the poor, even as a captive audience in schools. Others, however, see the poor as a market to be tapped. Usually, public schools attended by the poor are, given their lack of funding, even less able to resist any outside funding than are schools attended by the middle class. Two hundred dollars from a burger chain will buy basic supplies, pocket calculators, portable heaters, or book covers that a poor school could not otherwise afford. Given their financial need, where will poor schools draw the line on the commercialization of education?

No one imagines that a rigorous comparison of the thickness of Prego's and Ragu's spaghetti sauces is an adequate substitute for, say, a microscope and some prepared slides. To some schools, however, poverty and the lack of resources conspire to make a spaghetti sauce competition the most practical pedagogical option.

The commercialization of poor children's education is ironic: those persons who are least well placed to rely on commercial solutions to

life's difficulties will be precisely those most thoroughly indoctri-
nated into the belief that the best solutions are commercial ones.
Those least able to buy happiness in commercial markets will, given
the realities of school funding and our broader social structure, be
those most insistently told, in and out of school, that happiness is
for sale.

n o t e s

Notes to the Introduction

1. See Deborah Stead, "Corporations, Classrooms and Commercialism," *New York Times*, January 5, 1997, pp. 30, 32.

Notes to Chapter 1

1. Adam Smith, "Theory of the Moral Sentiments," p. 309 in L. A. Selby-Bigge, ed., *British Moralists*, vol. 1 (New York: Dover, 1965).
2. See Ronald K. L. Collins and David M. Skover, "Commerce and Communication," *Texas Law Review* 71 (1993): 697, 707.

3. 425 U.S. 748, 762 (1976) (quoting Pittsburgh Press Co. v. Pittsburgh Comm'n on Human Relations, 413 U.S. 376, 385 [1973]).

4. 447 U.S. 557, 561 (1980).

5. *Id.* at 566.

6. See Posadas de Puerto Rico Assocs. v. Tourism Co., 478 U.S. 328, 341 (1986).

7. Edenfield v. Fane, 507 U.S. 706 (1993). See also Ibanez v. Florida Dep't of Business and Professional Regulation, 114 *S. Ct.* 2084, 2089 (1994).

8. For further discussion, see the various opinions in 44 Liquormart, Inc. v. Rhode Island, 116 *S. Ct.* 1495 (1996).

9. City of Cincinnati v. Discovery Network, Inc., 507 U.S. 410 (1993).

Notes to Chapter 2

1. See "Regulations Restricting the Sale and Distribution of Cigarettes and Smokeless Tobacco Products to Protect Children and Adolescents," *Federal Register*, August 11, 1995, pp. 41314, docket no. 95N–0253.

2. See generally the discussion in Jef I. Richards, "Politicizing Cigarette Advertising," *Catholic University Law Review* 45 (1996): 147, 154.

3. For references to, as well as conflicting views of, some of the relevant literature, see, for example, Martin Duffy, "Econometric Studies of Advertising, Advertising Restrictions and Cigarette Demand: A Survey," *International Journal of Advertising* 15 (1996): 1; Jean J. Boddewyn, "Cigarette Advertising Bans and Smoking: The Flawed Policy Connection," *International Journal of Advertising* 13 (1994): 311; Rachel Nowak and Eliot Marshall, "New Studies Trace the Impact of Tobacco Advertising," *Science*, October 27, 1995, p. 573 (which discusses the work of the behavioral epidemiologist John Pierce), as well as much of the important work of Richard W. Pollay, including, for example, Richard W. Pollay et al., "The Last Straw? Cigarette Advertising and Realized Market Shares Among Youths and Adults, 1979–1993," *Journal of Marketing* 60 (1996): 1.

4. 127 *Dominion Law Reports 4th* 1 (1995).

5. The Canadian study is cited in RJR-MacDonald, Inc. v. Attorney General of Canada, 127 *Dominion Law Reports 4th* 1 (1995): 49–50. For relevant British studies, see, for example, Hilary Graham, "Cigarette Smoking: A Light on Gender and Class Inequality in Britain?" *Journal of Social Policy* 24 (1995): 509; Joy Townsend, Paul Roderick, and Jacqueline Cooper, "Cigarette Smoking by Socioeconomic Group, Sex, and Age: Effects of Price, Income, and Health Publicity," *British Medical Journal*, October 8, 1994, p. 134.

6. For supporting data, see, for example, Kathleen M. Macken et al., "Smoking Patterns in a Low Income Urban Population: A Challenge to Smoking Cessation Efforts," *Journal of Family Practice*, January 1991, p. 93; Jendi B. Reiter, "Citizens or Sinners?: The Economic and Political Inequity of 'Sin Taxes' on Tobacco and Alcohol Products," *Columbia Journal of Law and Social Problems* 29 (1996): 443, and "Smokers: The Young, the Poor, and the Less Educated," *The Women's Letter*, November 1990, p. 4; B. P. Zhu et al., "The Relationship Between Cigarette Smoking and Education Revisited," *American Journal of Public Health*, November 1996, p. 1582.

Notes to Chapter 3

1. For a discussion, see Peter Lipton, *Inference to the Best Explanation* (London: Routledge, 1991), chap. 8.

2. Greg Miller, "9 Firms Charged with Fraudulent Ads on Internet," *Los Angeles Times*, March 15, 1996, p. 1D.

Notes to Chapter 4

1. See, for example, Mary Williams Walsh, "German Court Bans Shocking Benetton Ads," *Los Angeles Times*, July 7, 1995, p. A6.

2. For further discussion, see Ian G. Evans and Sumandeep Riyait, "Is the Message Being Received? Benetton Analyzed," *International Journal of Advertising* 12 (1993): 291.

3. See, for example, R. George Wright, *Reason and Obligation* (Lanham, MD: University Press of America, 1994), chap. 5.

4. See Jane R. Eisner, "In a Blink, TV's Family Hour Has Been Replaced by Racier Fare," *Philadelphia Inquirer*, February 4, 1996, p. E5.

Notes to Chapter 5

1. Newton N. Minow and Craig L. LaMay, *Abandoned in the Wasteland: Children, Television, and the First Amendment* (New York: Hill & Wang, 1995), p. 54.

2. See 47 C.F.R. § 73.670 note 1 (1995).

b i b l i o g r a p h y

Abercrombie, Nicholas. "Authority and Consumer Society." In *The Authority of the Consumer*. Ed. Russell Keat. London: Routledge, 1994.

Abrahams, Ben. "Public Relations: Playing with Fire." *Marketing*, November 23, 1995, p. 47.

Abuhajheh, Alf. "Targeting a Captive Audience: Public Restrooms Are Latest Arena for Advertisers." *Miami Herald*, January 10, 1996, p. 7B.

Adolph Coors Co. v. Bensen, 2 *F.3d* 355 (10th Cir. 1993).

Ahrens, Frank. "It Adds up to Genius." *Washington Post*, January 26, 1997, p. F1.

Allen, Mike. "Testing Whether Internet Readers Will Pay." *New York Times News Service*, September 16, 1996 (1996 WL–NYT 9626000605).

"An Anti-Smoking Wheeze." *Economist*, August 19, 1995, p. 336.

Angell, David. "Laying the Track." *Internet World*, August 1996, p. 34.

Anheuser-Busch, Inc. v. Schmoke, 63 *F.3d* 1305 (4th Cir. 1995), vacated, 116 *S. Ct.* 1821 (1996).

Ansolabehere, Stephen, and Shanto Iyengar. *Going Negative: How Attack Ads Shrink and Polarize the Electorate*. New York: Free Press, 1996.

Appleyard, Brian. "Simply Shocking (They Hope)." *Independent*, August 30, 1995, p. 15.

Argyle, Michael. *The Psychology of Happiness*. London: Routledge, 1987.

Armstrong, Stephen. "Yobs on the Pitch." *Guardian*, January 1, 1996, p. 9.

Association of National Advertisers, Inc. v. Lungren, 44 *F.3d* 726 (9th Cir. 1994), cert. denied, 116 *S. Ct.* 62 (1995).

Auerbach, Joel. "For Teachers, a Screenful of Promise and Pitfalls: Amid the Hoopla, the Internet Delivers Some Uneasy—and Unwanted—Lessons." *Boston Globe*, March 24, 1996, p. 89.

Auerbach, Jon. "Premium Fees the Next Wave for Net Surfers." *Boston Globe*, April 18, 1996, p. 1.

Baird, Roger. "'Shocked' Contractors Force Benetton to Scrap Poster Ad." *Marketing Week*, July 12, 1996, p. 5.

Baker, C. Edwin. *Advertising and a Democratic Press*. Princeton, NJ: Princeton University Press, 1994.

———. "Advertising and a Democratic Press." *University of Pennsylvania Law Review* 140 (1992): 2097.

———. "Commercial Speech: A Problem in the Theory of Freedom." *Iowa Law Review* 62 (1976): 1.

———. "Realizing Self-Realization: Corporate Political Expenditures and Redish's The Value of Free Speech." *University of Pennsylvania Law Review* 130 (1982): 646.

Balbus, Isaac D. "Commodity Form and Legal Form: An Essay on the 'Relative Autonomy' of the Law." *Law and Society Review* 11 (1977): 571.

Baldini, Matthew. Comment: "The Cigarette Battle: Anti-Smoking Proponents Go for the Knockout." *Seton Hall Law Review* 29 (1995): 348.

Balkin, J.M. "Give Them Liberty to Give Us Death?" *Washington Monthly*, October 1995, p. 24.

Barber, Benjamin R. *Jihad v. McWorld: How Globalism and Tribalism Are Re-Shaping the World.* New York: Ballantine, 1996.

Barboza, David. "An Internet Newcomer Sells Space for Moving Ads." *New York Times News Service*, October 1, 1996 (1996 WL–NYT 9627502602).

Barker, Paul. "Why the Poor Smokers Bear the Tax Burden." *Times* (London), March 9, 1994, p. 14.

Baudrillard, Jean. "The Masses: The Implosion of the Social in the Media." Trans. Marie McLean. *New Literary History* 16 (1985): 577.

Bell, Daniel. *The Cultural Contradictions of Capitalism.* New York: Basic Books, 1976.

Bender, Thomas. Book Review: "Where the Suckers Moon." *Nation*, November 7, 1994, p. 542.

Bennet, James. "Among TV's Sales Pitches, Negative Ads Show a Scary Side." *New York Times News Service*, October 14, 1996 (1996 WL–NYT 9628800205).

Berkowitz, Harry. "FDA Blasted by Ad, Tobacco Industries." *Newsday*, August 11, 1995, p. A35.

———. "Sex Sells in Latest TV Commercials." *Newsday*, May 10, 1996, p. A55.

Besser, Howard. "A Clash of Cultures on the Internet." *San Francisco Chronicle*, August 25, 1995, p. A23.

———. "From Internet to Information Superhighway." P. 59 in *The Culture and Politics of Information.* Ed. James Brook and Iain A. Boal. San Francisco: City Lights, 1995.

BeVier, Lillian R. "The First Amendment and Political Speech: An Inquiry into the Substance and Limits of Principle." *Stanford Law Review* 30 (1978): 299.

Bhagwat, Ashutosh. "Of Markets and Media: The First Amendment, the New Mass Media, and the Political Components of Culture." *North Carolina Law Review* 74 (1995): 141.

Blasi, Vincent. "The Pathological Perspective and the First Amendment." *Columbia Law Review* 85 (1985): 449.

———, and Henry P. Monahan. "The First Amendment and Cigarette Advertising." *Journal of the American Medical Association*, July 25, 1986, p. 502.

Blim, John M. Comment, "Free Speech and Health Claims Under the Nutrition Labeling and Education Act of 1990." *Northwestern University Law Review* 88 (1994): 733.

Board of Trustees v. Fox, 492 *U.S.* 469 (1989).

Boccella, Kathy. "Shopping Down the Bunny Trail." *Philadelphia Inquirer*, April 4, 1996, p. C1.

Bocock, Robert. *Consumption*. London: Routledge, 1993.

Boddewyn, Jean J. "Cigarette Advertising Bans and Smoking: The Flawed Policy Connection." *International Journal of Advertising* 13 (1994): 311.

———. "Controlling Sex and Decency in Advertising Around the World." *Journal of Advertising*, December 1991, p. 25.

Bogart, Leo. *Commercial Culture: The Media System and the Public Interest*. Oxford: Oxford University Press, 1995.

———. "Freedom to Know or Freedom to Say?" *Texas Law Review* 71 (1993): 815.

———. *Strategy in Advertising: Matching Media and Messages to Markets and Motivations*. 3rd ed. New York: NTC Publishing Group, 1996.

Bolger v. Youngs Drug Products Corp., 463 *U.S.* 60 (1983).

Bollinger, Lee. *The Tolerant Society*. Oxford: Oxford University Press, 1986.

Boyle, James. *Shamans, Software, and Spleens: Law and the Construction of the Information Society*. Cambridge, MA: Harvard University Press, 1996.

Bredenberg, Al. "Caveat Spammor: Markets Are Trying to Legitimize Internet Junk Mail, or Spam, Through New Methods." *Internet World*, July 1996, p. 69.

Brent, Paul. "Distillers Pop Corks over Advertising Court Ruling." *Financial Post*, June 14, 1995, p. 3.

Brest, Paul. "Further Beyond the Republican Revival: Toward Radical Republicanism." *Yale Law Journal* 97 (1988): 1623.

Bridle, David. "Let's Make the Poor Cough Up." *Guardian*, March 9, 1994, p. 12.

"Brigadier Sees the Light over Advert on Dome of St. Paul's." *Daily Telegraph*, November 8, 1995, p. 5.

Britt, Donna. "Where There's Space, There's a Sponsor." *Washington Post*, March 22, 1996, p. D1.

Brubach, Holly. "Sackcloth and Ashes." *New Yorker*, February 3, 1992, p. 78.

Brueckner, Robert. "Taking on TV: TV Is a Bad Role Model for the Web." *Internet World*, July 1996, p. 59.

Bruton, Mike. "Amid Racial Polarity, Black Athletes Star as Salesmen." *Philadelphia Inquirer*, January 21, 1996, p. C1.

Buckley v. Valeo, 424 *U.S.* 1 (1976).

Budiansky, Stephen. "Tune in, Turn off, Drop Out." *U.S. News and World Report*, February 19, 1996, p. 30.

Bunting, Madeline. "The Abandoned Generation." *Guardian*, June 1, 1994, p. 18.

Butsch, Richard, ed. *For Fun and Profit: The Transformation of Leisure into Consumption*. Philadelphia: Temple University Press, 1990.

Cal-Almond Inc. v. United States Dep't of Agriculture, 14 *F.3d* 429 (9th Cir. 1993).

Campbell, Angus. "Subjective Measures of Well-Being." *American Psychologist* 31 (1976): 117.

Caragota, Warren. "Looking for Net Profit: Entrepreneurs Are Now Cruising the Internet." *MacLean's*, October 24, 1994, p. 38.

———. "Up in Smoke: Tobacco Industry Reaction to Canadian Supreme Court's 1995 Ruling on Tobacco Advertising." *MacLean's*, October 2, 1995, p. 34.

Carlill v. Carbolic Smoke Ball Co., (1893) 1 Q.B. 256 (1892).

Carrig, Eric. "Where to Reach Today's Young Adult Generation: Their Media Habits Center on Information Highway." *Advertising Age*, September 19, 1994, p. 23.

Cass, Ronald A. "Commercial Speech, Constitutionalism, Collective Choice." *University of Cincinnati Law Review* 56 (1988): 1317.

Central Hudson Gas and Electric Corp. v. Public Service Com'n, 447 *U.S.* 557 (1980).

Chandrasekaran, Rajiv. "FDA's Tobacco Ad Rules Face Lengthy Court Challenge." *Washington Post*, August 24, 1996, p. A9.

Chapman, Gary. "The 'Free Information Sandbox' Is Buried." *Los Angeles Times*, March 14, 1996, p. D2.

Chidley, Joe. "Tobacco's Soft Sell." *MacLean's*, December 25, 1995, p. 53.

"Cigarette Smoking Among Adults: United States, 1993." *Journal of the American Medical Association*, February 1, 1995, p. 369.

"Cigarette Smoking Among Adults: United States, 1992 and Changes in Definition of Smoking." *Journal of the American Medical Association*, July 6, 1994, p. 14.

Cimons, Marlene. "Cigarette Regulation Plan Challenged." *Los Angeles Times*, January 3, 1996, p. A11.

City of Cincinnati v. Discovery Network, 507 *U.S.* 410 (1993).

Clark, Eric. *The Want Makers: The World of Advertising.* New York: Viking, 1989.

Cleland, Kim. "Infomercials Hit the Web: Direct Sales Shops Move Their Expertise to Internet Sales." *Advertising Age*, August 7, 1995, p. 12.

Clomon v. Jackson, 988 *F.2d* 1314 (2d Cir. 1993).

Coase, R.H. "Advertising and Free Speech." *Journal of Legal Studies* 6 (1977): 1.

47 *Code of Federal Regulations* § 73.670, § 73.671 (1995).

Coffee, Brett B. "Environmental Marketing After Association of National Advertisers v. Lungren." *Fordham Environmental Law Journal* 6 (1995): 297.

Cohen, Joshua. "Freedom of Expression." *Philosophy and Public Affairs* 22 (1993): 207.

Collins, Glenn. "Coke's Blitz an Olympics Homestand." *Miami Herald*, March 29, 1996, p. C1.

———. "Tobacco Giants Seek Anti-Smoking Laws." *New York Times News Service*, May 16, 1996 (1996 WL–NYT 9613703606).

———. "Web Sites: Make Room for Yet Another Kitchen Appliance." *New York Times News Service*, September 16, 1996 (1996 WL–NYT 9625901809).

Collins, Ronald K. L., and David M. Skover. "Afterword: New 'Truths' and the Old First Amendment." *University of Cincinnati Law Review* 64 (1996): 1295.

———. "Commerce and Communication." *Texas Law Review* 71 (1993): 967.

———. *The Death of Discourse.* Boulder, CO: Westview, 1996.

————. "The Psychology of First Amendment Scholarship: A Reply." *Texas Law Review* 71 (1993): 819.

Confucius, *Analects of Confucius*. Trans. Arthur Waley. London: Allen & Unwin, 1938.

Conover, Kirsten. "Advertisers Aim to Cut Through Media Clutter." *Christian Science Monitor*, May 31, 1995, p. 12.

Cooper, Lane F. "The Commercialization of the Internet." *Communications Week*, April 1, 1996, p. 135.

Craswell, Richard, "Interpreting Deceptive Advertising." *Boston University Law Review* 65 (1985): 657.

Cross, Mary, ed. *Advertising and Culture: Theoretical Perspectives*. Westport, CT: Praeger, 1996.

Culf, Andrew. "Advertisers Get Warning on Use of Sex in Posters." *Guardian*, April 3, 1996, p. 10.

Davidson, J. Hugh. "Why Most New Consumer Brands Fail." *Harvard Business Review*, March–April 1976, p. 117.

Davis, Michael. "The Special Resiliency of Commercial Speech as Deus ex Machina." *Law and Philosophy* 6 (1987): 121.

De Abitua, Matthew. "Consumer Choice? Don't Buy It." *Guardian*, November 1, 1995, p. 10.

Diener, Ed, M. Diener, and C. Diener, "Factors Predicting Subjective Well-Being of Nations." *Journal of Personality and Social Psychology* 69 (1995): 851.

Dignam, Conor. "Console Game Ads: No Longer Child's Play." *Marketing*, October 5, 1995, p. 9.

Douglas, Torin. "Advertisers Jeopardize Image in Pursuit of Indecent Exposure." *Marketing Week*, February 2, 1996, p. 19.

Dourado, Phil. "Families Lose Their Appeal: Consumer Culture Is Changing." *Independent on Sunday*, February 10, 1991, p. 24.

Dowling, Paul J. Jr., Thomas J. Kuegler Jr., and Joshua O. Testerman. *Web Advertising and Marketing*. Rocklin, CA: Prima Publications, 1996.

Duffy, Martyn. "Econometric Studies of Advertising, Advertising Restrictions, and Cigarette Demand: A Survey." *International Journal of Advertising*, February 1996, p. 15.

Durning, Alan T. "Are We Happy Yet? How the Pursuit of Happiness Is Failing." *Futurist* 27 (1993): 20.

Dvorak, John. "The I-Way Is No Road to Riches." *PC Magazine*, April 9, 1996, p. 85.

Eagleton, Terry. "Where Do Postmodernists Come From?" *Monthly Review*, July 17, 1995, p. 59.

Eckhouse, John. "The High-Tech Future of Advertising." *San Francisco Chronicle*, November 21, 1992, p. B1.

Edenfield v. Fane, 507 *U.S.* 761 (1993).

Editorial, "Just Say No to Liquor Ads." *New York Times News Service*, November 13, 1996 (1996 WL–NYT 9631801801).

Editorial, "One Ban Hurts All Free Speech." *Advertising Age*, January 15, 1996, p. 112.

Edwards, Ellen. "The Children's Half-Hour Hostage to Toy Makers?" *Washington Post*, June 10, 1994, p. A1.

Edwards, Krista L. Comment: "First Amendment Values and the Constitutional Protection of Tobacco Advertising." *Northwestern University Law Review* 82 (1987): 145.

Edwards, Mark, and Stephen Armstrong. "Is Our Advertising Going the Wrong Way?" *Sunday Times*, July 16, 1995, p. 1.

Elliott, Stuart. "Ads for Women Are Put on a Pedestal, Showing How Times Change." *New York Times*, November 3, 1995, p. D13.

——— . "Advertising: Reviving Songs and Styles of the 1970s." *New York Times News Service*, May 7, 1996 (1996 WL–NYT 9612802201).

——— . "Calvin Klein Fragrance Campaign Emphasizes Youth." *New York Times News Service*, August 14, 1996 (1996 WL–NYT 9622702001).

——— . "Calvin Klein to Withdraw Child Jean Ads." *New York Times*, August 28, 1995, p. D1.

——— . "Distillers Chip Away at Ban on Commercials." *New York Times News Service*, May 3, 1996 (1996 WL–NYT 9612402202).

——— . "How to Focus a Sales Pitch in Cyberspace." *New York Times*, March 4, 1996, p. D1.

——— . "In the Competition Among Professional Athletes for Commercial Endorsements, N.B.A. Stars Rule." *New York Times*, February 15, 1994, p. D19.

———. "Liquor Industry Ends Its Ad Ban in Broadcasting." *New York Times Service*, November 8, 1996 (1996 WL–NYT 9631300209).

———. "Middle Age Catches up with the Me Generation." *New York Times*, January 2, 1996, p. C4.

———. "Ultrathin Models in Coca-Cola and Calvin Klein Campaigns Draw Fire and a Boycott Call." *New York Times*, April 26, 1994, p. D18.

———. "Whether in Asia, Latin America or the United States, Teen Agers in a Study Dress and Think Alike." *New York Times*, December 23, 1994, p. D6.

Ellsworth, Jill, and Matthew V. Ellsworth. *Marketing on the Internet: Strategies for the World Wide Web.* New York: Wiley, 1995.

Ellul, Jacques. *Money and Power.* Trans. LaVonne Neff. 2nd ed. Downers Grove, IL: Intervarsity Press, 1984.

Emerson, Ralph W. *Thoreau.* Pp. 475–90 in *The Oxford Authors: Ralph Waldo Emerson.* Ed. Richard Poirier. New York: Oxford University Press, 1990.

Emerson, Thomas I. "First Amendment Doctrine and the Burger Court." *California Law Review* 68 (1980): 422.

Emery, Vince. *How to Grow Your Business on the Internet.* 2nd ed. Scottsdale, AZ: Coriolis Group, 1996.

Enrico, Dottie. "Ads Target Graying Boomers: Products Aim at Hippier But Still Hip Buyers." *USA Today*, June 21, 1995, p. B1.

———. "High Tech Media May Reshape Ads." *USA Today*, March 13, 1995, p. B2.

———. "Lesson No. 1: Consumers Know Best." *USA Today*, March 11, 1996, p. B10.

Epictetus. *Discourses of Epictetus.* Trans. George Long. New York: A. L. Burt, 1885.

Epstein, Edward. "San Jose School Pulls Plug on Channel One and Its Ads." *San Francisco Chronicle*, April 20, 1996, p. A14.

Erasmus, Desiderius. *The Praise of Folly* (1668). Ann Arbor, MI: University of Michigan Press, 1958.

Evans, Ian G., and Sumandeep Riyait. "Is the Message Being Received? Benetton Analyzed." *International Journal of Advertising* 12 (Fall 1993): 291.

Ewen, Stuart. "Advertising and the Development of Consumer Society." In *Cultural Politics in Contemporary America*. Ed. Ian Angus and Sut Jhally. London: Routledge, 1989.

———. *Captains of Consciousness: Advertising and the Social Roots of the Consumer Culture*. New York: McGraw-Hill, 1976.

———, and Elizabeth Ewen. *Channels of Desire: Mass Images and the Shaping of American Consciousness*. Minneapolis: University of Minnesota Press, 1982.

Farber, Daniel A. "Commercial Speech and First Amendment Theory." *Northwestern University Law Review* 74 (1979): 372.

Farhi, Paul. "Children's Advertising: The Rules Not Followed." *Washington Post*, October 13, 1995, p. A33.

———, and Rajiv Chandrasekaran. "Web TV: Is the Internet Wave About to Come Crashing into Living Rooms?" *Washington Post*, January 4, 1997, p. C1.

Farley, H. Scott, and Brian R. Fraser. "Tobacco Advertising, Public Welfare, and Commercial Free Speech: Comparative Insights from the Canadian Experience." *American Journal of Trial Advocacy* 16 (1992): 497.

Feigin, Barbara. "Research Keeps Its Place in Line: Emphasis on Consumer Attitude Studies Continues." *Advertising Age*, September 7, 1992.

Feinstein, Jonathan S. "The Relationship Between Socioeconomic Status and Health: A Review of the Literature." *Milbank Quarterly* 71 (Summer 1993): 279.

Feldman, Heidi L. "Objectivity in Legal Judgment." *Michigan Law Review* 92 (1994): 1187.

First National Bank v. Bellotti, 435 *U.S.* 765 (1978).

Fiss, Owen M. "Free Speech and Social Structure." *Iowa Law Review* 71 (1986): 1405.

Flay, Brian R., J. K. Ockene, and I. B. Tager. "Smoking: Epidemiology, Cessation, and Prevention." *Chest*, September 1992, p. 277S.

Florida Bar v. Went-For-It, Inc., 115 *S. Ct.* 2371 (1995).

44 Liquormart, Inc. v. Rhode Island, 116 *S. Ct.* 1495 (1996).

Frank, Tom. "Hip Is Dead." *Nation*, April 1, 1996, p. 16.

Frean, Alexandra. "Women Insulted by 'Patronizing' TV Car Adverts." *Times* (London), February 10, 1996.

Freedland, Jonathan. "TV's Shame Game." *Guardian*, January 16, 1996, p. 16.

Freund, Charles Paul. "The New Face of Betty Crocker: Her Portrait as Drawn by Adam Smith's Invisible Hand." *Washington Post*, April 14, 1996, p. C5.

Fried, John J. "Junk Mail's Newest Frontier." *Miami Herald*, April 22, 1996, p. 19BM.

Friedman v. Rogers, 440 *U.S.* 1 (1979).

Fromartz, Samuel. "Just How Profitable Is Doing Business on Ballyhooed Web? Sales in Cyberspace Are Still a Ways Off." *Philadelphia Inquirer*, January 14, 1996, p. C3.

Fromm, Erich. *The Revolution of Hope: Toward a Humanized Technology*. Ed. Ruth N. Anshen. New York: Harper & Row, 1968.

Froomkin, A. Michael. "Flood Control on the Information Ocean: Living with Anonymity, Digital Cash, and Distributed Databases." http://www.law.miami.edu/~froomkin/articles/ocean1.htm.

Galbraith, John K. *The Affluent Society*. New York: NAL, 1958.

———. *The Culture of Contentment*. New York: Houghton Mifflin, 1992.

Gammon v. GC Servs. Ltd. Partnership, 27 *F.3d* 1254 (7th Cir. 1994).

Gardbaum, Stephen. "Liberalism, Autonomy, and Moral Conflict." *Stanford Law Review* 48 (1996): 385.

Garfield, Bob. "Ads R Us: From the Texaco Man to Mr. Whipple, TV Commercials Define Our Culture." *Washington Post*, February 26, 1995, p. C1.

———. "Come on, Calvin, Light My Fire: Pyro-Marketing Burns Us All." *Washington Post*, September 10, 1995, p. C1.

———. "In Defense of Commercials." *Advertising Age*, February 28, 1995, p. 24.

Garramore, Gina M. "Voter Responses to Negative Political Ads." *Journalism Quarterly* 61 (1984): 250.

Garvey, John H. Book Review: "The Sponsored Life." *Commonweal*, February 10, 1995, p. 7.

———. *What Are Freedoms For?* Cambridge, MA: Harvard University Press, 1996.

Gellene, Denise. "Internet Marketing to Kids Is Seen as a Web of Deceit." *Los Angeles Times*, March 29, 1996, p. A1.

"Generation Y: Inside the Mind of British Youth." *Independent*, January 23, 1995, p. 1.

Gitlin, Todd. *The Twilight of Common Dreams*. New York: Henry Holt, 1995.

Glantz, Stanton A., et al. *The Cigarette Papers*. Berkeley and Los Angeles: University of California Press, 1996.

Glossbrenner, Alfred, and Emily Glossbrenner. *Making Money on the Internet*. 1995.

Goffman, Erving. *Gender Advertisements*. New York: Harper & Row, 1976.

Goldman, Alvin I. "Epistemic Paternalism: Communication Control in Law and Society." *Journal of Philosophy* 88 (1991): 113.

Goldman, Robert. *Reading Ads Socially*. London: Routledge, 1992.

Goldstein, Amy. "Black Teens Smoke Less, but Why?" *Washington Post*, August 20, 1995, p. A1.

Gonyea, James C., and Wayne M. Gonyea. *Selling on the Internet: How to Open an Electronic Storefront and Have Millions of Customers Come to You*. New York: McGraw-Hill, 1996.

Goodyear, Mary. "The Five Stages of Advertising Literacy." *Admap*, March 31, 1991, p. 19.

Graff v. City of Chicago, 9 *F.3d* 1309 (7th Cir. 1993), cert. denied, 114 *S. Ct.* 1837 (1994).

Graham, Hilary. "Cigarette Smoking: A Light on Gender and Class Inequality in Britain?" *Journal of Social Policy* 24 (1995): 509.

Greenburg, Jan Crawford. "Tobacco Groups Seek to Snuff out Ad Rules." *Chicago Tribune*, February 15, 1996, p. B1.

Griffin, James. *Well-Being*. Oxford: Oxford University Press, 1986.

Gubernick, Lisa, and Luisa Kroll. "Gray Hair Is Cool: Suddenly Madison Avenue Is Using Grandma and Grandpa to Sell Computers and Cosmetics." *Forbes*, May 6, 1996, p. 116.

Gustafson, Robert, Johan Yssel, and Lea Witta. "Ad Agency Employees Give Views on Calvin Klein, Benetton Ads." *Marketing News*, September 23, 1996, p. 16.

Hafner, Katie, and Matthew Lyon. *Where Wizards Stay up Late: The Story Behind the Creation of the Internet*. New York: Simon & Schuster, 1996.

Hall, Charles W. "America Online Sues Internet Advertiser." *Washington Post*, April 11, 1996, p. B8.

Hall, Jane. "Cyberspace for Sale: From Madison Avenue to Silicon Valley, Companies Are Rushing to Market Products over the Internet." *Los Angeles Times*, May 21, 1995, p. D1.

Haran, Leah. "Madison Avenue Visits Dreamland." *Advertising Age*, March 18, 1996, p. C12.

Harrington, John. "Up in Smoke: The FTC's Refusal to Apply the 'Unfairness Doctrine' to Camel Cigarette Advertising." *Federal Communications Law Journal*, April 1995, p. 593.

Harwood, Richard. "Taking on Tobacco, Cautiously." *Washington Post*, September 14, 1996, p. A25.

———. "Speculating in Cyberspace." *Washington Post*, January 23, 1997, p. A17.

Hastings, Steve. "Advertisers Have to Invent New Ways to Entice Buyers." *Campaign*, May 14, 1993, p. 25.

Hatfield, Stefano. "Benetton Advertising: Should Brand Advertising Address Social Issues?" *Campaign*, October 6, 1995, p. 11.

———. "When They Just Don't Add Up." *Guardian*, August 11, 1995, p. 11.

Hecht, Brian. "Net Loss." *New Republic*, February 17, 1997.

Helberg, Daniel. "Butt Out: An Analysis of the FDA's Proposed Restrictions on Cigarette Advertising Under the Commercial Speech Doctrine." *Loyola of Los Angeles Law Review* 29 (1996): 1219.

"Hello, Good Buy." *Washington Post*, January 26, 1997, p. G6.

Henry, Jules. *Culture Against Man*. New York: McGraw-Hill, 1963.

Henry, William A. "The Meaning of TV." *Life*, March 1989, p. 66.

"High and Hooked: Molecular Biology of Addictions." *Economist*, May 15, 1993, p. 105.

Hilts, Philip J. *Smoke Screen: The Truth Behind the Tobacco Industry Cover-Up*. Reading, MA: Addison-Wesley, 1996.

Hine, Thomas. "A Car Named Desire: After a New Auto Is Made, It Can Really Begin to Take Shape." *Philadelphia Inquirer*, February 26, 1995, p. 25.

Hirsch, Fred. *Social Limits to Growth*. Cambridge, MA: Harvard University Press, 1976.

Hirschkop, Ken. "Democracy and The New Technologies." *Monthly Review*, July-August 1996, p. 86.

Honan, William H. "Scholars Attack Public School TV Program." *New York Times News Service*, January 22, 1997 (1997 WL–NYT 9702202804).

Hopkins, Claude. *My Life in Advertising* and *Scientific Advertising*. Reprint ed. 1995.

Horovitz, Bruce. "'Missed Opportunity' to Reflect Audience: Diversity Is Lacking, Minority Ad Execs Say." *USA Today*, January 30, 1995, p. B5.

————. "Sunglasses: Like, Cool, Man. $275 Buys You Protection . . . From Looking Like Everyone Else." *Philadelphia Inquirer*, June 2, 1994, p. C5.

Howkins, Alvin. ". . . And There Was Television." *New Statesman and Society*, July 29, 1994, p. 36.

Hutchinson, Allan C. "More Talk: Against Constitutionalizing (Commercial) Speech." *Canadian Business Law Journal* 17 (1990): 2.

Hutton, Will. "Happiness That Money Truly Cannot Buy." *Guardian*, December 13, 1994, p. 13.

Hwang, Suein L., and Alix M. Freedman. "Cigarette Makers Face the Threat of More Accounts from Insiders." *Wall Street Journal*, March 20, 1996, p. B1.

———— , and Timothy Noah. "Philip Morris Proposes Curbs on Sales to Kids." *Wall Street Journal*, May 16, 1996, p. B1.

Ibanez v. Florida Dep't of Business and Professional Regulation, 114 *S. Ct.* 2084 (1994).

Inglehart, Ronald. *The Silent Revolution*. Princeton, NJ: Princeton University Press, 1977.

In re Primus, 436 *U.S.* 412 (1978).

In re R.M.J., 455 *U.S.* 191 (1982).

"Interactive TV Ad Breaks New Ground." *Christian Science Monitor*, March 28, 1996, p. 12.

ITT Continental Baking Co. v. FTC, 532 *F.2d* 207 (2d Cir. 1976).

Jackson, Thomas H., and John C. Jeffries Jr. "Commercial Speech: Economic Due Process and the First Amendment." *Virginia Law Review* 65 (1979): 1.

Jacobs, Sally. "Man, Is She Angry! When It Comes to '90s Women, Madison Avenue Decides That Rage Sells." *Boston Globe*, November 7, 1995, p. 59.

Jacobson, Michael F., and Laurie Ann Mazur. *Marketing Madness: A Survival Guide for a Consumer Society.* Boulder, CO: Westview, 1995.

Janal, Daniel S. *Online Marketing Handbook: How to Sell, Advertise, Publicize, and Promote Your Products and Services on the Internet and Commercial Online Systems.* New York: Van Nostrand Reinhold, 1995.

Jhally, Sut. "Commercial Culture, Collective Values and the Future." *Texas Law Review* 71 (1993): 805.

Johnson, Steve. "Creeping Commercials: Ads Worming Way into TV Scripts." *Chicago Tribune,* March 24, 1996, p. 1.

Johnson-Cartee, Karen S., and Gary A. Copeland. *Negative Political Advertising: Coming of Age.* Mahwah, NJ: Erlbaum, 1991.

Johnston, David. "Federal Thrust Against Tobacco Gets New Vigor." *New York Times News Service,* March 18, 1996 (1996 WL–NYT 9607802404).

Jones, John Philip. *Does It Pay to Advertise? Cases Illustrating Successful Brand Advertising.* San Francisco: Jossey Bass, 1989.

"Juno Launches America's First Free Internet E-Mail Service." *Business Wire* 4191123, April 19, 1996.

Kalakota, Ravi, and Andrew B. Whinston. *Frontiers of Electronic Commerce.* Reading, MA: Addison-Wesley, 1996.

Kane, Pat. "In Thrall to New Age Thrills." *Guardian,* January 4, 1995, p. 12.

Kanner, Bruce. "Among Advertisers, It's Hooray for Hollywood." *Philadelphia Inquirer,* February 4, 1996, p. D1.

Kansas v. United States, 16 *F.3d* 436 (D.C. Cir. 1994).

Kant, Immanuel. *Lectures on Ethics.* Trans. Louis Infield. Indianapolis: Hackett, 1980.

Katona, George. *Psychological Economics.* New York: Elsevier, 1975.

Kemper, Vicki. "Paying the Piper." *Common Cause Magazine* 21 (Spring 1995): 4.

Kennedy, Duncan. "The Role of Law in Economic Thought: Essays on the Fetishism of Commodities." *American University Law Review* 34 (1985): 949.

Kennedy, Shirley Duglin. "Dilemmas Abound with Internet Ads: Technological Advance Allow Viewers to Bypass Advertising Altogether." *Information Today,* December 1996, p. 47.

Keynes, John M. "Economic Possibilities for Our Grandchildren." Pp. 358–71 in *Essays in Persuasion*. New York: Norton, 1963.

Kilborn, Peter T. "Clinton Approves a Series of Curbs on Cigarette Ads." *New York Times*, August 24, 1996, p. A1.

Kilbourne, Jean. "Brewers Should Stop Targeting Youth." *USA Today*, March 8, 1991, p. A6.

Kim, James. "IBM, Microsoft Prepare for On-Line Shopping." *USA Today*, June 12, 1996, p. B1.

Kirchner, Jake. "On the Web, You Get What You Pay For." *PC Magazine*, May 14, 1996, p. 37.

Klatton, Werner. "Media's Place in the Bumpy Nineties." *Admap*, December 31, 1990, p. 41.

Klausner, Manuel S. "The First Amendment and Commercial Speech." *George Mason University Law Review* 11 (1988): 83.

Kluger, Richard. *Ashes to Ashes: America's Hundred-Year Cigarette War*. New York: Knopf, 1996.

———. "A Peace Plan for the Cigarette Wars." *New York Times Magazine*, April 7, 1996, p. 28.

Koenig, Dorean M. "Joe Camel and the First Amendment: The Dark Side of Copyrighted and Trademark-Protected Icons." *Thomas M. Cooley Law Review* 11 (1994): 803.

Kong, Dolores. "Do Ads Lure Youngsters to Drink, Smoke?" *Boston Globe*, April 27, 1992, p. 41.

Kozinski, Alex, and Stuart Banner. "The Anti-History and Pre-History of Commercial Speech." *Texas Law Review* 71 (1993): 747.

———. "Who's Afraid of Commercial Speech?" *Virginia Law Review* 76 (1990): 627.

Kraft, Inc. v. FTC, 970 *F.2d* 311 (7th Cir. 1992), cert. denied, 113 *S. Ct.* 1254 (1993).

Kuhlengel, Kimberly K. Casenote: "A Failure to Preempt an Unfair Advertising Claim May Result in Undue Restrictions on Cigarette Manufacturers." *Southern Illinois University Law Journal* 19 (1995): 405.

Kuklin, Bailey. "Self-Paternalism in the Marketplace." *University of Chicago Law Review* 60 (1992): 649.

Kuntz, Mary. "The New Hucksterism." *Business Week*, July 1, 1996, p. 76.

Kurland, Philip B. "Posadas de Puerto Rico v. Tourism Company: 'Twas Strange, 'Twas Passing Strange; 'Twas Pitiful, 'Twas Wondrous Pitiful." *Supreme Court Review* 1986 (1987): 1.

Lane, Robert E. "Does Money Buy Happiness?" *Public Interest* 113 (1993): 56.

———. *The Market Experience*. Cambridge: Cambridge University Press, 1991.

Lapham, Lewis. "Yellow Brick Road." *Harper's Magazine*, November 1993, p. 10.

Lasch, Christopher. *The Culture of Narcissism*. New York: Warner Books, 1979.

———. *The True and Only Heaven: Progress and Its Critics*. New York: Norton, 1991.

Laver, Ross. "Plugging into the Future: Archaic and Slow, the Internet Is Still Not Ready for Prime Time, yet It May Soon Transform Life More Than the Computer Itself." *MacLean's*, January 29, 1996, p. 28.

Lawson, E. J. "The Role of Smoking in the Lives of Low Income Pregnant Adolescents: A Field Study." *Adolescence* 29 (Spring 1994): 61.

Lawson, Mark. "Buy Sexuality off the Shelf." *Guardian*, June 26, 1995, p. 11.

Leach, William. *Land of Desire: Merchants, Power, and the Rise of a New American Culture*. New York: Random House, 1983.

Lears, T. J. Jackson. *Fables of Abundance: A Cultural History of Advertising in America*. New York: Basic Books, 1994.

Lears, T. J. Jackson. "From Salvation to Self-Realization: Advertising and the Therapeutic Roots of the Consumer Culture, 1880–1930." In *The Culture of Consumption: Critical Essays in American History, 1880–1980*. Vol. 3. Ed. Richard Wightman Fox and T. J. Jackson Lears. New York: Pantheon, 1983.

Lebergott, Stanley. *Pursuing Happiness*. Princeton, NJ: Princeton University Press, 1993.

Leffler, Keith B. "Persuasion or Information? The Economics of Prescription Drug Advertising." *Journal of Law and Economics* 24 (1981): 45.

Leibenstein, Harvey. *Beyond Economic Man: A New Foundation for Microeconomics*. Cambridge, MA: Harvard University Press, 1976.

Leo, John. "The Official Column of Champions: The Selling of Official Sponsorships." *U.S. News and World Report*, November 27, 1995, p. 28.

Lessig, Lawrence. "The Path of Cyberlaw." *Yale Law Journal* 104 (1995): 1743.

Levine, Joshua. "Brands with Feeling: Products Are No Longer the Focus of Advertising." *Forbes*, December 16, 1996, p. 292.

Levine, Paul. Book Review: "Land of Desire." *Nation*, January 3, 1994, p. 25.

Lewis, Peter H. "Newcomers to Internet Are Older and Less Educated, Survey Finds." *New York Times News Service*, August 14, 1996 (1996 WL–NYT 9622700801).

———. "Online Service Blocks 'Junk' E-Mail Aimed at Subscribers." *New York Times News Service*, September 5, 1996 (1996 WL–NYT 9624803803).

———. "Technology for the Cybermarketing Age." *New York Times News Service*, September 18, 1996 (1996 WL–NYT 9626102804).

Lewis, Sinclair. *Babbitt*. New York: Viking Penguin, 1922.

Lipton, Peter. *Inference to the Best Explanation*. London: Routledge, 1991.

Loeb, Larry. "The Stage Is SET." *Internet World*, August 1996, p. 55.

Loper v. New York City Police Department, 999 *F.2d* 699 (2d Cir. 1993).

Loshin, Pete. "The Electronic Marketplace." *PC Today*, July 1996, p. 82.

Lowe v. SEC, 472 *U.S.* 181 (1985).

Luik, John C. "Tobacco Advertising Bans and the Dark Face of Government Paternalism." *International Journal of Advertising* 12 (Fall 1993): 303.

Lukács, George. *History and Class Consciousness*. Trans. Rodney Livingstone. Cambridge, MA: MIT Press, 1971.

Lynch, Daniel C., and Leslié Lundquist. *Digital Money: The New Era of Internet Commerce*. New York: Wiley, 1996.

Machina, Kenton F. "Freedom of Expression in Commerce." *Law and Philosophy* 3 (1984): 375.

Macken, Kathleen M., et al. "Smoking Patterns in a Low Income Urban Population: A Challenge to Smoking Cessation Efforts." *Journal of Family Practice*, January 1991, p. 93.

Maloof, Joel. *net.profit: Expanding Your Business Using the Internet*. Indianapolis: IDG Books, 1995.

Mander, Jerry. *Four Arguments for the Elimination of Television*. New York: Morrow, 1978.

"A Man's Guide to Buying Diamonds." *Scientific American*, April 1996 (inside back cover).

Marchand, Roland. *Advertising the American Dream: Making Way for Modernity, 1920–1940*. Berkeley and Los Angeles: University of California Press, 1985.

Marcotty, Josephine. "A Nation on Overtime." (Minneapolis) *Star Tribune*, September 5, 1994, p. A1.

Marcuse, Herbert. *Negations: Essays in Critical Theory*. Trans. Jeremy J. Shapiro. Boston: Beacon Press, 1968.

Marisetti, Raju. "P and G Steps up Ad Cyber-Surfing: Tide Could Have a Major Effect." *Wall Street Journal*, April 18, 1996, p. B10.

"Marketing Inner Beauty." *Futurist*, March–April 1994, p. 59.

Marsh, Harriet. "Tobacco Companies Cram in Pre-Ban Ads." *Marketing*, February 1, 1996, p. 8.

Marshall, Matt. "In Germany, a Backlash Hits Benetton: Store Owners Battle the Retailer over Ads and Store Policies They Say Are Costing Sales." *Washington Post*, February 9, 1995, p. D10.

Martin, Douglas. "New York Allows Companies to Shill in City Parks If They Make a Donation." *New York Times News Service*, May 19, 1996 (1996 WL–NYT 9613903800).

Martin, Ellen James. "Those Coupons Being Used at a Furious Clip." *Philadelphia Inquirer*, January 10, 1996, p. C1.

Marx, Karl. *Early Writings*. Trans. T. B. Bottomore. New York: McGraw-Hill, 1964.

Mathiesen, Michael. *Marketing on the Internet*. Gulf Breeze, FL: Maximum Press, 1995.

McChesney, Fred S. "Commercial Speech in the Professions: The Supreme Court's Unanswered Questions and Questionable Answers." *University of Pennsylvania Law Review* 134 (1985): 45.

McClure, K. Alexandra. "Environmental Marketing: A Call for Legislative Action." *Santa Clara Law Review* 35 (1995): 1351.

McGowan, David F. "A Critical Analysis of Commercial Speech." *California Law Review* 78 (1990): 359.

McKenzie, Diana J. P. "Commerce on the Net: Surfing Through Cyberspace Without Getting Wet." *John Marshall Journal of Computer and Information Law* 14 (1996): 247.

McLaughlin, Patricia. "Into Temptation: The Culture of Consumption Had to Lead Somewhere." *Philadelphia Inquirer*, May 1, 1994, p. 35.

Merritt, Sharyne. "Negative Political Advertising: Some Empirical Findings." *Journal of Advertising* 13 (1984): 27.

Mill, John Stuart. *On Liberty* (1859). New York: Macmillan, 1926.

Miller, Greg. "9 Firms Charged with Fraudulent Ads on Internet." *Los Angeles Times*, March 15, 1996, p. D1.

Miller, Stephen. "A Postmodern Age: What Is It?" *Current*, January 1994, p. 21.

Minow, Newton N., and Craig L. LaMay. *Abandoned in the Wasteland: Children, Television, and the First Amendment.* New York: Hill & Wang, 1995.

Miracle, Gordon E., and Terence Nevett. *Voluntary Regulation of Advertising: A Comparative Analysis of the United Kingdom and the United States.* New York: Free Press, 1987.

Mittal, Banwari. "Public Assessment of TV Advertising: Faint Praise and Harsh Criticism." *Journal of Advertising Research*, January–February 1994, p. 35.

Montaigne, Michel de. *The Complete Essays of Montaigne.* Trans. Donald M. Frame. Stanford, CA: Stanford University Press, 1958.

Montgomery, Kathryn C. "Children in the Digital Age." *American Prospect*, July–August 1996, p. 69.

Moody, Kim. "The Overworked American: The Unexpected Decline of Leisure." *Monthly Review*, October 1992, p. 50.

Moon, Richard. "Lifestyle Advertising and Classical Freedom of Expression Doctrine." *McGill Law Journal* 36 (1991): 76.

———. "RJR-MacDonald v. Canada on the Freedom to Advertise." *Constitutional Forum* 7 (1995): 1.

———. "The Supreme Court of Canada on the Structure of Freedom of Expression Adjudication." *University of Toronto Law Journal* 45 (1995): 419.

Moser v. Frohnmayer, 315 Or. 372, 845 P.2d 1284 (1993) (en banc).

Mowlana, Hamid. "The Communications Paradox: Globalization May Be Just Another Word for Western Cultural Dominance." *Bulletin of the Atomic Scientists*, July 17, 1995, p. 40.

Murdoch, Iris. *Metaphysics as a Guide to Morals.* New York: Viking Penguin, 1992.

Murray, Jeff B., and Julie L. Ozanne. "The Critical Imagination: Emancipatory Interests in Consumer Research." *Journal of Consumer Research*, September 1991, p. 129.

Myers, David G., and Ed Diener. "The Pursuit of Happiness." *Scientific American*, May 1996, p. 70.

National Commission on Egg Nutrition v. FTC, 570 *F.2d* 157 (7th Cir. 1977).

Nelson, K. P. "Women in Low Income Groups Smoke More: Canterbury 1976–92." *New Zealand Medical Journal*, April 26, 1995, p. 148.

"Net Profits." *Internet '96* (1996): 70.

"Netful of Junk?" *Washington Post*, April 14, 1996, p. C6.

"Netscape's Top Spot Now Paid Spot." *Cleveland Plain Dealer*, January 1, 1996, p. D4.

Neuborne, Burt. "The First Amendment and Government Regulation of Capital Markets." *Brooklyn Law Review* 55 (1989): 5.

———. "A Rationale for Protecting and Regulating Commercial Speech." *Brooklyn Law Review* 46 (1980): 437.

Nicholson-Lord, David. "Consumerism 'Undermining Western Society.'" *Independent*, May 19, 1994, p. 8.

Nickerson, Colin. "Cigarette Ads Are Back in Canada After 7-Year Absence." *Boston Globe*, February 23, 1996, p. 10.

Nissenbaum, Stephen. *The Battle for Christmas.* New York: McKay, 1996.

Noah, Timothy. "Study Says Minors Respond More to Cigarette Ads Than Do Adults." *Wall Street Journal*, April 4, 1996, p. B8.

Nowak, Rachel, and Eliot Marshall. "New Studies Trace the Impact of Tobacco Advertising." *Science*, October 27, 1995, p. 573.

Nugent, Lynne. "Notes from an Iron Cage: Humanism and the Commodity Fetish." *Humanist*, January–February 1994, p. 32.

Nussbaum, Martha C. Book Review: "The Empire of Fashion." *New Republic*, January 2, 1995, p. 29.

O'Barr, William M. *Culture and the Ad: Exploring Otherness in the World of Advertising*. Boulder, CO: Westview, 1994.

Ogilvy, David. *Confessions of an Advertising Man*. New York: Simon & Schuster, 1963.

————. *Ogilvy on Advertising*. New York: Random House, 1985.

"'Oh, Lord, Won't You Buy Me . . . '": Mercedes Puts Materialistic Spin on '60s Classic." *Miami Herald*, March 10, 1995, p. C1.

Ohmann, Richard. *Selling Culture: Magazines, Markets, and Class at the Turn of the Century*. London: Routledge, 1996.

Ohralik v. Ohio State Bar Ass'n, 436 *U.S.* 447 (1978).

Peel v. Attorney Registration and Disciplinary Comm'n, 496 *U.S.* 91 (1990).

Penn Advertising of Baltimore, Inc. v. Mayor and City Council of Baltimore, 63 *F.3d* 1318 (4th Cir. 1995), vacated, 116 *S. Ct.* 1821 (1996).

Perry, Michael J. "Freedom of Expression: An Essay on Theory and Doctrine." *Northwestern University Law Review* 78 (1984): 1137.

Pescovitz, David. "The Future of Electronic Shopping." *Wired*, January 1996, p. 4.

Pipher, Mary. *The Shelter of Each Other*. New York: Ballantine, 1996.

Pitofsky, Robert. "First Amendment Protections and Economic Activity." *George Mason University Law Review* 11 (1988): 89.

Pittsburgh Press Co. v. Pittsburgh Commission on Human Relations, 413 U.S. 376 (1973).

Polin, Kenneth L. "Argument for the Ban of Tobacco Advertising: A First Amendment Analysis." *Hofstra Law Review* 17 (1988): 99.

Pollay, Richard W. "Quality of Life in the Padded Sell: Common Criticisms of Advertising's Cultural Character and International Public Policies." *Current Issues and Research in Advertising* 9 (1986): 173.

————. "Targeting Tactics in Selling Smoke: Youthful Aspects of 20th Century Cigarette Advertising." *Journal of Marketing Theory and Practice* 3 (1995): 1.

———, and Katherine Gallagher. "Advertising and Cultural Values: Reflections in the Distorted Mirror." *International Journal of Advertising* 9 (Fall 1990): 359.

———, and Anne M. Lavack. "The Targeting of Youths by Cigarette Marketers: Archival Evidence on Trial." Pp. 266–71 in *Advances in Consumer Research*. Ed. Leigh McAlister and Michael L. Rothschild. Vancouver: University of British Columbia Press, 1993.

———, et al. "The Last Straw? Cigarette Advertising and Realized Market Shares Among Youths and Adults, 1979–1993." *Journal of Marketing* 60 (Spring 1996): 1.

"The Poor Die Younger." *Economist*, December 24, 1988, p. 69.

Posadas de Puerto Rico Assocs. v. Tourism Co., 478 *U.S.* 328 (1986).

Posner, Richard A. "Free Speech in an Economic Perspective." *Suffolk University Law Review* 20 (1986): 1.

Poster, Mark. *The Mode of Information*. Chicago: University of Chicago Press, 1990.

Postman, Neil. *Amusing Ourselves to Death*. New York: Viking, 1985.

Putnam, Robert D. "The Prosperous Community: Social Capital and Public Life." *American Prospect* 13 (1993): 35.

Radin, Margaret J. "Market-Inalienability." *Harvard Law Review* 100 (1987): 1849.

Randazzo, Sal. *The Myth Makers: How Advertisers Apply the Power of Classic Myths and Symbols to Create Modern Day Legends*. Burr Ridge, IL: Irwin, 1995.

Redish, Martin H. "The First Amendment in the Marketplace: Commercial Speech and the Values of Free Expression." *George Washington Law Review* 39 (1971): 429.

———. "Product Health Claims and the First Amendment: Scientific Expression and the Twilight Zone of Commercial Speech." *Vanderbilt Law Review* 43 (1990): 1433.

———. "Tobacco Advertising and the First Amendment." *Iowa Law Review* 81 (1996): 589.

Reed, O. Lee. "Is Commercial Speech Really Less Valuable Than Political Speech?" *American Business Law Journal* 34 (1996): 1.

"Regulations Restricting the Sale and Distribution of Cigarettes and Smoke-less Tobacco Products to Protect Children and Adolescents." *Federal Register*, August 11, 1995, p. 41314.

"Regulations Restricting the Sale and Distribution of Cigarettes and Smoke-less Tobacco to Protect Children and Adolescents." *Federal Register*, August 28, 1996, p. 44396.

"Regulations Restricting the Sale and Distribution of Cigarettes and Smoke-less Tobacco Products to Protect Children and Adolescents: Findings of the Focus Group Testing of Brief Statements for Cigarette Advertise-ments." *Federal Register*, December 1, 1995, p. 61670.

Reich, Robert B. "Preventing Deception in Commercial Speech." *New York University Law Review* 54 (1979): 775.

Reid, Tim. "Unfriendly Persuasion." (London) *Sunday Telegraph*, February 4, 1996, p. 3.

Reiter, Jendi B. "Citizens or Sinners?: The Economic and Political Inequity of 'Sin Taxes' on Tobacco and Alcohol Products." *Columbia Journal of Law and Social Problems* 29 (1996): 443.

Removatron Int'l Corp. v. FTC, 884 *F.2d* 1489 (1st Cir. 1989).

Resnick, Rosalind. "Sugar-Coated Spam." *Internet World*, August 1996, p. 32.

Rich, Frank. "Drug War on the Rocks." *New York Times News Service*, January 11, 1997 (1997 WL–NYT 9701002200).

Richards, Jef I., and Richard D. Zakia. "Pictures: An Advertiser's Expressway Through FTC Regulation." *Georgia Law Review* 16 (1981): 77.

Richardson, Scott. Comment: "Attorney General's Warning: Legislation May Now Be Hazardous to Tobacco Companies' Health." *Akron Law Review* 28 (Fall–Winter 1995): 291.

Richins, Marsha L., and Scott Dawson. "A Consumer Values Orientation for Materialism and Its Measurement: Scale Development and Validation." *Journal of Consumer Research*, December 1992, p. 303.

Rieff, David. "The Culture That Conquered the Earth: Why Conformist Consumerism Is America's Greatest Export." *Washington Post*, January 2, 1994, p. C1.

RJR-MacDonald, Inc. v. Attorney General of Canada, 127 D.L.R. 4th 1 (1995).

Robertson, Thomas S. *Consumer Behavior.* New York: Harper, 1970.

Roese, Neal J., and Gerald N. Sande. "Backlash Effects in Attack Politics." *Journal of Applied Social Psychology* 23 (1993): 632.

Romero, Dennis. "Memo to All Boomers: How Is It That You've Transformed the Rite of Turning 50 into a Celebration of Your So-Called Youth?" *Los Angeles Times*, February 9, 1996, p. E1.

Rosenberg, Howard. "For Whom the Taco Bell Tolls." *Los Angeles Times*, March 15, 1996, p. F1.

Ross, Chuck. "Marketers Fend off Shift in Rules for Ad Puffery." *Advertising Age*, February 19, 1996, p. 41.

Rothenberg, Randall. *Where the Suckers Moon: The Life and Death of an Advertising Campaign.* New York: Random House, 1994.

Rothstein, Edward. "Metaphors for Internet May Affect Its Use." *New York Times News Service*, October 28, 1996 (1996 WL–NYT 9630101802).

——— . " 'Push' Technology That Makes the Internet Come to You." *New York Times News Service*, January 20, 1997 (1997 WL–NYT 9701902411).

Rotunda, Ronald D. "The Commercial Speech Doctrine in the Supreme Court." *University of Illinois Law Forum* 1976 (1976): 1080.

Rousseau, Jean Jacques. *A Discourse on Inequality.* Trans. G. D. H. Cole. New York: Dutton, 1950.

Rowe, Jonathan. Book Review: "Marketing Madness." *Washington Monthly*, June 1995, p. 52.

Rubin v. Coors Brewing Co., 115 S. Ct. 1585 (1995).

Santiago, Denise-Marie. "Ads for Prescription Drugs Stir a Medical Controversy." *Philadelphia Inquirer*, January 15, 1996, p. F1.

Savan, Leslie. "Field of Teams: If You Name It, They Will Come." *Philadelphia Daily News*, May 2, 1996, p. 37.

——— . *The Sponsored Life: Ads, TV, and American Culture.* Philadelphia: Temple University Press, 1994.

Scanlon, T. M. "Freedom of Expression and Categories of Expression." *University of Pittsburgh Law Review* 40 (1979): 519.

Schauer, Frederick. "Commercial Speech and the Architecture of the First Amendment." *University of Cincinnati Law Review* 56 (1988): 1181.

————. *Free Speech: A Philosophical Enquiry*. Cambridge: Cambridge University Press, 1982.

Schelling, Thomas C. "Addictive Drugs: The Cigarette Experience." *Science*, January 24, 1992, p. 430.

Schiller, Herbert I. *Culture, Inc.: The Corporate Takeover of Public Expression*. Oxford: Oxford University Press, 1989.

Schlag, Pierre. "This Could Be Your Culture: Junk Speech in a Time of Decadence." *Harvard Law Review* 109 (1996): 1801 (reviewing Ronald K. L. Collins and David M. Skover, *The Death of Discourse*).

Schnably, Stephen J. "Property and Pragmatism: A Critique of Radin's Theory of Property and Personhood." *Stanford Law Review* 45 (1993): 347.

Schor, Juliet. "Why (and How) More People Are Dropping out of the Rat Race." *Working Woman*, August 1995, p. 14.

Schudson, Michael. *Advertising, the Uneasy Persuasion: Its Dubious Impact on American Society*. New York: Basic Books, 1984.

Schwartz, Barry. *The Costs of Living: How Market Freedom Erodes the Best Things in Life*. New York: Norton, 1994.

Schwartz, John. "Dole Tobacco Stand Draws Fire: Ex-Surgeon General Criticizes Candidate's Comment on Addiction." *Washington Post*, June 22, 1996, p. A3.

————. "New Cigarette Clears the Smoke, but the Heat Is Still On." *Washington Post*, May 27, 1996, p. A3.

————. "Smoke, Letters and Documentation: Tobacco Companies Swamp FDA with Final Comments on Regulation." *Washington Post*, January 3, 1996, p. A20.

————. "Teen Smoking Still Rising, CDC Says." *Washington Post*, May 24, 1996, p. A24.

Scitovsky, Tibor. *Human Desire and Economic Satisfaction*. New York: New York University Press, 1986.

————. *The Joyless Economy*. Oxford: Oxford University Press, 1976.

Scott, Michael D. "Advertising in Cyberspace: Business and Legal Considerations." *Computer Law* 12 (1995): 1.

SEC v. Wall Street Publishing Institute, Inc., 851 *F.2d* 365 (D.C. Cir.), cert. denied, 489 *U.S.* 1066 (1988).

Seelye, Katharine Q. "Trickle of TV Liquor Ads Releases Torrent." *New York Times News Service*, January 12, 1997 (1997 WL–NYT 9701200205).

Sellers, Patricia. "To Avoid a Trampling, Get Ahead of the Mass." *Fortune*, May 15, 1995, p. 201.

Settles, Craig. "A Dose of Reality: Too Many People Believed the Web Was Paved with Gold." *Internet World*, July 1996, p. 63.

Shalit, Ruth. "The Oppo Boom: Smearing for Profit Takes Off." *New Republic*, January 3, 1994, p. 16.

Shapero v. Kentucky Bar Ass'n, 486 *U.S.* 466 (1988).

Shapiro, Joseph. "Teenage Wasteland?" *U.S. News and World Report*, October 23, 1995, p. 84.

Sharkey, Alix. "Take a Look at These Images from Television Commercials—They Look Harmless Enough—Now Look Again." *Independent*, January 20, 1996, p. 6.

Sharpe, Robert J. "A Comment on Allan Hutchinson's Money Talk: Against Constitutionalizing Commercial Speech." *Canadian Business Law Journal* 17 (1990): 35.

Shiner, Roger A. "Advertising and Freedom of Expression." *University of Toronto Law Journal* 45 (1995): 179.

———. "Freedom of Commercial Expression." P. 91 in *Free Expression: Essays in Law and Philosophy*. Ed. W. J. Waluchow. Oxford: Oxford University Press, 1994.

———. "The Silent Majority Speaks: RJR-MacDonald Inc. v. Canada." *Constitutional Forum* 7 (1995): 8.

Shiffrin, Steven. "The First Amendment and Economic Regulation: Away from a General Theory of the First Amendment." *Northwestern University Law Review* 78 (1983): 1212.

Shorris, Earl. *A Nation of Salesmen: The Tyranny of the Market and the Subversion of Culture*. New York: Avon, 1994.

Simon, Todd F. "Defining Commercial Speech: A Focus on Process Rather Than Content." *New England Law Review* 20 (1985): 215.

Smith, Adam. "Theory of the Moral Sentiments." Pp. 251–357 in *British Moralists*. Vol. 1. Ed. L. A. Selby-Bigge (1897). New York: Dover, 1965.

Smith, David A. "Buying Power: Thoughts on the Crisis of Commodification." *Tikkun*, September–October 1994, p. 63.

Smith, Marlin H. Note: "The Limits of Copyright: Property, Parody, and the Public Domain." *Duke Law Journal* 42 (1993): 1233.

"Smokers: The Young, the Poor, and the Less Educated." *The Women's Letter*, November 1990, p. 4.

Smolla, Rodney. "Information, Imagery, and the First Amendment: A Case for Expansive Protection of Commercial Speech." *Texas Law Review* 71 (1993): 777.

Soper, Kate. *Troubled Pleasures: Writings on Politics, Gender and Hedonism.* London: Routledge, 1990.

Spain, William. "Talk Shows Heed Loud Dissension from New Voices." *Advertising Age*, January 15, 1996, p. 28.

Span, Paula. "The TV Ads That Hit the Spot: Among Viewers, Dogs and Celebs Have Commercial Appeal." *Washington Post*, January 7, 1989, p. G1.

"Speeding up 'Net Traffic." *Newsday*, March 19, 1996, p. B23.

Spencer, Herbert. *The Man Versus the State.* Ed. Eric Mack. Indianapolis: Liberty Fund, 1982.

Stabiner, Karen. *Inventing Desire.* New York: Simon & Schuster, 1993.

Star, Alexander. Book Review: "Fables of Abundance." *New Republic*, March 20, 1995, p. 38.

Stead, Deborah. "Corporations, Classrooms and Commercialism." *New York Times*, January 5, 1997, sec. 4A, p. 30.

Stefik, Mark. *Internet Dreams: Archetypes, Myths, and Metaphors.* Cambridge, MA: MIT Press, 1996.

Steiker, Jordan M. "Creating a Community of Liberals." *Texas Law Review* 69 (1991): 795.

Steinberg, Steve G. "Toll Roads May Be the Future Route of the Internet." *Los Angeles Times*, January 25, 1996, p. D2.

Stepp, Laura Sessions. "Panel Sounds Alarm About Adolescence: Youths Found Adrift in Age of Discovery." *Washington Post*, October 12, 1995, p. A1.

Sterne, Jim. *World Wide Web Marketing: Integrating the Internet into Your Marketing Strategy.* New York: Wiley, 1995.

Stets, Dan. "Computer Expert Warns of Internet Reaching Overload." *Atlanta Constitution*, January 14, 1996, p. R05.

Stobart, Paul, ed. *Brand Power*. New York: New York University Press, 1994.

Stone, Christopher D. "Theorizing Commercial Speech." *George Mason University Law Review* 11 (1988): 95.

Strauss, David A. "Constitutional Protection for Commercial Speech: Some Lessons from the American Experience." *Canadian Business Law Journal* 17 (1990): 45.

Sugarman, Carole. "Truth in Labeling, but What About Advertising?: Controversy over FTC's Plans to Keep Product Claims Consistent with FDA's New Labels." *Washington Post*, May 31, 1994, p. Z16.

Summers, Lawrence H., and Chris Carroll. *Why Is U.S. National Saving So Low?* Washington, DC: Brookings Institution, 1987.

Sunstein, Cass. Book Review: "Abandoned in the Wasteland." *New Republic*, August 21, 1995, p. 38.

——— . Book Review: "Fatal Tradeoffs: Public and Private Responsibilities for Risk." *New Republic*, February 15, 1993, p. 36.

——— . "The First Amendment in Cyberspace." *Yale Law Journal* 104 (1995): 1757.

"Sweden: Space, the Final Frontier for Advertising." *Independent*, August 12, 1995, p. 6.

Swisher, Kara. "Curbs on Cyberspace Ads Proposed: Trade Groups Offer Guidelines as FTC Workshop Airs Privacy Issues." *Washington Post*, June 5, 1996, p. F1.

——— . " 'Web' Opens up a World of On-Line Commerce." *Washington Post*, March 26, 1995, p. H1.

Tarsney, Peter J. Note: "Regulation of Environmental Marketing: Reassessing the Supreme Court's Protection of Commercial Speech." *Notre Dame Law Review* 69 (1994): 533.

Tawney, R. H. *The Acquisitive Society*. New York: Harcourt, 1920.

Taylor, Lester D., and Daniel Weiserbs. "Advertising and the Aggregate Consumption Function." *American Economic Review* 62 (1972): 642.

Teague, John H. "Marketing on the World Wide Web." *Technical Communication*, May 1995, p. 236.

"That's Web Biz." *Internet '96* (1996): 76.

Thoreau, Henry D. *Walden and Other Writings*. Ed. Brooks Atkinson. New York: Modern Library, 1950.

Timmins, Nicholas. "Poorest Families More Likely to Smoke." *Independent*, March 9, 1994, p. 1.

Townsend, Joy, Paul Roderick, and Jacqueline Cooper. "Cigarette Smoking by Socioeconomic Group, Sex, and Age: Effects of Price, Income, and Health Publicity." *British Medical Journal*, October 8, 1994, p. 923.

Trachtenberg, Jeffrey A. "'It's Become Part of Our Culture.'" *Forbes*, May 5, 1986, p. 134.

"Trends in Smoking Initiation Among Adolescents and Young Adults: United States, 1980–1989." *Journal of the American Medical Association*, August 16, 1995, p. 528.

Tully, Shawn. "Teens: The Most Global Market of All." *Fortune*, May 16, 1994, p. 90.

Tushnet, Mark. "Decoding Television (and Law Review)." *Texas Law Review* 68 (1990): 1179.

———. "New Meaning for First Amendment." *ABA Journal*, November 1995, p. 57.

Twitchell, James B. *Adcult USA: The Triumph of Advertising in American Culture*. New York: Columbia University Press, 1996.

———. *Carnival Culture*. New York: Columbia University Press, 1992.

"The Unhealthy Poor." *Economist*, June 4, 1994, p. 55.

United States v. Edge Broadcasting Co., 509 *U.S.* 418 (1993).

United States v. National Association of Broadcasters, 536 *F. Supp.* 149 (D.D.C. 1982).

United States v. National Association of Broadcasters, 553 *F. Supp.* 621 (D.D.C. 1982).

Van Alstyne, William. "Remembering Melville Nimmer: Some Cautionary Notes on Commercial Speech." *UCLA Law Review* 43 (1996): 1635.

Veblen, Thorstein. *The Theory of the Leisure Class* (1899). New York: B. W. Huebsch, 1924.

Veenhoven, Ruut. *National Wealth and Individual Happiness.* Pp. 9 and 19 in *Understanding Economic Behavior.* Ed. Klaus G. Frunert and Folke Olander. Norwell, MA: Kluwer, 1989.

Verhovek, Sam Howe. "Halloween: The Making of a Mercantile Event." *New York Times News Service,* October 24, 1996 (1996 WL-NYT 9629800401).

Virginia State Board of Pharmacy v. Virginia Citizens Consumer Council, 425 *U.S.* 748 (1976).

Viscusi, W. Kip. *Smoking: The Risky Decision.* Oxford: Oxford University Press, 1992.

Wagner, William J. "The Contractual Reallocation of Procreative Resources and Parental Rights: The Natural Endowment Critique." *Case Western Reserve Law Review* 41 (1990): 1.

Walker, Charles E., Mark A. Bloomfield, and Margo Thorning, eds. *U.S. Savings Challenge: Policy Options for Productivity and Growth.* 1990.

Walker, Leslie. "The Internet's Tale Is Radio, Revisited: A Debate over Interaction Covers Familiar Ground." *Washington Post,* December 16, 1996, p. F17.

Walsh, Mary Williams. "German Court Bans Shocking Benetton Ads." *Los Angeles Times,* July 7, 1995, p. A6.

Waters v. Churchill, 114 *S. Ct.* 1878 (1994).

Weber, Max. *Economy and Society.* Vol. 1. Ed. Guenther Roth and Claus Wittich. Berkeley and Los Angeles: University of California Press, 1978.

———. *The Protestant Ethic and the Spirit of Capitalism.* Trans. Talcott Parsons. New York: Simon & Schuster, 1958.

Webster, Nancy Coltun. "Marketing to Kids: In Tune with High-Tech as Early as 2, Youngsters Control Future of Market Success." *Advertising Age,* February 13, 1995, p. S1.

Wehling, Bob. "The Future of Marketing: What Every Marketer Should Know About Being Online." *Vital Speeches,* January 1, 1996, p. 170.

Wells, Melanie. "Procter and Gamble Tells Ad Agencies to Diversify." *USA Today,* April 26, 1996, p. B2.

———, and Dottie Enrico. "Bathroom Humor a New Fixture in Advertising." *USA Today,* June 15, 1995, p. B1.

Welz, Gary. "The Ad Game: Industry Analysts and Agencies See the Web Advertising Market Exploding." *Internet World,* July 1996, p. 51.

Wernick, Andrew. *Promotional Culture: Advertising, Ideology and Symbolic Expression*. Thousand Oaks, CA: Sage, 1991.

Werther, William B. "Toward Global Convergency." *Business Horizons*, January–February 1996, p. 3.

Whatley, Michael. Note: "The FDA v. Joe Camel: An Analysis of the FDA's Attempt to Regulate Tobacco and Tobacco Products Under the Federal Food, Drug and Cosmetic Act." *Journal of Legislation* 22 (1996): 121.

Wheat, Jack. "Professor Studies Targeting of Minorities by Advertisers." *Miami Herald*, February 5, 1996, p. B5.

While, D., et al. "Cigarette Advertising and Onset of Smoking in Children: Questionnaire Survey." *British Medical Journal*, August 17, 1996, p. 398.

Williams, Lucy A. "The Ideology of Division: Behavior Modification Welfare Reform Proposals." *Yale Law Journal* 102 (1992): 719.

Williams, Raymond. *Television: Technology and Cultural Form*. New York: Schocken Books, 1974.

"Wispa Gets Reprimand from Pulpit." *Media Week*, November 10, 1995, p. 3.

Wolfson, Nicholas. *Corporate First Amendment Rights and the SEC*. Westport, CT: Greenwood Press, 1990.

Wood, Ellen Meiksins. "What Is the 'Postmodern' Agenda?: An Introduction." *Monthly Review*, July 17, 1995, p. 1.

Wood, James. "Sold Out." *New Republic*, October 21, 1996, p. 42.

Wood, Valerie D. "The Precarious Position of Commercial Speech." *Harvard Journal of Law and Public Policy* 19 (1996): 612.

Wordsworth, William. *The Poetry of William Wordsworth*. Ed. Alan Gardiner. New York: Penguin, 1990.

Wright, J. Skelly. "Politics and the Constitution: Is Money Speech?" *Yale Law Journal* 85 (1976): 1001.

Wright, R. George. "Free Speech and the Mandated Disclosure of Information." *University of Richmond Law Review* 25 (1991): 475.

——— . "Freedom and Culture: Why We Should Not Buy Commercial Speech." *Denver University Law Review* 72 (1994): 137.

——— . *The Future of Free Speech Law*. Westport, CT: Greenwood Press, 1990.

————. *Reason and Obligation*. Lanham, MD: University Press of America, 1994.

Wulf, Steve. "Generation Excluded: A Report Chides America for Neglecting Adolescents." *Time*, October 23, 1995, p. 86.

Wuthnow, Robert. "Pious Materialism: How Americans View Faith and Money." *Christian Century*, March 3, 1993, p. 238.

Young v. New York City Transit Authority, 903 *F.2d* 146 (2d Cir.), cert. denied, 498 *U.S.* 984 (1990).

"Young People Talk with FDA Commissioner About Smoking." *FDA Consumer*, January–February 1996, p. 22.

Young, Scott. "Taking Measure: In the Brave New World of Web Advertising, Numbers Alone Don't Tell the Story." *Internet World*, July 1996, p. 66.

Zauderer v. Office of Disciplinary Council, 471 *U.S.* 626 (1985).

Zhu, B. P., et al. "The Relationship Between Cigarette Smoking and Education Revisited." *American Journal of Public Health*, November 1996, p. 1582.

index

243